WORLD OF HERBS

WORLD OF HERBS

RECIPES, REMEDIES AND DECORATIVE IDEAS

LESLEY BREMNESS

based on a series directed by
Nicholas Ferguson and produced
by Saskia Sutton

EBURY PRESS
in association with
CHANNEL FOUR TELEVISION COMPANY LTD
LONDON

To J. Roger Lowe

First published by Ebury Press
an imprint of Century Hutchinson Ltd
Brookmount House
62–65 Chandos Place
London WC2N 4NW
in association with Channel 4

WORLD OF HERBS was produced by Blossom Productions for
Channel 4 Television

British Library Cataloguing in Publication Data
Bremness, Lesley
  World of herbs.
  1. Herbs
  I. Title
  641.3'57

  ISBN 0-85223-821-5

Phototypeset in Baskerville by Textype Typesetters, Cambridge
Printed and bound by Mackays of Chatham, Plc, Kent

CONTENTS

Acknowledgments   6

Useful Addresses   7

Introduction   9

1 HERB SEEDS   18

2 HERB LEAVES   51

3 HERB FLOWERS   82

4 ROOTS AND BULBS WITH
HERBAL PROPERTIES   112

5 ESSENTIAL OILS   145

Suggested Further Reading   170

Index   172

ACKNOWLEDGMENTS

I would like to thank John and Caroline Stevens of Suffolk Herbs for seed information and Joy Larkcom for sharing the experience gained from her charming pottager of salad herbs, flowers and unusual vegetables.

A posy to Sonia Beresford-Hobbs, garland maker, and to Henry Head of Norfolk Lavender. Thanks also to John Stephen from the Cotswold Perfumery Ltd. Christine Hack contributed beautifully prepared recipes using herbal seeds, flowers and roots while Craig Jarvis and Andrew Jacka provided the 'herbal leaf' recipes from Craig Jarvis' country restaurant, Ravenwood Hall, in Suffolk. Many thanks to John and Ciona Hall for their information on eastern and western medicinal herbs, and to a Chinese colleague Cao Heng, for research assistance on culinary and medicinal herbs and gardens in China.

A bouquet to Patricia Davis, who kept me buoyant while writing this book with aromatherapy treatments and, in addition, supplied information about the practice of aromatherapy. Gratitude also to Dr Annie Coxon, neurologist, for sharing her perceptions on the use of aromatherapy in the management of stress.

Thanks to my family who were good-humoured recipients of herbal experiments; to my eldest son Toby Lowe for casting a critical literary eye on my efforts, to young J. J. who didn't complain when his birthday party was postponed, to Rory and Cameron who tolerated late collections from school and most of all to my husband, J. Roger Lowe, for his unfailing support.

USEFUL ADDRESSES

When writing to any of these addresses please enclose a large stamped addressed envelope.

The Herb Society (presently moving their office)
PO Box 415
London SW1P 2HE
(They have a list of herb nurseries in Britain noting those who supply mail order and a list of Herb Gardens open to the public)

The British Herb Trade Assoc
Farnham Court
Church Rd
Farnham Royal
Slough SL2 3AW
(Please include a large SAE. They publish a list of member nurseries and sell a map of nurseries and herb gardens open to the public)

The National Trust
36 Queen Anne's Gate
London SW1H 9AS
(Several National Trust gardens include a herb garden)

Henry Doubleday Research Assoc
Ryton Gardens
Ryton-on-Dunsmore
Coventry CV8 3LG
(National Centre for Organic Gardening and can supply seeds of *Tagetes minuta* and comfrey plants)

British Herbal Medicine Assoc
Lane House
Cowling
Keighley
W Yorkshire
DB22 0LX

The British Migraine Assoc
178a High Road
Byfleet
Weybridge
Surrey
(Publish a leaflet on feverfew)

British Homeopathic Assoc
27a Devonshire Street
London W1N 1RJ

The Institute for Complementary Medicine
14 Upper Harley Street
London NW1 5HE
(For information on practitioners of Chinese or western herbalism)

Natural Medicine Society
Regency House
97–107 Hagley Road
Birmingham B16 8BR
(For those who wish to protect the use and availability of all plant medicines)

The International Federation of Aromatherapists
46 Dalkeith Road
Dulwich
London SE21 8LS

The National Institute of Medical Herbalists
148 Forest Road
Tunbridge Wells
Kent
(School of herbal medicine)

London School of Aromatherapy
PO Box 780
London NW6 5EQ

SUPPLIERS

Herb Seeds

John Chambers
15 Westleigh Road
Barton Seagrave
Kettering
Northamptonshire NN15 5AJ

Suffolk Herbs
Sawyer's Farm
Little Cornard
Sudbury
Suffolk CO10 0NY

Essential Oils

Body Treats Ltd
Ground Floor Suite
15 Approach Road
Raynes Park
London SW20 8BA
(They supply some organically grown oils, particularly lavender)

Norman and Germaine Rich
2 Coval Gardens
London, SW14 7DG
(Wide range, some organic)

Shirley Price Aromatherapy
Wesley House
Stockwell Head
Hinkley
Leicestershire LE10 1RD

Other Suppliers

Norfolk Lavender Ltd
Caley Mill
Heacham
King's Lynn
Norfolk PE31 7JE

Baldwins
173 Walworth Road
London SE17
(For dried herbs and herbal cosmetic ingredients)

Culpeper Ltd (Mail Order)
Hadstock Road
Linton
Cambridgeshire CB1 6NJ

Neal's Yard Apothecary
2 Neal's Yard
London WC2

The Cotswold Perfumery Ltd
Bourton-on-the-Water
Gloucestershire
(Supplies ethyl alcohol)

INTRODUCTION

Herbs are plants which enhance our lives, as they serve and delight us. The group of plants encompassed by the word 'herb' has stretched and shrunk through the ages like an elastic band. The changes run parallel to our relationship with nature. The closer we are to nature, the more plants we consider valuable and hence are considered to be herbs. To the early races and the aboriginal groups still close to nature, almost all plants were considered herbs as they were useful. The whole earth was a continuum in which everything was connected in a profound way. The Cree Indians, for example, say the following when collecting medicinal plants: 'Oh great spirit of the heavens, we beg of you and Mother Earth with her great gifts, that this remedy will do good to those who suffer, we are very thankful.'

In the opening chapter of Genesis, verse 11, the Bible says: 'And God said "Let the earth bring forth grass, the herb yielding seed, and the fruit tree yielding fruit..."' Here, 'herb' appears to include any plant that is neither grass nor a tree; a large range similar to those today classified as herbaceous. Indeed, the two words have the same root.

All the early civilizations valued a large number of herbs. Chinese, Indian, Assyrian and Egyptian cultures each had medical and mystical treatises about the healing and sacred properties of several hundred plants. There were many herbs used for flavouring food, beauty treatments, crafts and celebrations but less is written about these. The recognition of a large number of herbs continued through Greek and Roman societies to Europe and Charlemagne who, in 812 AD, ordered a set list of herbs to be grown on all the imperial farms in his empire.

In sixteenth-century Britain, a wide range of plants were still considered to be herbs, and were roughly divided into four groups. First were the pot herbs, those added to the cooking pot for bulk which

9

included plants like carrots, onions and leeks. (The word 'vegetable' only came into its present meaning around 200 years ago. Before this it was still connected to the meaning of vegetation. Early additions of Mrs Beeton's famous cookery book speak of pot herbs.) Then there were 'sallet' herbs: those used to create a salad, historically a much more adventurous dish than present day efforts, as illustrated by John Evelyn's treatise in 1699 of 72 suitable salad herbs and instructions for their preparation. The third group comprised the sweet herbs used as flavourings, probably the closest to the more recent meaning of the word herb. Several retained this in their names such as sweet cicely, sweet woodruff and sweet marjoram. Finally, there were 'simples'; single herbs used as medical treatments or mixed together to create 'compounds'. The first physic garden in North America was created by a Quaker 'so lads and lasses could know simples'.

What caused the dramatic reduction in the number of plants we call herbs so that by the early to mid-twentieth century the number was reduced to only a few seasoning herbs such as parsley, sage, rosemary, thyme, mint and chives? Part of the answer lies in the effect of science on western development in general and on our relationship with nature and useful plants in particular.

In ancient times it was accepted that a divinity could provide certain individuals with a special knowledge of nature.

In the thirteenth century BC, there lived in Greece a healer who many felt was divinely inspired. His name was Asclepius and he was skilled in the use of herbs. He designed a healing system which by changing old thinking patterns could transform individuals. In this he seems to have understood and treated aspects of stress. Many miracles of healing were attributed to Asclepius and his three healing daughters: Hygieia, Iaso and Panacea. Eventually he was deified and healing temples sprang up across Greece.

The first step towards healing for the crowds who came for treatment was to experience beauty. Stunning sites were chosen for these temple-hospitals and famous architects and artists were commissioned to create and furnish them. The first day's attendance also involved a theatre visit where several thousand would share the emotional richness of soul-charging tragedies; and then have a herbal massage to relieve the emotions. Following days included music, poetry, athletics and fresh air; herbal tonics, compresses and massage; discussions with philosophers, and a visit to the House of Comedians as the Greeks discovered the releasing power of humour.

When a patient felt 'ready' he was sent to the sacred statue of Asclepius to offer a part of himself for healing. The priest or priestess-healer then gave specific herbal remedies. Finally, the visitor would be ready for the 'temple sleep' known as the 'incubation' in a special dormitory, the 'abaton', which slept 240 people. During this time, the thoughts and feeling of their inner turmoil would come to a head (from this the word came to mean the time taken by disease germs to develop before symptoms appear). Deep in the night the priest and priestess would return dressed as Asclepius and Hygieia and carry on a dialogue with the patients about their ailments. Then the priest-healers told the patients to 'Dream the dream of Asclepius'.

By then, each patient was likely to have a potent dream. Some awoke healed and these cures are recorded on many tablets. A celebration ceremony was held in honour of Asclepius and each person's dream was interpreted on many levels. Patients were offered insights into their lives and most departed healthier with an increased sense of their own potential.

The system of Asclepius was practised in Greece for several hundred years and there are temple remains at Cos, Athens and, the most famous, at Epidaurus. Some of his ideas continue today in therapy centres and health resorts.

The inspirational aspect of science is again represented in the work of philosopher and mathematician Pythagorus whose ideas on harmony, theorems of geometry and discoveries about the vibrations of sound were the result of meditation. In the sixth century BC, Pythagorus set up a university to teach the key to universal harmony, both natural and social. Herbs played an important part in the cleansing and restorative routine which preceded advanced learning. Poultices were the favourite method of applying herbs to create a longer, continuous contact with the plants. Pythagorus is said to have held the medical properties of the sea onion in such high regard that he wrote an entire volume on the subject. Herbs were also used in the special high energy food mixture created for his long sojourns alone for contemplation. Poppy and sesame seeds, sea onion skin, daffodil flowers and mallow leaves were mixed in a paste of barley and peas (note: daffodil bulbs are poisonous).

Scholarship flourished in Classical Greece in which the natural world was still considered man's dominant partner. The major contribution of Hippocrates (460–377BC) was to place a scientific framework of diagnosis and treatment around western medicine. He was one of the Aesclepiadae, a group of physicians named after Aesclepius. From him the Hippocratic Oath, a code of conduct for the medical profession, is still honoured by doctors throughout the world. He tried to eliminate the idea of disease as being punishment from the gods and considered food, occupation and climate important factors in disease. He wrote 'Our natures are the physicians of our diseases', and that patients should help their bodies to heal themselves by diet and plant medicines.

Aristotle was one of the world's greatest scholars with interests ranging over the entire natural world including ethics and metaphysics. He championed accurate observation and disciplined theorizing. He organized biological science and wrote many plant descriptions. Philosophy, botany and healing were closely linked; it was a golden age for enquiring minds.

Aristotle's friend and pupil, Theophrastus (372–286 BC), inherited Aristotle's school and garden. Starting with his master's notes and augmented by observation from his own travels and the reports of other colleagues, Theophrastus made the first western attempt to establish a scientific classification of plants.

In honour of Alexander the Great, Alexandria was established and around 300 BC the cultural centre of the Mediterranean shifted to this city. A medical school was established which very soon became world famous, attracting scholars and their works from many countries willing to share ideas. Mithridates, the king of Pontus in Persia from 120 to 63 BC sponsored work on poisons and, in fact, his name has come to mean an antidote to poison. Then, around 60–77 AD Dioscorides travelled through this area as a surgeon with Nero's army and investigated 600 plants including cannabis, hemlock and peppermint which he listed in his *De Mataeria Medica*. This five-volume text became the leading pharmacological reference book for 15 centuries. Galen (130–201 AD) began his career as a physician in the school of gladiators in Alexandria and went on to found, and give his name to, galenic pharmacy, the science of using botanical drugs and the mixing of herbal preparations to treat specific conditions.

Perhaps the highpoint of herbal knowledge was reached around the time of Hypatia (370–415). The sum of human knowledge had been collected and translated at the famous university library in Alexandia. Hypatia was a child prodigy, tutored by the finest scholars of her day. She became famous for her knowledge in the fields of mathematics, astronomy and natural sciences and was eventually appointed head of the University of Alexandria and a government advisor. In her popular lectures, Hypatia tried to effect an intellectual reawakening of the concepts of the Greek deities, particularly the feminine Earth Mother because she could see that respect for the Mother Goddess would return respect and power to women. But she was anathema to the Catholic Church and the Bishop of Alexandria despised her. He did not have the power to openly criticize her so he directed a group of fanatical monks to attack her on her way to deliver her weekly lecture. They viciously hacked her to pieces and burnt the remains. A few years later the same fate befell the Great Library of Alexandria with an incalculable loss of ancient texts from Egypt, Greece, and other Mediterranean cultures.

This could be considered a pointer to the Dark Ages to come. Whereas steps had been taken to rise above the superstitions and ignorance of the past by free-thinking scholars, they were now forbidden to think outside the boundaries imposed by the Catholic Church. The result of this intellectual stifling had such a crippling effect on thinkers and scientists that later, when they were free from these restrictions, the backlash of their treatment resulted in a condemnation of all metaphysical ideas. Ripples still affect objective judgement of the natural sciences, inspirational thought and complementary medicine today.

For example, in his *Natural Medicine*, Brian Inglis reports a cholera outbreak in 1854 which spread through Europe. A homoeopathic hospital had been set up in London and its wards were given over to the care of cholera patients. The newly formed Board of Health inspected the results of all London hospitals and discovered the mortality rate of cholera patients in all the other hospitals was 50 per cent but in the homoeopathic hospital it was only 16.4 per cent. Embarrassed by this information they omitted it from their report to parliament. When a young member, Lord Grosvenor, noted the omission it was reluctantly revealed. When asked the reason for suppressing it, the committee said they were concerned that if the information was made public, 'They would give an unjustified sanction to an empirical practice alike opposed to the maintenance of truth and to the progress of science.'

Through the Dark Ages there was some contact with Arab cultures which had preserved the Greek heritage and made advances in medicine. The court physician, Avicenna (980–1037), an outstanding student of all the natural sciences of his day: philosophy, astronomy, logic, geometry, metaphysics as well as medicine, produced his '*Canon of Medicine*' which became a standard university textbook for 600 years. His second volume describes 811 medicinal plants and minerals from India, Tibet and China and their effect on the human body.

From India, where skills in surgery and mathematics were highly developed, some knowledge filtered through the Arab connection, especially the Indian numerical system of nine digits plus a zero. But the special study of India is that of higher consciousness and, in this, European thought is so deficient that it is scarcely aware of what it is lacking in, though this science may have a more important role to play in the future.

There was also a little contact with China and the Far East through traders like Marco Polo and later through missionaries. The West remains curiously ignorant of its debt to China, though, in that the three main inventions which Francis Bacon declared were crucial to the transformation of European society – the magnetic compass, gun powder and the printing press – all came from China. From the Far East also came spices awakening new culinary zest in the rather basic fare of the times and these fetched high prices.

There was the occasional spark of light during Europe's Dark Ages. One was the writing of Hildegarde of Bingen, an abbess, scientist, musician, herbal healer, prophetess and visionary. In her two works, *Physica* and *Causa et Cure*, she was probably the first to use common names along with Latin names for herbs.

But early in the fifteenth century, the general economy of Europe had been weakened by the Black Death; universities were in decline and the Church was disintegrating. Apart from isolated examples of free thinking, dogma dominated religion, philosophy, medicine and many other branches of learning, including herbalism.

By good fortune, several ideas matured concurrently. The first area of fresh thinking in Europe came in the Renaissance of Italy where artists rediscovered classical Greek and Latin thinking and their human, as opposed to divine, centered universe. The visual arts and their craftsmen rose in social esteem and artists became people of wide cultural interests, examplified by Leonardo Da Vinci.

At the same time, in a mining area of southern Germany, practical mathematics was being used to develop skills in metallurgy. Along the trade route from this area to the weaving centres of Flanders, these skills were used to create the alloy metals suitable for making the replaceable bits of type for the printing press of Gütenberg. Once developed, the press spread rapidly along the trade routes. Herbals were among the first books published and there was an explosion of learning from this newly available information.

World travel routes were being discovered. The desire for spices introduced from the Orient (spice is another word whose meaning shifts; it was then defined as any exotic comestible from the Far East, like flavourings, condiments and drugs), and the lucrative business involved, led to a search for new sources of these products and new trade routes by the Spanish and Portuguese. The resulting world exploration brought the 'discovery' of the Americas and Australia. This long-distance travel demanded higher standards of astronomy and mathematical instruments and science filled the need. On the return currents, new plants were introduced from the New World and the Far East along with their herbal uses.

In the sixteenth century, the Protestant Reformation curbed the religious stranglehold on scientific thinking and sparked off wars in which the gentlemen officers needed higher levels of scientific learning. This reduced the amount of class snobbery against engineering and surgery paving the way for a more generally acceptable new 'scientific', that is measurable, view of the world.

But many scientific discoveries were made by those who still held metaphysical beliefs. In 1600, the Englishman William Gilbert explained why a compass needle moved, saying that the earth was a giant, weak magnet. He also set out to prove that the world's soul was embodied in that magnet. In 1609, Kepler discovered the elliptical orbits of the planets around the sun while searching for cosmic harmonies, and another Englishman William Harvey, interested in the concept of the human as a microcosmic image of the world movements, established the circulation of the blood.

This blend of scientific observation within an intuitive philosophy was best exemplified by Paracelsus, the 'medical Luther' of the sixteenth century. He combined metallurgy with mysticism and was the most successful chemist of his day. He seemed to have extra-sensory perception and was famous for many miraculous cures. He developed a treatment for syphilis with small doses of mercury and showed that 'miner's disease' (silicosis) came from breathing metal vapours and was not, as previously thought, a punishment from mountain spirits. This did not please the mine owners. He stated that each plant had a mark which indicated its medicinal use. He foresaw homoeopathy when he declared 'what makes a man ill also cures him if given in small doses' and he is said to have cured many people in the plague town of Stertzing with a minute dose of their own excretia in a bread pill. He also did pioneering work in what was later called psychiatry, work acknowledged by Carl Jung.

Paracelsus loudly declared, 'Reason is a Great Open Folly, Imagination is Creative Power. Resolute Imagination can accomplish all things; He who is born in imagination discovers the latent forces of Nature.' This so irked those who argued for the power of logic that his surname, Bombast, became the adjective it is today.

The new philosophy of the seventeenth century propounded that objects and occurrences like storms were just ordinary things without human or divine properties. We dismissed the threatening gods of volcanoes and hurricanes but with them went the comforting spirits of trees and herbs. Then followed the so-called scientific revolution. Before, during, and after this time, irrespective of labels, enquiring minds continued to investigate the world around them and this is true science. The scientific revolution was not a change in this activity but rather a change in how science viewed itself and the cosmos. It changed the perception of the universe from that of a living whole to a dead machine and perhaps this is the inherent flaw which led to lifeless products. There was a string of new inventions with the industrial revolution but with them came canned food with synthetic flavourings and cosmetics with chemical preservatives to extend the shelf-life of cheaper ingredients. There were synthetic perfumes (the first famous one was Chanel No. 5), chemical dyes, household cleaning products and medical drugs, all previously made from herbs. Scientists learned to analyse the components of herbs to select the active ingredients and synthesize them, and then businessmen convinced the public and doctors that the synthetics were preferable. Herbs had been tainted with images of witchcraft, superstition, and folk lore and gradually the use and even the knowledge of herbs faded away in the great admiration for laboratory science.

Eventually the pendulum began to swing back. The mid-twentieth century brought the dropping of atomic bombs and caused fears that scientific knowledge, if given over to business or the military while scientists exercise no social responsibility, will create moral problems. In the late twentieth century, there is further disquiet. Because the scientific revolution literally dismissed the heart and soul from the universe, the lack of awareness and respect for the entity of the earth has brought us near-fatal pollution.

There was a reaction against the growing sterility of science as early as the French revolution by a group who called for 'Science for the people' and in Germany a romantic reaction called *Naturphilosophie* was led by the poet Goethe and the philosopher Schelling. They condemned the lack of soul in dry, experimental science and proposed a philosophy of nature which attempted to synthesize the physical and spiritual world. One adherent, the Danish physicist Hans Christian Orsted, in his search to demonstrate the unity and polarity of the forces of nature, discovered electromagnetism in 1820. Julius von Mayer, a physician with a similar goal, developed the notion of the conservation of energy in 1841.

Eventually a bitter feud developed between the 'dead universe' scientists and *Naturphilosophers* and though the opinion of the 'dead universe' scientists prevailed, they were so haunted by the *Naturphilosophie* that they reacted by ridiculing all non-conformist ideas so further reinforcing the dry inhuman aspect of their approach which was so distasteful to artists like Goethe. It meant, too, that when something like acupuncture was shown to work, the 'dead universe' scientists had no mental process to cope with the information.

Now we are returning to a more balanced middle ground, some scientists – especially physicists – find common ground with ancient philosophies such as Taoism with regard to understanding the forces of the universe. As we again draw closer to nature our concept of a herb has expanded in line with its original meaning.

The ideas of physicists like David Bohm in *Wholeness and the Implicate Order*; the explanation of new areas of research in physics written for the lay-person by Gary Zukav in *The Dancing Wu Li Masters*, and most especially the extraordinary and beautiful concept of *Gaia*, by James Lovelock, which shows how the earth is a self-regulating entity maintaining an environment in which our concept of life is sustainable, reinforce the inter-relation of all things. As if to reinforce the value of the intuitive side of science, even the beauty and fragrance of herbs have been shown to have a beneficial effect on our health and this was my introduction to herbs.

My gardening began with a strong desire to grow things but with only a vague notion of how to begin. As a child in Edmonton, Canada, I made the classicially terrible dog's dinner rock gardens. I hauled home large stones where the pile was tolerated but the donated plants usually died as I had no understanding of how to nurture them.

Despite my ignorance and failure, the desire to grow things remained. In my first balcony flat in London, I grew a row of sweet peas in plastic coffee cups, intoxicated with the idea of creating a wall of the sweet-scented flowers. But I just dug the soil from a large, communal shrubbery and in the hard, caked soil they too quickly expired.

When a visitor gave me my first gardening book, *The Small Garden* by CE Phillips I was amazed to discover the depth of my ignorance. From then on I read every gardening book I could get. However, a streak of Prairie Puritan re-emerged in my first 'proper garden' and at first I only grew vegetables.

Then I began to learn about herbs. These, too, were useful plants, but also beautiful. A door opened and I gave way to their voluptuous energy. As I began learning more, other interests were woven in. In my teens, I had fluctuated between wanting to be an astronomer and an artist, settling for design as a sort of middle ground. Herbs satisfied both these interests. A scientific attitude helps the understanding of the nutritional and medical properties of herbs while designing a herb garden, collecting and using their aromatic and colourful leaves and flowers, gladdens the heart of the artist latent in us all.

This gardening experience had wider benefits. The earthiest of subjects, it still gives me great pleasure to have my hands in healthy friable soil and to marvel at the mysteries of germination. There is the physical exercise of gardening and the benefits to health and appearance of using herbs. Emotions benefit, too, as frustrations drop away in the company of herbs and there is the soothing effect of a massage with aromatic plant essences. Mentally, the calming atmosphere of a herb garden is an excellent place to sit and solve problems.

Sitting in a herb garden, surrounded by plants which appeal to the head as well as the heart, plants with herbal links with the past, thoughts also move to the future. Understanding expands from the personal to wider issues with concern for holistic health and ecological issues. It eventually encompasses the implications of the fact that we share one planet and all our futures are linked.

Now the word 'herb' is more an expression of cultural attitudes and activities than a precise category. Herbs are persuasive teachers and they will open as many doors for exploration as you allow them to.

1
HERB SEEDS

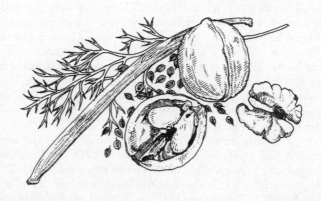

Our long and intimate association with seeds is revealed in archaeological digs which show seeds both in the digestive tract of our ancestors and in the culinary and craft debris of their living quarters. Seeds have always been an important dietary source of protein, minerals and trace elements and the seeds of fat hen (*Chenopodium album*), a common weed and reasonable salad herb, were found among the stomach contents of the mud-preserved Iron Age Tollund Man in Sweden. Another seed from prehistoric finds is that of marsh mallow or the wild hollyhock (*Althaea officinalis*). These grow encased in a ring called a cheese and if picked at their plumpest and sprinkled on a salad, they will add a mildly flavoured nutty texture.

Mustard seed has also been in use for thousands of years both as a condiment and as a medicine. Ancient Greek physicians held this seed in such high esteem for its ability to relieve respiratory congestion and pain that they attributed its discovery to the legendary healer Aesclepius. The Greek philosopher and botanist Theophrastus (372–286 BC) and Dioscorides, a physician and botanist writing in the first century AD, paid tribute to mustard as well as aniseed and dill seed. In the same century in Rome the loquacious Pliny, in his 37 volumes of Natural History, noted 40 remedies with mustard as chief ingredient.

It was also a culinary favourite of the Romans who named mustard from 'mustum', the 'must' or newly-fermented grape-juice in which they steeped the seed, and 'ardens' for fiery. Indeed, the Romans cooked an

18

encyclopaedic range of animal and vegetable species and seemed to find the idea of a dish served unadorned as uncomprehensible. They made complicated sauces with interesting, if unusual, mixtures of herbs and spices and mustard seed was one of the main ingredients in their extravaganza of flavours.

Recipes from the first-century Roman Cookery Book of Apicius include mustard in a coating for preserved meat and turnips, mixed with pine kernals and cumin to serve with boiled beets and green beans; in a sauce with lovage and thyme for boiled ostrich; in a sauce with coriander, mint and dates for boiled crane or duck; mixed with caraway, dates and wine in a stock for wood-pigeons, served with dates and dill seed on chicken; pounded with caraway, pepper and salted sea-urchin as a stuffing for sow's udder; in a sauce with celery-seed, caraway, savory, safflower and onions to pour over meat slices; mixed with grilled coriander, celery, caraway, dill seed and toasted almonds to serve on wild boar boiled in sea-water and wine with bay leaves; and in recipes for venison, veal, hare, prawns, electric ray and tuna-fish, usually in a sweet sour mixture of vinegar or wine and honey. One can only marvel at their digestive system and sympathize with their need to serve little cakes of digestive seeds at the end of their extraordinary meals.

The Romans probably taught the Celts how to use mustard seed by soaking it in new wine with enough honey to make a consistency suitable for rolling into tiny balls. Later generations made variations, often adding cinnamon and soaking the seeds in vinegar instead of wine.

Love Potions

Mustard was often used in a poultice to bring blood to the surface to relieve congestion and this ability to rouse the system to activity earned mustard seed a place in love potions. Coriander seed was also considered to have such powers for the Persians who developed an elaborate charm to return an erring husband. 'Mix cloves, cinnamon and coriander in a large jar; recite over this seven times backward the 'Yasin' chapter of the Koran; then fill the jar with rose water. Immerse a shirt of the husband and a piece of paper with the name of the truant on all four angles in to the jar and place it over a fire. As soon as boiling begins, the husband is on his way home.'

Caraway was believed to prevent departures so it, too, was used in love potions. The same principle is employed by today's pigeon fanciers who claim that a tame pigeon will always return if there is baked caraway seed bread in its dove cote. Cardamom was yet another seed used in love philtres as it was considered to be an aphrodisiac by the Greeks and Romans. Perhaps this was simply because it makes the breath sweeter. The use of cardamom (a Greek word for 'spice plant') is recorded in Sanskrit, eighth century BC. It is also listed as one of the 400 simples noted by Hippocrates in the fifth century BC and is still used by Arabs in curries or as candy and sometimes chewed to relieve indigestion.

Seed Use Today

Today, our most important food staples come from seeds: the grains of rice, wheat, soya, corn, barley and oats. Traditional herbal activities include seeds grown for cosmetic, household and medicinal uses. The favourite domestic use is undoubtedly still as seasoning. Flavouring seeds include aniseed, caraway, coriander, cumin, dill, fennel, fenugreek, lovage, mustard, poppy, sesame and smallage (wild celery) which can all be grown in a temperate climate although the annuals aniseed, cumin, fenugreek and sesame require a long, hot summer.

Many seeds are used to flavour foods and the strongly aromatic ones are commonly called spices, especially if they come from the Far East. However, the word is imprecise and any definition is immediately followed by exceptions. It now generally refers to highly flavoured plant parts excluding leaves but including bark (cinnamon) and roots (ginger) which are used in cooking. From the early meaning there still lingers the implication that they come from distant countries.

When first introduced, pungent seeds like peppercorns, cloves and nutmeg, transformed existing tastes and soon demand for these new spices exceeded supply resulting in expanding trade routes.

THE FUNCTION OF SEEDS

The survival of the species is nature's strongest call and the production of seed is the plant kingdom's main response. Quite simply, seeds are formed in the ovary of a flower after it has been fertilized by pollen and there they ripen to become a model of perfect packaging.

Inside the protective seed coat, each seed contains an embryo which is the beginning of a new plant. There is also enough stored food for the embryo to establish itself in the soil. This food is often stored in the two seed leaves (cotyledons) surrounding the embryo in the seed. The two sections are easily visible in such seeds as peas and beans and in these plants they are large and nutritious enough for us to make use of them as food.

Small seeds, such as chamomile, have less food reserve and therefore less strength to grow any distances through the soil and that is why they must not be deeply buried when sown – give them only a light sprinkling of soil to anchor them.

It would be difficult to design a seed-sized computer capable of performing all the functions of a seed. Apart from storing the genetic information for future growth and reproduction it also incorporates a mechanism for dispersal. Though a few herb seeds just drop where they ripen, most have evolved a more sophisticated system.

Methods of Dispersal

Tiny black poppy seeds (*Papaver* species) stay in their pepper-pot shells until the stems bend enough in the wind to allow the seeds to escape through small holes around the rim. This can take them 24 to 36 in (60 to 100 cm) away from the mother plant. Dry seed pods of the witches broom (*Cytisus scoparius*) suddenly twist open and jerk their seed a little further away. Meadow crane's bill (*Geranium pratense*) develops a hair trigger and when touched by wind or animal it catapults the seed to a new location. Others have hooks or spines that catch on passing animals. Once you have brushed by a ripened plant of the medicinal hound's tongue (*Cynoglossum officinale*) or viper's bugloss (*Echium vulgare*), the seed burrs will remain in your memory and elsewhere! Aiming to travel further afield, the seed of thistles and dandelions have exquisite parachutes attached and the papery wings of maple seed are famous as the helicopter archetype. Some seeds take a packaged flight; seeds in fleshy berries are eaten by birds and a few survive intact to be deposited complete with fertilizer.

Seed Dormancy

A seed also needs to be able to recognize when the time is suitable to begin growing. With some seeds, this means continuous monitoring until certain temperatures or light levels are registered as acceptable for germination. The chemical computer in a seed is also sensitive to moisture levels and the composition of gases in the soil. By giving each factor its own level of importance the seed can compromise where necessary.

Most seeds have a built-in period of dormancy, up to several years for some species. The shortest time is reserved for those seeds which have evolved in climates that remain constant throughout the year such as tropical areas or for seed produced early in the season when the seed will have all summer to become established. The downy seeds of willow blow

along the river in early summer with a good chance of taking hold even though they have a life-span of only one week. Angelica seeds also germinate best when they have just ripened and only a few will maintain their viability (their ability to germinate), over the winter.

Stratification

Some seeds, like those of sweet cicely (*Myrrhis odorata*), bluebells (*Endymion nonscriptus*), juniper (*Juniperus communis*), violets (*Viola odorata*) and sweet woodruff (*Asperula odorata*) have a hard coat to protect them during winter. In fact, they actually need a cold period to eventually break down the outer coat, the period of stratification. Such seeds therefore need to be planted in autumn so that they will be ready to germinate the following spring. If this is not possible, the winter experience can be substituted by mixing the seed with damp sand in a polythene bag or container and placing in a refrigerator (not a freezer) for 6 to 8 weeks. Then move the seeds to a warmer place (about 60–65°F or 25°C) until the first green shoot appears. At the first sign of growth, plant the seedlings into pots of suitable compost in a cold greenhouse, or outdoors if the weather is suitable. As with all young seedlings, try to avoid sudden changes in temperature.

Scarification

Scarification is sometimes confused with stratification but scarification refers to a treatment to speed the germination of the seeds of leguminous species – those whose roots fix nitrogen in the soil as they grow, such as sweet peas, melilot, clovers and sainfoin. The hard seed coat is not broken down by cold temperatures, but instead by moisture. It takes several weeks for water to penetrate the seed coat but this time can be reduced by carefully rubbing the seed with sandpaper or nicking it with a knife, taking care not to damage the delicate embryo inside.

Germination Triggers

Some seeds germinate in response to the length of daylight and the soil temperature. Tiny poppy seeds and winter savory will only begin to grow either in the presence of strong light or large temperature fluctuations, both of which occur only when the seed is on or near the surface. This ensures that it has enough food in its tiny reservoir to reach the light. This is also why earth moving, which brings buried seed up to the surface, gives a crop of poppies the following summer and why the battlefields of Flanders produced their heartwarming display during the First World War.

When a seed registers that adequate conditions for germination have arrived, it allows moisture to penetrate the seed coat which swells the seed leaves inside until they push open the seed. The embryo divides into two parts, sending first a radicle downwards in response to gravity to anchor the plant in the soil. When this begins to grow root hairs the seed sends a shoot upward into the light to grow leaves.

SOWING SEEDS

Armed with the understanding of how a seed functions it is easier to see the reasons for particular requirements in order to achieve successful growth. Spring is the primary time of sowing and if you are sowing outdoors it is necessary to wait for the proper weather conditions or you may loose a frustrating number of seedlings. Watch the spring soil for weed germination as an indication that the soil has warmed up enough. Having spent my early gardening years impatiently sowing seeds too soon, I now like to wait until the first flush of weeds has germinated, both as a soil temperature check and so that I can remove them before sowing my seeds.

Herb plants can be divided into annuals: those which grow, flower and die in one growing season; biennials which begin to grow in one season, overwinter and then flower and die the following year and perennials which live for several years. Herbaceous perennials are those which die back to their roots each autumn and send up new growth each spring. Several plants behave in a way to muddy the edges of these definitions. Hardy annuals like chervil, borage and calendula will sometimes overwinter and flower the following spring if they are about 6 in (15 cm) high in the autumn and have not yet produced any flowers. This means that with a little foresight you can have the sky blue flowers of borage, the golden petals of calendula and fresh chervil leaves for your spring salads. Occasionally biennials like foxglove, woad and evening primrose that have become large plants in their second year, will send new side shoots from the base to grow on in the third year instead of dying as scheduled.

All annual and biennial herbs are grown from seed. Of the perennials, though, many are easier to propagate by methods other than seed; for example, rosemary, sage, tarragon and lavender from cuttings or mint

23

and sweet woodruff from runners. Other perennials are worth growing from seed as they are easy to germinate. This group includes catnep, chamomile (flowering), chives, fennel (green and bronze), feverfew, good King Henry, hyssop, lovage, marjoram (French), oregano, rue, sage (common), salad burnet, sorrel, sweet cicely, thyme (common), Welsh onion, winter savory, and wormwood. Indeed, growing from seed may be the only way to obtain many of the wild flower herbs and unusual herbs from abroad.

It is also worth remembering that if you are likely to require only one plant of a herb such as lovage, angelica or sweet cicely, it is probably cheaper and easier to purchase it.

Herbs which can be used in abundance outdoors like parsley, and perhaps coriander leaf ('cilantro' is the coriander variety to grow for more leaf production), dill for flowering heads, florence fennel and salad herbs, can be sown in rows or scattered in patches in the vegetable garden. Several plants of chives and sorrel can be located in the herb garden or with perennial vegetables like asparagus or rhubarb.

Sowing and Germinating Seeds Outdoors

Mark out a shallow drill with the rake handle. Sow the seeds thinly, including the tiny ones, say 3–5 per inch or ½–1 cm apart. Cover lightly with ¼–½ in (6–12 cm) of soil; even less for small seeds like poppy and summer savory. Tap in gently with the back of the rake head to ensure the seeds make contact with as much soil as possible. Label your row with the seed packet or a waterproof marking (pencil is waterproof and sunbleach proof).

In very dry weather, water the seed drill (not the surrounding area) before sowing until it is muddy. Drop the seed in this moist soil and then cover with *dry* soil, as this prevents evaporation and should keep the seed moist until it has germinated.

Once the seeds have germinated, thin the seedlings to 2–4 in (5–10 cm) by pinching out the surplus at ground level to avoid disturbing neighbouring roots. The thinnings of suitable herbs can be used in salads or soups. Parsley requires a high temperature to germinate quickly because in its natural biennial cycle it would seed in high summer giving sturdy young plants to overwinter and flower the following year. In hot weather it will germinate in two weeks, but if planted in spring, parsley can take up to seven weeks.

Sowing and Germinating in Trays

Sowing in trays or pots is also a good idea for rare or expensive seeds that it is necessary to keep an eye on, and for those herbs whose seedling appearance may be unfamiliar.

To have seeds germinate at a time of our choosing it is necessary to simply supply the conditions which would trigger germination in their natural state. Usually this means moisture and warmth, and later, light and ventilation. For each herb seed it is a question of learning the right balance.

Start with a clean seed tray or pot. Sterilize used containers in a disinfectant if you suspect there may have been any disease in the previous soil or plant occupants. Buy a seed compost or make your own by mixing two parts sterilized loam (rich garden soil), one part fine peat and one part coarse sand with a dash of fertilizer. As most seed contains enough food to get the seedlings started, the dash is only necessary to tide them over until they are transplanted. Blend the mixture well and shake through a ⅜ in (8 mm) sieve.

A shallow tray that is 2 in (5 cm) deep is best for small seeds though any pots are acceptable. Add your compost to within ¼ in (6 mm) of the top. Give the container a sharp tap to settle the soil and then press gently with a flat board or lid. This should leave your final soil level about ½ in (12 cm) from the rim. A tray- or pot-sized board with a grip handle on the top is something a child could construct in a woodworking class and would be a valuable luxury for a keen gardener.

If the soil is very dry, water it first and leave it to drain. Then sow the seed thinly and evenly. Sieve a fine layer of compost over the top making the layer only as deep as the diameter of the seed.

Label and date your tray and cover with a sheet of glass or clear plastic. Add newspaper if it will be in direct sunlight. Seeds should be checked daily for germination at which time they must be moved into gentle light and given air. Do this by lifting the glass along one edge for two days. Then remove the glass but shade the seedlings from bright sun for a few more days.

When they need watering, water gently with a fine rose. Begin by watering off the edge of the tray, move evenly over it and end off the other end of the tray to avoid heavy splashes on the soil surface. Or better still, water from below by setting the pot in water just long enough for the surface to appear damp.

POTTING ON

If seeds are sown in small, individual pots, soilblocks or trays with divisions, the plants will suffer no check when moved to a larger container. They will gain perhaps a week's growing time over plants potted on in the traditional way which causes some root disturbance. When the first pair of true leaves has developed, tease out the seedling, keeping soil around the roots if possible and pot on to a small, individual container. A soil-based mixture is best and the growing plant will now require a fertile medium. The traditional potting mixture (John Innes no. 2) is made up of seven parts sterilized loam, three parts peat and two parts grit or sharp sand with nutrients added. (The difference between sharp sand and soft or builder's sand is important. Grains of sharp sand have rough facets which create tiny air spaces and drainage routes in the soil whereas builder's sand has a smooth, rounded surface and fills in tiny air spaces creating the opposite effect.)

Herbs grown in containers can be planted out whenever the ground is not frozen. Prepare an area larger than the container, water it well, line it with a crumbly soil similar in consistency to the soil in the container so the roots will get away more easily. Remove the plant from container carefully and spread the roots if they appear cramped. Fill in with a similar soil, press down gently and water in. Tuck in your label nearby for reference. If planting a Mediterannean type herb such as rosemary, thyme, santolina, savoury, lavender or sage, in heavy clay soils, add a small bucket of grit to the planting area, working it in at least 12 in (30 cm) deep to improve the drainage.

Handling plants over a period of time you will develop a 'feel' for different types. You will recognise the silver plants – the artemisias, curry plant and lavender – that like sun and dryish sandy soils; the resinous-leaved Mediterranean herbs like rosemary, thymes and sages that want sun and ample space for a good root run in light soil. You will respond to the lush leaved plants like angelica, sorrel and mint with a moisture retentive soil, and to those herbs like parsley, chives and comfrey, which give us valuable nutrients, you will supply a fertile soil in return.

HARVESTING SEEDS

Seeds are collected both for their use in recipes and for future propagation. Pick them on a warm, dry day when they are fully ripe. This is when seeds have turned from green to buff, brown or black and are hard with paper-dry pods.

Collect them in paper bags. Shake the seeds directly into a bag, or if they do not fall easily, snip the whole stalk with the seed head and separate later. For propagation, choose seeds from the best plants – either the most vigorous or most highly scented or with greatest leaf production, whichever trait you value in that herb. From umbellifera herbs, save seeds from the top centre seed head as these are said to have the highest germination rate. Dry sunflower heads whole and separate the seeds for storage when they become loose. Keep each variety separate and have a pen with you to label the bags.

Dry for a further two weeks indoors to ensure no moisture remains. Lay them loosely on paper or hang the stalks upside down with a box below to catch the seeds. Then rub the seeds from their stalks or pods and store in airtight jars for culinary use, labelling with the variety and date.

Store seeds for propagation in paper packets or envelopes and place all the envelopes in a large container with a packet of silica gel crystals. These will absorb moisture in the air which might otherwise trigger germination. Aim to keep them dry, dark and at a cool, even temperature indoors. There are cards available now with chemical charts like litmus paper which read the level of moisture in the air by turning pink when damp. These can be stored with the seeds to act as a constant monitor.

DESIGNING A HERB GARDEN

If you have the good fortune to have the space for a herb garden, you have the pleasurable task of designing it. It is the ultimate artistic venture as you are dealing with shape and form in three dimensions, with texture and with colour – and with the evocative powers of scent. You can also take a tip from the ancient Chinese garden builders and consider sound such as wind playing solar chords through stems. And over all of this, there is the changing panorama created by consecutive seasons.

Try to choose a site with at least three quarters of the area in sun to allow you to grow the widest range of herbs. Most herbs, like vegetables, prefer a slightly alkaline soil and most need good drainage. If the site is open, consider a wide break – either a wall or hedge of herbal trees or shrubs – to create privacy, confine the perfumes for your pleasure, and give a settled atmosphere where bees and butterflies can work undisturbed.

Paths are important in planning and their design and material will create the style of your garden. Herbs are such exuberant, generous plants that they need some form of discipline as a contrast. A geometric path design offers just such as contrast, gives the garden a pattern in winter months and, of course, provides access to your plants. Select the path materials with care. Grass, gravel or wood chippings can look attractive but require some upkeep. Hard surfaces last longest and old materials, old bricks and stone slabs offer the most beautiful colours. But sadly they are not easily obtained and often very expensive.

If buying hard materials, think carefully about the colours. Take a large bottle of water with you to garden centres so that you can test colours in the wet. This is where the crudeness of many concrete products shows up. There is really no excuse for the lack of hard surfaces with good textures and subtle colours – except that so many people continue to buy them.

Think about planting in all three dimensions. Tall plants or features such as a pergola or arch can focus interest and block out unsightly views. They can also be used to lift scented flowers and leaves to nose height and above. And finally, perhaps the most important feature, plan to include a seat in your garden.

The choice of plants for a herb garden is enormous. Place your favourites first, in the sun or shade as appropriate, with scented plants near the seat. New culinary and aromatic plants will want a space as you discover them. Most herbs are easy to move around in spring or autumn so changes and adjustments are not a problem.

OIL EXTRACTS

The high oil content of many seeds provides us with a rich source of useful oils. Edible vegetable oils are used for frying, roasting, marinades and salad dressings. Those with a light texture and little scent are used in cosmetic recipes and for massage. 'Drying' oils, such as linseed, have industrial applications and are used by oil painters while many other oils are used commercially in soap-making.

Oils are extracted from seeds by pressing and the best culinary oils are 'cold pressed'. As its name suggests, no heat is involved and the resulting oil is considered superior in nutritional content and flavour. The seed residue left after oil extraction is known as 'oilcake' and often makes a valuable contribution to livestock feed. Essential oils, used in perfumery, are extracted by distillation and treated separately in Chapter 5.

Almond

Sweet almond oil is expressed from the seed of both sweet and bitter almonds. It has a mild, nutty, sweet flavour which can be used for salad dressings but its main use is in cosmetic preparations.

The sweet almond (*Prunus amaygdalus* var. *dulcis*) is a small tree of southern Europe and western Asia which can be grown in sheltered areas of Britain. The edible nut is an important culinary ingredient used whole, flaked and ground. Of all nuts, almonds have the largest share of world trade.

The bitter almond (*Prunus amygdalus* var. *amara*) is a small native tree of Mediterranean countries. This variety is the chief source of 'oil of bitter almonds' which has a distinctive strong taste used as a flavouring. It is not a pressed oil but a flavouring created by mixing ground nuts with water. The bitter almond flavour only develops at the mixing stage in a reaction similar to that when making mustard. An enzyme is released which creates two new substances: benzaldehyde (or oil of bitter almonds) plus about 2–4% hydrocyanic acid (prussic acid). Both taste of bitter almonds, but the prussic acid is deadly poisonous. Fortunately it is highly volatile and evaporates completely when heated but crude sources of bitter almond flavouring may be poisonous and are best avoided.

Apricot Kernel and Peach Kernel

The oils from both of these seeds have the same properties as sweet almond oil but are more expensive.

Avocado (*Persea americana*)

The oil from this tropical plant is used mainly for skin care. It is rich in vitamins A, B, D and lecithin which gives the oil skin healing properties particularly helpful for dry skins.

Carrot (*Daucus carota*)

The extraction of carrot oil needs expert attention as it mainly consists of water with tiny amounts of oil in suspension. It is a treasure chest of vitamins, being rich in A, B, C, D, E and F and is used externally for skin care products. Carrot oil has some screening effect against the sun's UVA rays which accelerate wrinkle formation.

Coconut Palm (*Cocos nucifera*)

This is a tall handsome, tropical tree which tolerates salty sandy soils. It produces a fruit with a fibrous exterior and a seed inside, the coconut. Within unripe nuts is a thin layer of white flesh and a refreshing, nutritious, watery liquid called 'coconut milk'. As the nut ripens, the flesh absorbs most of the liquid. Recipes calling for coconut milk (such as in some Indian curries), are not referring to this but instead to a liquid made by macerating shredded coconut flesh in hot water and squeezing out the cream. The white flesh is sometimes available as edible coconut but most often it is dried when it becomes known as copra. Coconut oil is extracted from the copra and mainly used in soap and cosmetics.

Corn (*Zea mays*)

Corn is an annual crop which takes from 3 to 5 months to mature. This is the familiar corn-on-the-cob, or sweet corn, plant. Commercial 'corn-flour' is a finely ground form of the maize meal and 'corn flakes' are made from pre-cooked, flaked and toasted maize grain. Maize is a good source of starch but its protein has a lower nutritional value than other cereals.

The oil expressed from the seeds is reasonably priced with a mild taste. It is a good oil for frying but most cooks consider it too heavy for mixing in a salad dressing. It is an acceptable massage oil though not first choice. Vegetable oils on their own keep quite well but once essential oils have been added they tend to oxidize and turn rancid after a month or two. Corn oil has the least keeping qualities so if it is required for storage in mixtures, add 5% wheatgerm oil to double its storage time.

Evening Primrose (*Oenothera biennis*)

This biennial is an introduced wild flower with soft yellow fragrant flowers which open at twilight. An oil is pressed from the seeds which contains gamma-linoleic acid and is proving very useful medicinally.

Grapeseed (*Vitis vinifera*)

This oil is extracted from the seeds of various grapes. One of the oldest cultivated plants on earth, the grapevine (giving us grapes, wine and raisins), has a long pedigree. But the oil from the seeds has only been extracted on a large scale in the last few years. It is a fine, clear, light oil, almost tasteless and odourless and very low in saturated fats. Though a little more expensive than the most common cooking oils, it is very pleasant in salad dressings and marinades and has a high smoke point which makes it useful for frying.

Groundnut or Peanut (*Arachis hypogaea*)

This plant is an annual, with yellow pea flowers belonging to the legume family. It prefers a light soil and subtropical climate to develop its crop in 4–5 months. The flower stalks push into the soil where the seeds – or peanuts – develop underground. The highly nutritious seeds contain Vitamins B and E, 30% protein and 40–50% oil.

Peanuts are familiar eaten fresh or roasted and salted and they are used whole in the recipes of tropical countries where they are grown. Peanut butter is made by removing the skin and germ and grinding the roasted nuts. The oil pressed from the nuts is usually refined, making it virtually tasteless and this makes it popular for cooking and salads and one of the most important oils used for making margarine. It has a high smoke point so it is good for frying. The oil is also used for packing fish like tinned sardines and tuna. Cosmetically, if unrefined, its distinctive colour and oilier feel make its less favoured for massage and lotions.

Hazelnut (*Corylus avellana*)

This native shrub yields a nut oil with a distinctive flavour that is low in saturated fats. As it is more expensive than most other oils it is usually reserved for special salads.

Jojoba *(Simmondsia chinensis)*

This is a tender, shrubby evergreen 2–8 ft (60 cm–2.4 m) tall which grows in semi-arid land. The seeds contain a scentless, clear, waxy oil which is very stable because it is indigestible to bacteria and humans. This liquid wax has the same properties which made sperm whale oil so valuable so now there is no longer any reason for killing the whales. As it dissolves sebum, it is good for acne and gives a satin smooth feel to the skin. It is much used in shampoos, creams and lotions.

Linseed *(Linum usitatissimum)*

Linseed is the seed of flax, the source of linen. Flax is a graceful upright annual, 1–2 ft (30–60 cm) high, with delicate blue flowers and it grows well in this country in deep, moist loam. Linseed oil has been used medicinally as a laxative and by veterinaries as a purgative for sheep and horses. The seed is used in bird-feed mixtures and the oil-cake is used as a fattening food for cattle, but neither the seed nor the oil is used for human consumption.

The oil is important to the paint and varnish industry and valued by oil painters. When mixed with oil paints it makes the colours easier to manipulate on the canvas and when it dries it gives a slight glaze to the colours which helps display the richness of the pigments – like the difference between a stone wet and dry.

Mustard *(Sinapis species)*

Various annual varieties of mustard seed are pressed to give an edible yellow oil. It has a strong pungent flavour when raw but sweet when heated to a light haze and gives a regional flavour to certain Bengal and Kashmir dishes. It is also used by watch repairers as a frost proof lubricant.

The pressed oil should never be confused with essential oil of mustard which is distilled from the seeds. The essential oil is deadly and connected with the making of mustard gas.

Olive *(Olea europaea)*

The olive is a small, slow-growing, evergreen tree that has been valued and cropped since prehistoric times. Moses exempted men from military duty who worked at its cultivation. The word oil comes from the Latin for olive, so close is the association of oil with olives. Olives are very bitter and need to be washed in water several times and soaked in brine to reduce the bitterness. Mediterranean markets offer a wide range of varieties and styles of preparation of both the green (unripe) and black (ripe) olives. They can be found flavoured with garlic, fennel, thyme and other herbs as well as the more common stuffing of sweet red pepper.

The tree originated in the Mediterranean and prefers a well-drained soil in a dry area of sub tropical or warm temperate climate. It can be grown in sheltered areas of Britain and with a good summer will occasionally produce fruit.

Olive oil is pressed from the fresh ripe fruit and has long been used medicinally. Internally it found favour as a laxative, as a mechanical antidote to irritant poisons, and in enemas. Externally it is a good vehicle for liniments, a valuable skin lubricant for massaging painful muscles and joints.

Olive oil has a distinctive taste particularly suited to Mediterranean dishes, marinades, salads and some special recipes like pesto and ratatouille. It comes in several grades depending on the quality of olives used and the method of extraction. 'Virgin' olive oil is extracted by mechanical means and usually cold pressed. The first pressing gives the best oil so these are usually labelled 'first cold pressing'. Subsequent pressings to extract more oil sometimes use heat. 'Extra virgin' oil is pressed from the best quality olives, just ripened. Some less well-flavoured olive oil is refined to create a more neutral taste and remove some of its colour. This is labelled just olive oil. This is cheaper and with its milder flavour is suitable for ordinary cooking.

Pine Nut (*Pinus pinea* and 17 other species)

Pine kernels, taken from the cones during the winter have been used for centuries by Mediterranean peoples. Indeed, the shells of the nuts were found in the debris of Roman legions stationed in Britain. The taste is delicate with a hint of pine resin but, as the pine nuts are fairly expensive, the oil extracted from them is even more so. At present, it is the most expensive of the vegetable oils. This distinctive-tasting oil can be used to dress vegetables and baste a roast as well as flavouring a salad dressing, particularly for a Greek salad.

Poppy Seed (*Papaver rhoeas*)

Poppy seed oil is extracted from the seed of the wild, or corn, poppy. It has been used as a substitute for olive oil and occasionally used to adulterate olive oil. The second pressing yields an oil with similar qualities to linseed and is used by artists. It is more refined than linseed and not so yellow, so when mixed with oil paints it makes the pigments flow more easily and they dry to become richer colours.

Pumpkin (*Cucurbita pepo* and *C. moschata*)

The seeds of pumpkin are rich in fats and proteins and have been valued by the Chinese for centuries. They are usually roasted or deep fried and salted. The oil pressed from them has a strong flavour and is nutritious, but of the vegetable oils it has the highest amount of saturated fats. It is fairly expensive, so its unusual taste is used for special recipes or salad dressing.

Rape (*Brassica napus*)

This is an annual herb in the wallflower family which has been cultivated since ancient times. Its other name, 'Cole' (or 'Coleseed'), is preferred by many because of the second unfortunate meaning of the word rape. It grows 3 ft (1 m) high with flowers of such an intense yellow that fields of them can be painful to the eyes. Some people experience unpleasant symptoms from the pollen in areas such as East Anglia where large amounts are grown.

On a small scale, young leaves can be used like mustard greens in spring salads. Both the plant and seed cake are widely used as cattle food.

Of the vegetable oils, rape seed oil has the highest percentage of unsaturated fats with a good balance between poly- and mono-unsaturated fats. As a very inexpensive oil with a neutral flavour, it represents good value for frying, basting food in preparation for roasting or grilling, and for marinades. Commercially it is used for oiling loaves of bread before baking. It is also the main, and sometimes the only, ingredient of 'blended' oils. A little soya oil is usually the second partner.

Safflower (*Carthamus tinctorius*)

This is an annual herb, native to India but some varieties can be cultivated in Britain on poor, dry soil in full sun. It reaches 3 ft (1 m) with shaggy heads of loose, orange florets and these give a good yellow dye with water, or a red dye with alcohol. The petals can be used as a saffron substitute for colouring rice but the flavour is slightly bitter. An infusion of the petals has been used as a laxative and to reduce perspiration and fevers.

The cooking oil extracted from the white seed, like that of rape, is low in saturated fats and has a neutral taste suitable for salad dressings. It has a high smoke point which makes it an excellent choice for deep frying and stir-frying though it is currently 2½ times the price of rape seed oil.

Sesame (*Sesamum indicum*)

Sesame is an annual plant which takes 3–5 hot months to mature. It grows to a height of 6 ft (2 m) with white, pink or mauve flowers. When harvested, the whole plant is cut and dried upright. As they dry, the seed capsules split open at the top and then the plants are turned upside down and the small seeds are shaken out onto cloths. They are usually creamy white but may be brown, black or red. In Europe, the seeds are used to decorate cakes and bread. African families stew the seeds in savoury dishes and Japanese recipes make use of ground sesame seed. In the Middle East the confectionary 'halva' is properly made with ground sesame seed which gives it that rich, nutty taste. Finely-ground seeds are also used to make tahina, a paste rather like a runny peanut butter used in a range of savory and sweet dishes. It is thickened and extended to a sort of mayonnaise consistency by beating in water drop by drop and with added garlic and lemon juice it becomes a delicious dip for crudities and bread.

Modern varieties of sesame seed can contain as much as 60% oil and when highly purified it has little taste and smell. It is not so prone to rancidity in warm climates as other oils and this makes it very useful in hot countries. The unrefined oil has a distinctive flavour which is valued in special Oriental dishes and used in salad dressings.

Soya or Soybean (*Glycine max*)

This is an annual herb of the pea or legume family with 5000 years of recorded cultivation in China. Now there are over 1000 varieties in cultivation ranging in size from a bushy 1½ (50 cm) to 6 ft (2 m). Efforts have been made to develop a variety acceptable for a northern summer season such as Britain's. I managed a small crop when I succumbed to the advertising for a new variety but the soybeans are so inexpensive to purchase that it was more a novelty than an economic exercise.

This bean, rich in oil and protein, is one of the world's most important food crops and often used as a meat substitute. It is one of several beans used in Chinese cookery as bean-sprouts. It is the source of a high protein, low carbohydrate flour which is mixed with wheat flour in baked products and also used to make ice-cream. Soy-milk, extracted from the seeds, is available in China and Japan and recommended as an invalid food. The bean is also fermented to make 'tofu', a curd cheese with many variations, and flavoured slabs are sold on the street corners of China as a sweet snack.

The most well known product from soy beans is soy sauce, the dark brown, savoury, salty sauce available in every Chinese restaurant. It was introduced to Japan from China in AD 500 and arrived in the West 1300 years later to become one of the ingredients in Worcestershire sauce. It is made by extracting the liquid from a fermented mixture of salted, cooked soy beans and wheat or barley flour. Besides being an important flavouring in many Oriental dishes, it is also useful in marinades and barbeque sauces. Refined soya oil is the least expensive cooking oil.

Sunflower (*Helianthus annuus*)

The sunflower is a striking annual which can reach 12 ft (3.5 m) or more. It has large yellow flowers sometimes 12 in (30 cm) across which are enjoyed by bees and thereby make a contribution to honey. Sunflowers happily grow in temperate climates, including that of Britain, and are grown commercially in parts of Russia, Argentina and Canada. It has such a great capacity for taking up water that is sometimes planted in areas to help drain soils. Large tracts of marginal land can be seen in the Netherlands planted with sunflowers. Little is wasted of the plant; leaves and stems contain fibres which can be used in paper-making or are fed to livestock along with the residual oilcake.

Sunflower seeds contain about 40% oil. They are very nutritious and often eaten raw or roasted and salted in their shells. They are fed to poultry and are an important ingredient of bird-feed mixtures for cage birds.

After soybean oil, sunflower oil is the least expensive and with its neutral flavour, light yellow colour and high percentage of unsaturated fats is good value for salad dressings and shallow, deep and stir-frying. It is also employed in the manufacture of varnishes and soaps.

Walnut (*Juglans regia*)

The oil expressed from walnuts is rather expensive but its delicious nutty flavour, easily identified with walnuts, makes a very special salad dressing ingredient.

Wheatgerm

Extracted from the kernel of grains of wheat, this oil is a natural anti-oxidant. It is not used in cooking but in skin care as it is nourishing, rich in vitamin E and especially good for dry skins. It is rather too rich and heavy, too 'oily', and probably too expensive to be used on its own for massage but is added to other massage oils to extend their keeping qualities.

COSMETIC USES

Several of the above oils, especially sweet almond and grapeseed, are used in massage because their fine molecules can penetrate the skin. The larger molecules of mineral oils do not pass the skin barrier and their presence can rob the body of fat-soluble vitamins, two attributes which make them unsuitable for skin lotions. Unfortunately, they are often chosen by cosmetic firms because they are cheaper and have an unlimited shelf life. However, they have a use where a barrier cream is required, such as a protective hand cream or a salve to protect a baby's bottom from nappy rash.

Creams are made of a combination of an oil, a wax and a water-based liquid mixed together to form an emulsion. This combination, with minor variations, has been the basis of skin creams since the first recipe recorded by the Greek physician Galen (131–201 AD). His major contribution was the introduction of 'polypharmacy', a system of mixing herbal preparations to treat specific conditions. His recipe for skin cream was made with olive oil, bees wax and rose water and it is still an excellent nourishing cream, though a little 'heavy' for modern tastes. In the sixteenth century, the oil used was coleseed (or rape) and from this came the name cold-cream.

Skin Cream based on Galen's recipe

Used as a cleansing or nourishing night cream (with the addition of an essential oil), this recipe incorporates rose water which benefits the circulation of all skin types, particularly sensitive skins. An essential oil can be added to alleviate specific skin conditions: try sandalwood or chamomile for dry skin, lemon or ylang-ylang for oily skin or frankincense or jasmine to aid rejuvenation (see Chapter 5 for further information).

½ oz (15 g) white beeswax
3 fl oz (90 ml) sweet almond oil
4 tbsp (60 ml) triple strength rose water
3 or 4 drops of essential oil (optional)

Melt the wax over low heat and warm the oil and beat into the wax. Then warm the rose water, and dribble this into the warm wax/oil mixture beating it as you go. Stir the essential oil into the cream before it has set. Pour into a clean jar choosing one with a wide mouth because the cream solidifies as it cools. Cap and label with your recipe and date.

The main benefit of making your own creams is that you control the ingredients. You can choose the finest quality nourishing ingredients and be sure of their freshness and purity. You can add herbal extracts and essential oils to suit your exact requirements and the only drawback I have found with home made creams is that without special equipment it is difficult to achieve the light whipped effect of modern daycreams.

If you have very sensitive or allergic skin you can substitute ingredients and find which are acceptable to your skin. Even the top quality ingredients will still cost a small fraction of the cost of commercial products. To make 75 ml of a moisture cream using the best quality ingredients costs about 35 pence or a little more if a few drops of rose oil are included.

Breath Sweetener

Dill seed can be chewed to sweeten the breath as can cardamom seed, which will help mask garlic odours. Serve a few in a small dish at the end of a meal as they will help aid digestion, too.

Black Hair Dye

Walnut shells make an excellent dye for dark hair. Crush a handful of the green outer shells of unripe walnuts (*Juglans nigra*) in a pestle and mortar. Leaves can also be used. Add a pinch of salt, cover with water and soak for three days. Then add three cups of water and simmer for five hours adding more water if necessary to maintain at least one cup of liquid. Strain and reduce to one cup by boiling. This gives a dark brown stain which will add richness to brown hair and help mask grey hair. Cool to body temperature and pour through clean hair catching the rinse in a bowl. Repeat as many times as possible until the colour fades from the liquid. Using gloves, pat the hair dry with an old towel as some colour may come off. The colour is cumulative so the more you use the stain, the stronger the colour will become.

Hair Growth

The seed of fenugreek is currently the subject of medical and cosmetic research. It contains certain components which influence hormones and appear to have a part to play in hair growth. The Chinese have produced several hair growing products which have gained world-wide fame for reducing some forms of baldness. One of two sample packets I purchased in China has a distinct smell of fenugreek though they do not list their ingredients.

Dill Seed and Horsetail Nail Bath

The mineral salts in dill seed and the high content in silicic acid in horsetail combine to make a useful treatment for strengthening the nails.

2 tbsp (30 ml) crushed dill seed
2 tbsp (30 ml) fresh or dried chopped horsetail
1 cup water

Boil the two herbs in the water for 15 minutes over medium heat to reduce the liquid by half. Cool to blood heat and soak finger nails for 10-15 minutes. Repeat three times a week with warm solution until nails are stronger. Strain any solution to be kept and store in the fridge for a few days but make it fresh each week.

HOUSEHOLD USES

Fabric Dyes

The seed of fenugreek yields a yellow fabric dye and the seed heads of sweet joe pye (*Eupatorium purpurea*) give a pink-red dye. The boiled green husks of walnuts give a yellow dye.

Mouse Bait

Aniseed makes very good bait for mousetraps. Local cholesterol-conscious mice definitely prefer it to cheese.

Pan Cleanser

Bruised mustard seed is useful for freeing a cooking pan of food odours. Sprinkle 1 tsp (5 ml) of crushed seed in the pan, add a little water, shake the mixture around for a few minutes, then wash out the pan with boiling water.

MEDICINAL USES

Dietary and Digestive Aids

For anyone on a salt-free diet, dill seed, which is rich in mineral salts and smallage (wild celery), are useful substitutes.

Several herb seeds are excellent aids to digestion. The 'four warming seeds' form a special carmative mixture which reduces flatulence. The mixture includes equal parts of aniseed, caraway, coriander and fennel. An old English custom of serving a small dish of caraway seeds with roast apples is still practised at Trinity College, Cambridge and some London

Livery dinners. Dill, too, is an excellent aid to digestion, especially for babies and is an important ingredient in gripe water. Dill water is easy to make but ensure everything is properly sterilized and be certain you have the correct seed. Infuse ½ oz (15 g) of bruised dill seed in a cup of boiling water for ¼-½ hour. Give baby a teaspoon at room temperature when required. For adult indigestion, take a tablespoon when needed.

Mustard Poultice

A mustard poultice is used to relieve pain and mitigate inflammation in rheumatism, arthritis, muscular pain, congested lungs and chilblains. It works by drawing blood to the surface and increasing circulation around the lungs but it can irritate delicate skins.

It is made by crushing the seed and mixing it with a little boiling water to make a paste. Cool a little before applying. Normally a poultice is applied directly to the skin as hot as can be comforably tolerated so that the herb has direct contact with the skin to speed its function. But as mustard can irritate tender skins it is applied between two layers of gauze. Cover with plastic and then a folded towel to maintain the heat. When cool, replace with hot gauze or a hot-water bottle over the plastic. Stop if the skin becomes too red or uncomfortable.

Note that it is not suitable for a swelling caused by a sprain. Such a swelling should, instead, have a cold compress of the leaves of comfrey or St John's wort.

Evening Primrose

Oil extracted from the seed of evening primrose (*Oenothera biennis*) contains gamma-linoleic acid (GLA) which has many curative properties. It is taken in capsule form for scaly dry skin, psoriasis, some causes of dandruff, premenstrual tension and menopausal discomfort. GLA lowers levels of cholesterol and blood pressure and seems to reduce the risk of thrombosis. It is currently being researched for its effectiveness in controlling symptoms of multiple sclerosis and other degenerative diseases.

CULINARY USES

Sprouting seeds

These are seeds which are placed in a container and given moisture and warmth to germinate and swell until the first shoot emerges. The seed uses the food stored within it to begin growth and in the process the stored fats and starches are converted into sugars, proteins, vitamins and minerals. It is easy to see that once germinated, they are a highly nutritious food source. Because the stored food is limited, they quickly reach a peak time for appearance and nutritional value. After this they would normally draw on earth and sunlight for growth. If there is insufficient sun, they begin to turn brown at the ends and become bitter. They should be used at this point or rinsed and stored in a refrigerator to halt growth. Given a daily rinse this should prolong their usable life for a few days.

Sprouted seed can be added to sandwiches and salads and are especially useful in the winter when less fresh greenery is available. They can be cooked in stir fried dishes as they are in the Orient or added to soups and stews. Alfalfa, aniseed, clover, fennel, fenugreek, lentils, mung beans and soya beans; seeds of the cabbage family like cauliflower, radish, salad rocket and cabbage; and several grains: barley, buckwheat, unpolished brown rice and wheat can be sprouted. Most take 3–5 days, though fennel and mung beans can take 6. Each has its individual fresh flavour and crunchy texture.

To sprout seed:

Select clean, healthy seed, say a tablespoon to begin with. Soak them overnight in warm water to speed the process of germination. Choose a clean container with a wide shallow base to allow seeds to germinate more evenly and with space to increase fourfold. Rinse and drain the seed and spread them out over the base. Cover to retain the moisture. If they are sprouted in the dark, the shoots will be crisper and whiter like the traditional Chinese bean sprouts, and if they are grown in light they will be softer and greener. The room or cupboard temperature should be between 60 and 70°F (15 and 21°C) with a 5°F (3°C) leeway up or down. Sprouting will happen more quickly in the warmer temperatures and give less time for disease to develop.

The secret of success is rinsing which must be done each morning and evening. Rinsing performs two functions; it carries away the waste-products of germination, keeping the seeds clean and preventing them from becoming sour, and it keeps the air fresh and circulating as the warmth and moisture needed for germination would otherwise create a perfect environment for moulds. Either pour the seed into a sieve to rinse thoroughly or fill the sprouting container with warm water, slosh around and pour the water off through a muslin cover to drain the seeds.

Seeds of the legume family (peas, beans, lentils, alfalfa, clover, and fenugreek), contain small amounts at toxic substances which could be damaging if consumed regularly or in large quantities. These are best eaten in moderation or cooked to destroy the toxins. Chinese mung beans and soya beans come into this category but they are the least toxic of the family.

Bread and Biscuits

Many herb seeds are used in bread, biscuits and other baked products, both in the dough and sprinkled on the surface. Records show ancient Greeks used aniseed and cumin in their bread. Caraway gives its distinctive flavour to the bread of middle Europe. Dill, fennel seed, lovage seed and sunflower seed are found in specialist bread recipes and deserve a wider audience, while poppy and sesame seeds are universally popular.

Fruit Salad

Aniseed and green sweet cicely seeds add flavour, crunchy texture and a hint of fun to fruit salads.

Salads

Mustard is important in many salad dressings while celery seed and smallage (wild celery), dill, sunflower and sesame seeds can be used in salads. Browned sunflower and sesame are especially tasty and they can be browned on a baking sheet in the oven without extra fat as the seeds are oily themselves.

Spices

Because of their strong flavour, spice seeds should be used sparingly, at least until you are familiar with their effects. Generally they have little nutritional value, but they enhance the flavour of other ingredients in the cooking pot. In small amounts they often aid digestion by activating the lower digestive glands but very large amounts can be harmful. Many spices help to preserve food by inhibiting the growth of bacteria, an important quality in hot countries.

Where possible buy your seeds whole and grind them when needed with a pestle and mortar or a spice mill as this will give you a much richer

flavour than buying a powder. Seeds should be stored in dark jars or containers away from strong heat and moisture. If stored whole they will last many seasons, but once ground they slowly lose their pungency.

Pickling Spice

Many aromatic seeds are used in pickles and preserves, particularly white mustard seed, allspice, cardomom seed, cloves, mace (seed coat of nutmeg), and black peppercorns.

Unripe green walnuts make a superb pickle. Pick them at the green stage when they can still be pierced with a knitting needle (usually about mid-summer). Wear gloves as they stain skin.

Make a brine of 6 oz (175 g) sea salt to 2 pts (1.2 l) water, bring to the boil and cool. Cover walnuts with cold brine and soak for four days. Put a plate on top to keep walnuts immersed. Drain, make a new brine and repeat for four more days stirring frequently.

Remove walnuts from brine, wash in cold water and then spread in the sun for several days to turn black, turning at least once for even exposure. Prick each walnut several times with a darning needle and pack into quart jars.

Heat the vinegar with a muslin bag of whole pickling spice . Allow 1 tbsp (15 ml) spice for each quart of walnuts. Cover vinegar and boil for 10 minutes. Allow it to cool and then remove spices. Pour over walnuts, add 1 tbsp (15 ml) sugar to each bottle. Screw down, label and date. Leave 2 months before using.

DILL PICKLES
gherkins or small cucumbers 3–5 in (7.5–12.5 cm) long
dill, flowering seed heads and leaves
garlic
coarse salt
white vinegar
water

Scrub freshly-picked cucumbers and soak overnight in cold water. Place a clove of garlic and a flowering head of dill in each clean sterilized jar. Pack gherkins into jars whole or cut in quarters lengthwise. For 2 quart jars of pickles prepare the following liquid:

3 fl oz (75 ml) salt
8 fl oz (225 ml) white vinegar
24 fl oz (675 ml) water

Bring this mixture to the boil and pour hot liquid over cucumbers. Seal. Label and date. Keep in a cool place six weeks before using.

PICKLED NASTURTIUM SEEDS

These are a useful substitute for capers and can be used on pizzas and savoury snacks.

Pick nasturtium seeds on a dry day while they are still green (as soon as the flowers have dropped). Steep for 24 hours in brine (4 oz [100 g] salt to 1½ pts [900 ml] water). Thoroughly dry the seeds and pack into small jars. Make strong spiced vinegar to fill the jars using white wine vinegar and salt and a selection from tarragon leaves, mace, nutmeg, shalots, garlic, peppercorns and horseradish slices. Pour in hot vinegar and seal. They will be ready for eating in one month. Once opened it is best to use up the contents quickly.

Mustard

This is a higly complex seed worth looking at more closely. Mustard is grown in three varieties: black, brown and white. Black seed has the strongest flavour, whereas brown seed, although similar to black, is a little less pungent. It is usually chosen by growers because it has a smaller, neater plant size which makes it more convenient to harvest. White seed has less flavour but more heat and the strongest preserving qualities so it is used in pickles and mayonnaise to help stabilize the emulsion. Black mustard may be native to England but it is generally conceded that white is not. White was probably left behind by Romans.

All mustard varieties have no scent when they are whole seeds, they only have a bitterness. The desirable aromatic pungency is only released when the seeds are ground and soaked in a liquid which allows a chemical reaction to take place. When seeds are soaked in water, they become somewhat mucilaginous from material in cells just underneath the outer shell and enzymes are released creating a pale yellow volatile oil which is acid in reaction and so penetrating in effect as to make it a tear gas. This provides the pungency and flavour.

When making mustard sauce, use black or brown seed. Buy powder or grind seed (to release enzymes which produce the flavour), make a paste with cold water to activate enzymes and leave for ten minutes before use. Boiling liquid will kill the enzymes, salt and vinegar may inhibit them, but these can be added after the flavour has been developed. Because the sulphur in the oil causes discolouration on metal, wooden serving spoons are used with mustard.

Dijon mustard is made from black seed with the husks removed, and white wine and spices. It is used in French cooking. 'French mustard' is Bordeaux mustard, is dark as the entire seed is used, and is heavily flavoured with vinegar, sugar and tarragon. German mustard is similar, mixed with Rhine wine.

English powder is the most pungent. It is mainly black and brown seed with some white seed, and a little wheat flour is added to absorb the mustard oil (but not in the USA and some other countries which do not allow the addition of wheat flour) and turmeric is also added for colour. Many new mustards, mixed with wines, herbs and spices are now available.

Blended Seed Mixtures

Several seeds are often blended together to give a distinctive taste. Curry powder is one such mixture but the recipe varies in different provinces of India and also varies for individual dishes, unlike the standard powder which is offered for sale in Britain. For that reason and the significant improvement in flavours, a better dish is obtained by mixing your own. Coriander seed, cardamom seed, and cumin are commonly used along with black pepper, chilli, ginger and turmeric; some forms add fennel, fenugreek, mustard and poppy seed plus cinnamon, clover, nutmeg, allspice and curry leaves (karipatta, not the silver-leaf *Helichrysum angustifolium* of British gardens). Curry powder is 'hot' or 'mild' depending on the amount of peppery spices used.

CURRY POWDER

1 oz (25 g) each of coriander seed, cardamom seed, ginger
3 oz (75 g) turmeric
½ oz (15 g) cumin
¼ oz (7 g) best cayenne

Powder finely and mix together.

TANDOORI MIX

This is a blend of spices which results in an orange colour. It is used to flavour roast and grilled meat in Northern India and Pakistan where the coated meat is cooked in a clay oven or tandoor. Ingredients vary but can include cardamom, coriander, cumin and peppercorns plus turmeric, chilli powder, garlic, cinnamon, ginger and nutmeg. Crushed aromatic seeds mixed with breadcrumbs can also be used to make an appetizing coating for poultry, fish and lamb chops.

Curry Dishes

KOFTAS *(Serves 4–6)*
Indian meat balls in a curry sauce, served with spiced rice and spinach.

1 lb (450 g) lean lamb/chicken/beef
2 large garlic cloves
1 in (2.5 cm) square piece of peeled fresh ginger
1 fresh green chilli
1 small onion
1 tbsp (15 ml) ground coriander
1 tsp (5 ml) garam masala
½ tsp (2.5 ml) ground cumin
juice of ½ lemon
1 egg
salt, freshly ground black pepper
vegetable oil
4 green cardamom pods
6 cloves
approx 1 in (2.5 cm) of cinnamon sticks

Mince first five ingredients, then mix in a food processor until slightly gelatinous (vigorous beating with a wooden spoon will achieve the same effect). Add seasoning, then beat again incorporating lemon juice and egg. Shape into balls about 1½ in (3.25 cm) in diameter.

Pour vegetable oil to a depth of ¼ in (6 mm) into straight-sided, shallow pan. Heat carefully and then add cardamom pods, cloves and cinnamon stick. When the seeds have expanded well the oil is ready for frying the meat.

Lower the meat balls carefully into the hot fat and fry, turning with a perforated metal spoon so that they are browned on all sides. (This is merely intended to brown the meat, not to cook it through.)

Lift from the fat and drain on kitchen paper. Strain the oil and reserve for making the sauce.

KOFTA SAUCE
(Serves 4–6)

strained vegetable oil
2 small, finely chopped onions
1 large garlic clove
2 large tomatoes deseeded and chopped
1 tsp (5 ml) turmeric
1 tbsp (15 ml) ground coriander
1 tsp (5 ml) ground cumin
1 tbsp (15 ml) paprika
1 tsp (5 ml) salt
½ pt (300 ml) plain yogurt

Garnish
pinch of freshly ground cardamom seeds
1 tbsp (15 ml) toasted sunflower seeds

Fry finely chopped onion in the strained oil until transparent and very lightly golden. Slightly increase heat, then add the garlic, previously mashed with salt, plus chopped tomato and spices.

Fry for about five minutes shaking the pan occasionally to prevent sticking. Now add yogurt and stir thoroughly. Gently lower the meat balls into the sauce, cover the pan and allow to simmer for about ½ hour.

Remove meat balls to a serving dish, pour sauce over and then garnish with freshly ground cardamom seeds and toasted sunflower seeds.

SPICED RICE
(Serves 4–6)

Try to find Basmati rice for this dish, its flavour blends best with Indian food. But any good quality, long-grain rice will do.

8 oz (225 g) Basmati rice
1 oz (25 g) butter
¾ pt (450 ml) cold water
1 tsp (5 ml) salt
1 bay leaf, and some cumin seeds
1 in (2.5 cm) of cinnamon stick

Wash rice well under running cold water in a fine sieve or muslin cloth.

Melt the butter in a large saucepan then toss the drained rice in this for a few moments. Add the water and salt. Bring to the boil, cover, lower the heat to a simmer, and cook for about 20 minutes.

Drain the rice of any excess water, then add the bay leaf, cumin seeds and cinnamon stick. Cover the pan with a cloth, being careful not to let it drape onto the hot plate. Place lid over the cloth and keep pan on a very low heat for about 5 minutes, or until the rice is quite fluffy and dry.

SPICY SPINACH *(Serves 4–6)*
1½ lbs (675 g) good fresh spinach
1 oz (15 g) butter
1 tsp (5 ml) cumin seeds
1 tsp (5 ml) ground coriander
salt, freshly ground black pepper

Wash spinach in a sink full of cold water. Agitate gently in the water to allow any grit to fall to the bottom. Drain, then rinse again. After draining the second time, shake the leaves dry in a cloth. Push the spinach into a large heavy-bottomed pan, there is no need to add water as the damp leaves provide enough and they also give off plenty of liquid as they cook.

Place the covered pan over a moderate heat, shaking it occasionally to distribute the cooking leaves. Turn out the spinach into a strainer and press out as much liquid as possible. Chop roughly.

Melt the butter in the saucepan, add spices and allow the flavour to develop for a few minutes, keeping the pan at a low heat. Now add the chopped spinach, turn up the heat and stir with a metal fork as the spinach cooks.

The increased heat will help evaporate the lingering wateriness in the spinach, but keep stirring to avoid any risk of burning.

Arrange on a serving dish, surrounded with spiced rice.

Dinner Party Dishes

CROWN ROAST OF LAMB *(Serves 4–6)*
Ask your butcher to prepare two best ends of neck as a rack or as a crown, the centre of which can be filled with a stuffing or with potatoes tossed in butter, chopped parsley and dill seed heads.

To achieve a pretty, marbled effect on the platter, arrange random groups of steamed and skinned broad beans with braised garlic cloves around the base of the lamb.

2 prepared best ends of neck
1 heaped tbsp (20 ml) toasted fennel seeds
2 tbsp (30 ml) melted butter
salt, freshly ground black pepper

Lightly toast fennel seeds under the grill. Sprinkle them onto a sheet of grease proof paper. Brush the lamb with melted butter, season with pepper and salt, then roll the meat gently around on the fennel seeds until the lamb has been fairly well covered.

Place in an oven, heated to 425°F (218°C) Mark 7. After 15 minutes lower oven to 375°F (190°C) Mark 5 and allow to roast for a further half hour. The ideal is to achieve a roast with a baby pink interior and a succulent but well roasted exterior. Use the juice from the meat to mix with the braised garlic.

BRAISED GARLIC

This method of preparing garlic transforms the pungent flavour usually associated with this bulb, to a sweet, melting experience. Wonderful with lamb.

A few cloves, cooked in this way can be mashed into gravy as a flavour enhancer, or incorporated into the juice of casseroled meats, etc.

Immerse 2 dozen cloves of garlic in a small pan of boiling water. Allow to simmer gently for about 5 minutes, drain and run under cool water. The skin can then be easily removed by squeezing the end of the clove.

Melt 1 tbsp (15 ml) of dripping or lard in the bottom of a small casserole, gently lay in the garlic cloves then add about an inch of vegetable or meat stock. Season with a little salt and pepper. Braise in a moderate oven for about 1 hour.

When the cloves are tender, remove from oven and strain off excess stock. For serving in the manner described (on the serving dish with broad beans), pour the juice from the roasting pan over the strained cloves and then arrange attractively as desired.

CORIANDER MUSHROOMS   (Serves 4)
8 oz (225 g) button mushrooms
thinly shredded zest and juice of 1 lemon
olive oil
2 large cloves thinly sliced garlic
2 tbsp (30 ml) coriander seed lightly crushed
2 bay leaves
salt, freshly ground black pepper
small bunch fresh coriander or parsley

Trim back mushroom stalks to the level of the cap and lightly dust off any compost or dirt. (Only wash if absolutely necessary and then dry very gently.) Squeeze lemon juice into a bowl and swill the mushrooms round in it.

Pour oil to a depth of approximately ¼ in (5 mm) into large frying pan, heat gently and add garlic, coriander seed and bay leaves. As the perfume of the seeds and leaves begins to rise from the heated oil, add mushrooms. Allow mushrooms to warm and not fry in the scented oil, shaking the pan occasionally to make sure that all the mushrooms are well coated. Simmer until the juices from the mushrooms run into the warm oil. At this point transfer the contents to a shallow bowl and when cooled slightly season to taste. Then add chopped coriander or parsley and garnish with lemon zest.

Barbeque

PORK SKEWERS
(Serves 4–6)

Marinaded pork, barbecued over charcoal and small branches of juniper, served with juniper sauce.

1½ lbs (675 g) lean pork
3 large tomatoes
1 large onion
1 red or green pepper
bay leaves
salt, ground black pepper

Marinade
juice of 1 lemon
8 fl oz (225 ml) of white wine
2 fl oz (50 ml) olive oil
1 dozen crushed juniper berries
1 tsp (5 ml) crushed cumin seeds
1 tsp (5 ml) black pepper corns

Mix all marinade ingredients together then add pork, sliced into good sized cubes. Cover, and allow to marinate for at least 6 hours.

To prepare for cooking – thread the pork onto skewers, attractively arranged between sliced tomato, onion, peppers and the occasional bay leaf. Season with salt and freshly ground pepper. Cook for 20 minutes turning frequently.

BARBEQUE SAUCE
2 oz (50 g) butter
½ dozen finely sliced spring onions
8–10 crushed juniper berries

Melt butter in a small pan, add the onions and allow to soften over a gentle heat. Do not allow the butter to colour. Add crushed berries and keep over a low heat or place in a dish in a very low oven. When skewers are cooked, brush liberally with this sauce before serving.

Desserts

ORANGES WITH SWEET CICELY　　　　　　　　　　*(Serves 6)*
8 good oranges
1 lb (450 g) sugar
½ pt (300 ml) water
1 tbsp (15 ml) Kummel
24 young green sweet cicely seeds

First pare the zest from two of the fruits and cut into fine strips. Simmer them in some boiling water for 5 minutes and drain.

Dissolve sugar in the water, bring to the boil and boil for 1 minute without stirring. Add the zest and continue to cook for a further minute.

Now peel the oranges with a sharp knife and detach as much of the pith as possible. Cut down between the membranes to remove segments. Do this over a bowl in order to save the juice that will certainly drip from your hands!

Pour the cooled syrup over the orange segments and then add Kummel. Ten minutes before serving add the cicely seeds. Try to use a glass bowl as the orange and bright green colouring of this pretty dish make for a lovely summery effect.

RHUBARB SCENTED WITH CARDAMOM　　*(Serves 4–6)*
1 lb (450 g) rhubarb
6 oz (175 g) demerara sugar
10 cardamom pods
½ pt (300 ml) thick yogurt (*e.g.* Greek)

Roughly chop rhubarb, rinse and then put in a heavy saucepan with the sugar and lightly crushed cardamom pods. Cook very slowly allowing the fruit to give up its own juice and to ensure a good infusion of flavours. Allow to cool, then remove the cardamom pods.

Spoon alternate layers of yogurt and fruit into tall glasses and decorate with a sprig of mint.

2
HERB LEAVES

The leaf is the part of a herb plant most commonly used, and from it we have culinary, cosmetic, medicinal, aromatic, decorative and household uses. There is also the odd, unexpected encounter – for example, painters like Gainsborough and Constable used parsley leaves as a model for trees in their landscape paintings. Also, a desire for aromatic herb leaves can claim to have affected history. In the sixteenth century, Cardinal Wolsey's palace at Hampton Court began to outshine Henry VII's so charges were drawn up against him which included extravagant expenses. A major complaint concerned his purchase of vast amounts of the aromatic leaves of sweet flag (*Acorus calamus*) for strewing on the floors of his many rooms.

A herb garden appeals to all the senses and leaves are the major contributor to these pleasures as they offer such a wide range of colours, textures, sizes and scents. For me the greatest of these is their fragrance. Some are sweet like bergamot, chamomile, eau-de-cologne mint, sweet myrtle and southernwood; some are savoury like tarragon, thyme and sage; some are clean and fresh like lemon verbena, spearmint, angelica and the apple-scented leaves of sweet briar after a light rain; some have a medicinal scent, like camphor leaf, and some are pungent, like wormwood and santolina.

To smell a leaf, it is usually necessary to press it hard enough to break the cell walls of the tiny glands holding the aromatic essential oils, thus releasing them to the air. Usually a gentle rubbing will suffice. In some leaves, though, like sweet myrtle, the scent pockets are deeply imbedded so a little more pressure is required to release the spicy orange fragrance. Hot sun will draw the scented essence from the leaves of several herbs as they evaporate to create a protective aura around the plant in certain conditions. Hence the summer aroma of marjoram and thyme on the hillsides of Greece.

There are several different leaf scents within a single species, for example, among the thymes we find the scent of common thyme, lemon thyme, the caraway scent of *Thymus herba barona*, the sweet-piny scent of *Thymus azoricus* and the fruity sweetness of *T. vulgaris* 'Fragrantissimus'.

In herbs, leaf sizes range from the tiny ¹/₁₀ in (2 mm) leaves of *Mentha requinii*, (the Corsican mint) to the 3 ft (1 m) elephant ears of Elecampane *Inula helenium*), the herb Helen of Troy was collecting when she was abducted.

Then there is the texture of herb leaves: the sensuous, velvety leaves of the marsh mallow plant; the knobbly leaves of sage, and the rough leaves of comfrey and borage with their prickly hairs.

For a spectrum of leaf colour, herbs would be difficult to surpass. We find bright green lemon balm; the steely blue of Jackman's blue rue; the silver of curry plant; the strong yellow of golden moneywort or creeping Jenny (*Lysimachia nummularia aurea*); the vibrant purple of dark opal basil; plus a full range of variegated leaves. *Salvia tricolor* has pink, cream and green leaves while a leaf of the variegated form of purple sage can display purple, dark green, pink, peach and cream.

THE FUNCTION OF LEAVES

A leaf is a factory for photosynthesis; the most important process for life on the planet as it provides all our food (the entire food chain depends on plants), much of our energy (oil, natural gas and coal begin as organic material) and some of our oxygen (a by-product of photosynthesis). A leaf accomplishes this by trapping sunlight which excites the green molecules of chlorophyll in the leaf.

There is beautiful meaning in the word chlorophyll; *chloros* is Greek for green, and *philo* means loving or *philos* means beloved. So, we have beloved green or green love, a poetic summation of herbs and their offerings.

When the green molecules of chlorophyll are excited by sunlight, the leaf converts water, which it draws up from the soil via the roots and carbon dioxide inhaled from the air through tiny holes in the leaf called stomata, into sugars (food for the plant) and oxygen which it exhales back through the stomata to our benefit.

Each stomata opens into an internal air sack which links with others creating a spongy 'lung' inside the leaf. On a dry, hot day there is more water vapour in the leaf than outside so it passes out through the stomata. This process is called transpiration. In hot weather, a birch tree standing in open ground with 200,000 leaves has been found to loose 100 gallons of moisture a day. Though the stomata can close to a fine slit, which they usually do at night, transpiration still occurs as the evaporation cools the air around the plant.

The water lost by transpiration is replaced by absorption through the roots. If the loss is greater than the intake, because the ground is dry or too cold, or a plant has just been transplanted and the roots have not yet caught hold, or it has no roots because it is a cutting, then the plant withers and may die. Some assistance is offered by mist spraying the leaves. Herbs do not absorb moisture through their leaves, or at least very little, but the mist will stop the transpiration of the existing moisture in the leaf.

Sometimes a large-leaved herb like sweet basil will wilt in the day, even when the soil is damp, because the water transpires more rapidly than it can be taken up by the roots. Misting the leaves at the hottest, dryest time of day will help, but the plant will revive at night when the air is cooler because absorption has time to catch up with transpiration.

In winter the lack of sunlight makes it unnecessary for leaves to remain on the plant and in autumn the centre of the herb will reabsorb some of the goodness in the leaf. This process diminishes their flavour and therapeutic values and also causes changes in the pigments or colours. A few thymes take on a bronze tint after a cold spell but sages tend to turn mottled and unattractive. It is mainly the leaves of trees and shrubs that give such a farewell blaze of colours. Following the leaf changes, the plant grows a layer of tissue over the base of each leaf stalk cutting off the water supply. When the leaf is dry a gust of wind will finally separate it from the plant.

With a variegated plant such as gold variegated sage, the pale yellow or white areas are not photosynthesizing as this only happens in the green areas, so these plants are weaker. This is why they usually need more sunlight and also why, if a stronger green shoot appears, it should be removed – otherwise it will dominate the variegated part and eventually replace it.

Several herbs have evergreen leaves which give plant colour and form to the herb garden in winter. These include: bay (green and gold), box (dwarf and variegated), chamomile (perennial forms), curry plant (*Helichrysum angustifolium*), feverfew (green and gold), hyssop, lavender, rosemary, rue, sage, santolinas, southernwood, sweet myrtle (*Myrtus communis* 'Tarentina'; said to be hardy though I find it only hardy in sheltered spots), thyme, wall germander (*Teucrium chamaedrys*), wild strawberry and winter savory. These plants should be called 'winter-green' rather than 'evergreen' as they replace their leaves in the spring. But with some of these plants, like hyssop and a few lavenders, (sometimes called semi-evergreen), their leaves barely hang-on over the winter. Towards the end of the leaf cycle, in late winter, they look a little dismal so you would not want to feature them in your winter planning.

Several other herbs appear green throughout the winter in mild seasons because they produce new shoots in the autumn which over-winter. Varieties of marjoram and oregano, angelica, fennel, salad burnet, sorrel, welsh onion and everlasting onion offer these occasional young autumn leaves which can all give an unexpected fillip to winter salads.

DESIGNING WITH HERB LEAVES

Hedges

Some of the evergreen herbs can be used to create a hedge in a garden. Box is excellent, though dwarf box is very slow growing. Its roots seldom expand outward so it does not encroach on neighbouring plants. Rosemary and curry plant are very attractive but are best grown in sheltered areas as a cold winter kills parts or all of the plants. Lavender, santolina and southernwood also offer good colours plus scent. They are a little hardier than rosemary and curry plant but will still be damaged by a severe winter. Shrubby thymes and the upright wall germander are reliable plants reaching a height of around 12 in (30 cm).

Decide before planting whether you wish to let the plants grow to their natural height (this would suit rosemary, though a little clipping will encourage bushy side growth), or whether to clip them to a set height and width which suits the santolina and box. Herbs whose flowers are valued, like lavender, are allowed to flower and are then clipped. When planting, as a rough guide, plant the herbs a distance apart which is two-thirds of their eventual height. For example, plant 3 ft (1 m) lavenders 2 ft (60 cm) apart.

Knot Gardens

The various colours of evergreen herb leaves can be used to make the pattern of woven ribbons of plants found in a knot garden. Similar to the effect of a formal path design in a garden of herbs, the geometric patterns of a knot garden give a rich contrast to the exhuberant informality of many herb plants; an oasis of clipped discipline among the carefree and bountiful wild plants. It can be the focal point of your herb garden or a feature on its own. Even a small knot garden, well kept, gives an air of maturity to an entire garden.

It is wise to start with a small area as it needs regular tending to keep it looking good. About 6 x 6 ft (2 x 2 m) is the smallest into which you can thread a pattern of plants, though at this size the plants need to be clipped down to 6 in cubed (15 cm^3) bands which is difficult to maintain. An 8 x 8 ft (2.5 x 2.5 m) or 9 x 9 ft (2.75 x 2.75 m) area will allow for ribbons 9–12 in cubed (22.5–30 cm^3).

For pattern inspiration, look to old herbals or the art and artifacts of cultures which featured geometric styles such as North and South American Indians, Arabic and Chinese decorations or Hindu mandalas. It is important to achieve a balance between a simple and an intricate plan. A pattern of separate geometric beds is called a *parterre* and even though they can be very elaborate, as in some French gardens, to me they don't have the extra dimension of the movement that is created by interlocking flowing ribbons of plants, weaving over and under each other to create the pattern. I have found that three colours of plants within an outer border of box give the richest pattern which remains distinct. Box is a perfect plant because it responds so beautifully to clipping and grows slowly. To achieve a colour range, santolina is a good choice because it, too, clips well and offers a silver leaved form (*S. incana* or *S. chamaecyparissus*), a green form (*S. virens*) and a willow coloured form (*S.* 'Lemon Queen'). Using three varieties of one species should give uniform growth and leaf size.

Plan your pattern carefully on grid paper making sure you mark the thickness of the ribbons of herbs and show which ribbon crosses 'over' and which crosses 'under'. Keep this drawing for future reference when you come to clip the herbs. Choose a site in full sunlight with excellent drainage and, if necessary, incorporate extra grit to a depth of 18 in (45 cm). Be meticulous about clearing the weeds from the area. Mark your design out carefully with chalk or sand and use a card template for small repeated shapes. Set plants 6–9 in (15–22.5 cm) apart. When they are large enough to clip, you can shape each plant into a square or curved section. Make the first cutting in late spring to encourage bushy growth and emphasize the movement of one ribbon 'crossing' over another by clipping a gentle humpback shape to the 'top' ribbon. If the 'lower' ribbon of herbs is clipped to slope downward before it stops either side of the 'upper' ribbon, it encourages the illusion of passing underneath. Make the last clipping in late summer so that the new growth will have time to harden before the first frosts.

PROPAGATION

Many herbs can be propagated from leaf and stem cuttings by taking a shoot of the plant and rooting it to form a new plant. This method guarantees the same characteristics of the parent plant, such as leaf and flower colour, flavour and habit of growth, and is necessary for named varieties of species. Plants from seed are more variable. For example, common sage can be grown from seed but the purple or gold leaf form needs to be grown from cuttings. Cuttings are classified in three groups:

softwood, semi-hardwood and hardwood.

Softwood cuttings are taken from the current season's growth which has not yet hardened. The ideal time is either late spring, from new growth, or late summer, after flowering. Use sturdy, healthy pieces 2–4 in (5–10 cm) long with several leaves and without flowers or flower buds. If you are propagating a coloured leaf form, select a shoot with good colouring. For most plants cut just below a leaf node (the junction of leaf to stem) because there is a group of special cells which promote growth located there. Make a clean cut without ragged edges. Remove the leaves from the lower third taking care not to peel the stems which might allow entry to infections.

Softwood cuttings wilt quickly and must be planted soon after cutting. Open ground, in a sheltered spot out of constant sunlight, is always suitable for planting cuttings. Work in extra peat and sand to create the loose open soil which favours root formation. The base of the cutting can be dipped in hormone rooting powder to encourage root formation but for most herbs it is not necessary. If you do use a rooting compound, shake off the excess powder as too much can be more detrimental than using none. The leaves must be sprayed or misted twice a day for the first few days and thereafter on dry days because they will transpire moisture from their leaves but will not have roots to draw up replenishing supplies. They normally take about six weeks to root with soil temperature as the main determining factor. Sage and pelargoniums (scented leaf geraniums) take four weeks.

Alternatively, cuttings can be grown in containers, which gives greater control over their environment and flexibility in their positioning. Aim for a minimum soil temperature of 55–64°F (13–18°C); 'warmer is quicker'. When the cuttings have begun to grow, pot on into individual pots with nutrients supplied, or plant outdoors giving them a sheltered position with some sun, though avoid strong mid-day sun at first. As with all plant dealings try to avoid shocks for the herb like sudden changes of temperature, light levels, etc., make any change a gradual procedure.

Semi-hardwood cuttings are taken from new growth which has begun to firm up at the base. These are usually taken mid-summer to mid-autumn from shrubby herbs such as rosemary and sweet myrtle. Follow instructions as for softwood cuttings.

Hardwood cuttings are taken from the woody parts of shrubs and trees in mid- to late autumn and given the winter to slowly develop roots, usually outside in the open ground. Follow details as for softwood cuttings.

Herbs to grow from cuttings

Bay (needs bottom heat; *i.e.* warmed soil), box (can take a year or longer to root), curry plant, hyssop varieties, lavender varieties, lemon verbena (in May), marjorams, myrtle, pelargoniums, rosemary varieties, rue varieties, sage varieties, santolinas, tarragon (French), thyme varieties (take small cuttings, 1–1½ in [2.5–4 cm]), winter savory and prostrate winter savory (take small cuttings, 1–1½ in [2.5–4 cm]) and wormwood varieties. Choose soft, semi-hard or hardwood cuttings depending on the time of year you are working and the available material.

HARVESTING LEAVES

A few fresh leaves can be picked whenever required in the growing season and a serving of evergreen leaves can be picked any time of the year. But for leaves destined for storage it is important to pick them at the time of optimum flavour and therapeutic qualities. This is affected by the time of day and season of the year. The best time for most leaves is morning when the dew has evaporated but before the sun has fully ascended. Damp leaves may go mouldy but the hot sun draws out the valuable plant essences. The best season is just before the plant flowers because after this some of the goodness from the leaves goes into flower and seed production.

Make certain you are confident of the variety you are picking, especially if collecting plants from the wild. This is essential both for safety (you won't wish to poison anyone) and for conservation (don't mistakenly pick an endangered species).

Pick only healthy leaves without blemish, yellowing or insect damage. When picking leaves from a perennial herb, try to leave at least two thirds of the leaves on the plant so it can continue to grow. Chives can be cut down to 2 in (5 cm) which will allow regrowth. With tall plants like marsh mallow, pick the upper portions. For small-leaved plants like marjoram and thyme cut whole stems to dry and then separate the individual leaves later.

PRESERVING

As soon as a leaf is separated from its mother plant, individual cells start to die as their supply of moisture and nutrients is cut off. Enzymes which previously helped to create active constituents now begin to break down these substances so flavour and medicinal virtues deteriorate on a sliding scale. One of the beauties of growing your own herbs is that you can have the freshest and most flavoursome herbs by picking them at the last minute. If this is not possible, herbs can be kept in good condition for a few days by placing them in the refrigerator, with air in a tightly closed plastic bag. This works well with a bunch of parsley. Putting herbs in a jar of water out of sunlight will help for a few hours but it is keeping a moist atmosphere around the leaves which maintains them longest.

For leaves to be stored, the sooner the drying or freezing begins, the more flavour and green colour can be preserved. The speed of the dry process is limited, however, because the moisture must be removed gradually from a leaf. Drying in an oven evaporates the water too quickly and the essential oils responsible for flavour and fragrance, are lost.

Freezing retains colour and flavour well and is a fast and convenient method for culinary herbs although some medical herbalists say it is not suitable for therapeutic herbs. It is very useful for the delicate-leaved herbs which do not dry well, like basil, chervil, chives, fennel, parsley, salad burnet, sweet cicely and tarragon. If they are from your own garden and have not been sprayed nor grown near car fumes, or made unsuitable by animals or children, you can probably judge that it is not necessary to wash them. Just pack them in plastic bags singly or in mixtures, such as a bouquet garni, and label.

Some people recommend blanching (dipping the leaf in boiling water to reduce the surface bacteria), which may be necessary for long-term storage and for large leaves like sorrel. But it is also said that ten minutes of boiling is necessary to kill all bacteria so it seems to me that its value would be minimal and it would not improve the flavour of the herb. If you wish to do it, rinse in cold water after dipping and pat or shake dry.

Herbs such as chives and parsley can be chopped and put in an ice-cube, topped up with water. When the cubes are frozen, remove them from the ice-cube tray and pack them in bags to store in the freezer. A normal ice-cube holds 1 tbsp (15 ml) of chopped herb and 1 tbsp (15 ml) of water. The frozen cube can be added to soups, stews or other liquid dishes or, if the water is unsuitable, place the cube in a sieve overnight to melt the ice and drain the herb.

The traditional method for preserving leaves, however, is to dry them. Many dry well, including mint, bay, rosemary, sage, thyme, savory, and hyssop. Lay the leaves on muslin stretched over a box to allow air to circulate. Place them in a dust-free, warm, ventilated room out of direct sunlight as this will cause essential oils to evaporate. Hang stems of leaves such as rosemary, marjoram, savory and thyme in small bunches (say ten stems), stem upwards, and place an open paper bag over them if the area is dusty.

Bay is unusual in that it is one herb leaf which is better dry than fresh because the changes which take place when the leaf is detached from the plant improve its flavour rather than diminish it. It reaches optimum flavour four or five days after being picked after which it is somewhat reduced.

The ideal drying environment is a temperature of 90°F (32°C) for the first 24 hours and 75–80°F (24–26°C) thereafter. Leaves will take about four days at these temperatures. Allow one to two weeks at cooler temperatures for thick leaves.

When completed, the leaves will be paper dry but hopefully still green. Remove them from their stems and keep whole until required as this will retain flavour longer. Store in dark, airtight, glass bottles away from sunlight, moisture, dust and excessive heat. Metal and plastic containers are not advisable as they may affect the chemistry of a herb. Certain leaves such as marsh mallow and lady's mantle are hygroscopic when dried which means they absorb moisture from the air. This can reactivate their enzymes enough to cause chemical deterioration so avoid storing these for too long. The moisture-absorbing property of these herbs is, however, put to good use when used in soothing skin creams.

Most dried herbs deteriorate after a year, but by then the next year's crop is available. Put old sweet herbs in with pot pourri and sprinkle pungent herbs on seed trays to discourage mice. Failing that, add them to the compost heap.

The flavour of herbs can also be preserved in substances which absorb flavours such oils, fats and alcohols (including vinegar which is made from alcohol). For culinary purposes vegetable oils and vinegars can be flavoured with herbs to add an extra dimension to recipes.

Infusing an oil with herbs

Use one part herb to eight parts oil (by volume). Use unheated vegetable oil without a strong flavour such as sunflower or safflower although the matter is open to experimentation: olive is interesting infused with basil for special recipes like pesto and a dressing for sliced tomatoes.

Pound clean, fresh herbs in a mortar. Add a little oil and mix well. Pour into a clean glass jar with the remaining oil, cover and store for two weeks, stirring or shaking daily. Strain and bottle. Decorate with a sprig of the herb used.

If you are feeling creative, experiment with a blend of two or three herbs, steeped in succession. Savoury herbal oils can be used in salad dressings, marinades, for browning meats, softening vegetables and stir frying, but begin with small amounts until their individual strengths become familiar.

Sweet almond and grape seed oil can be used to infuse sweet scented leaves for use in cosmetic recipes.

Savoury herb leaves best used for oils are basil, fennel, marjoram, mint, rosemary, tarragon, thyme, savory and the garlic bulb. Purple basil and bronze fennel give subtle burgundy/purple shades to the oil. Good sweet herb leaves for oils are young bergamot leaves, eau-de-cologne mint, lemon verbena, and sweet myrtle leaves (bruise the leaves first).

Infused Vinegars

Loosely fill a glass jar with bruised fresh leaves of the selected herb. Use cider vinegar or wine vinegar and have it warm but not hot. Pour into a jar of leaves right to the top and cap with an acid-proof lid (cleaned pickle or mayonnaise jars and lids are suitable). Place on a sunny window ledge, or if that is not available, a warm place and shake daily for two weeks. Test for flavour; if a stronger taste is required strain and save the vinegar and repeat with fresh herb leaves. When satisfied, save as it is or strain through two layers of muslin and rebottle. You can add a fresh sprig of the herb for identification and visual appeal but expect this to make the flavour a little stronger. Use in salad dressings, marinades, gravies and sauces. Even more than herbal oils, these herbal vinegars can be more potent than anticipated (especially homemade tarragon vinegar), so begin by adding a few drops to your normal vinegar until you familiarize yourself with their effects.

Basil, bay, chervil, dill, fennel, lemon balm, marjoram, mint, rosemary, savory, tarragon and thyme can all be used. Purple basil and bronze fennel give stunning rich shades of ruby and burgundy to the vinegars.

Herb butters and cheese

The composition of fats make these products excellent vehicles for absorbing the flavours of herbs. The method called *enfleurage* involves layers of fats combined with layers of flowers to absorb their delicate perfumes. Butter and soft cheeses can be treated in the same way.

Choose strongly-flavoured herbs such as chervil, chives, garlic, parsley, rosemary, sage, salad burnet, tarragon and thyme.

Use about 2 tbsp (30 ml) finely chopped fresh herbs to ½ lb (225 g) of butter or vegetable spread. Soften the butter and beat the herbs in until smooth. Set aside for two hours to allow the herb flavour to permeate the butter. Shape into moulds if desired and chill before serving.

HERBS FOR HEALTH AND BEAUTY

When the primary aspects of lifestyle are in order, the individual qualities of many herbs can be used to enhance the appearance of our skin and hair. Herbs have a part to play in creating a healthy diet, by offering sugar and salt substitutes, caffeine-free drinks, and even massage oils for exercized muscles.

Herbal Nutrition for Skin Care

Raw materials required by the body to neutralize elements which cause ageing and loss of elasticity in the skin include Vitamins A, beta-carotene, C, and E, some amino acids and selenium.

A rich source of Vitamin A can be found in fresh dandelion leaves, most beneficial taken raw in salads and sandwiches. Vitamin A is also present in watercress, American landcress and parsley. (A little parsley each day is highly beneficial but avoid an excess as it contains apiol, an alkaloid harmful in large quantities.) Vegetables with Vitamin A include Swiss chard and seakale beet, broccoli, carrots, spinach, turnip tops, tomatoes and radishes while kale is almost as rich in the vitamin as cod liver oil. Fruits with orange-coloured skins, including apricots, oranges and peaches, contain a little Vitamin A.

Vitamin E should be taken with Vitamin A as the body needs one to make use of the other. Vitamin E is present in leafy, green herbs and vegetables, in wheatgerm, green peas and beans. It is most useful taken with Vitamin B2 and they are found together in wheatgerm, kale, Swiss chard, cress and legumes.

Herbs containing Vitamin C include the leaves of dandelion, watercress, lady's smock and nasturtium, and the fruits of strawberries, blackcurrants, grapes and apples of which Bramley's seedling has the highest Vitamin C content. Of the vegetables, tomatoes, curly kale and broccoli are rich in Vitamin C.

Skin Care – Using Herbal Extracts

Skin is constantly under attack from external agents such as the sun's ultraviolet radiation, environmental radiation, drying winds, cigarette smoke, air pollutants, including ozone and sulphur dioxide, pesticides, heavy metals, petrol fumes, some cosmetic ingredients and several household chemicals.

The first line of defence is to avoid as many of these pollutants as possible. The second is to clean, protect and nourish the skin with pure herbal products. To extract the useful properties of herbs four methods have been developed.

1. **Pulverize**. Use a pestle and mortar (or blender) to mash, grind or bruise the plant parts breaking the fibres to make the essential oils or other therapeutic parts more accessible.
2. **Infusion**. Put 1½ handfuls of fresh herbs or 1 oz (25 g) dried herbs in

61

a china, glass or enamel pot (avoid aluminium or copper). Boil 1 pt (600 ml) of pure water (rainwater, mineral water or distilled water), pour over the herb immediately, then cover with a lid to stop the therapeutic vapours escaping. Steep for at least 30 minutes, then filter through a fine plastic strainer or coffee filter. It will keep for up to three days in the the refrigerator.

3. **Decoction**. This system is generally used for the tougher parts of herbs such as roots, stems and seeds. 1 oz (25 gm) of the herb, chopped if necessary, is put into a pyrex or enamel saucepan and boiled with 1 pt (600 ml) of pure water. Bring to the boil then simmer gently for 30 minutes by which time the liquid should be reduced by half. If more has evaporated, top-up with water to make ½ pt (300 ml). Cool, strain and bottle. Store in the refrigerator and use within three days.

4. **Maceration**. This method is used for herbs which would loose some of their valuable properties if heated. It involves steeping the herbs in oil, vinegar, wine or alcohol, often in the presence of sunlight to speed the process. Some of the herbal properties will be released within a few hours but most require two or three weeks with daily stirring or shaking of the oil, vinegar or alcohol to have the maximum absorbtion. Some herbalists leave the plant parts macerating until the liquid is needed.

Macerations required for aromatic purposes can be judged by scent or taste. If the aroma is insufficient after two weeks, the first plant parts are removed and fresh plants are added, repeating the process. As the liquids used have preserving qualities, macerations will keep several months.

Herbal Baths

The easiest way to use herbs to benefit our skin and well-being is to add a handful to the bath or sprinkle in a few drops of the herb's essential oil. Herbs can be chosen for deep cleansing action, to stimulate the circulation, or to relax the body for a peaceful night's sleep. They can be added to improve specific skin conditions, or just for the pleasure of their fragrance.

Dismiss the desire to fling the leaves into the water with romantic ideas of Ophelia. They cling to you and clog the drain. Instead put a generous handful of fresh or dried herbs in the centre of a handkerchief and tie up the corners to make a bag. Amounts are not critical. Use a single herb or a mixture of those which have the therapeutic properties you prefer. By adding fine ground oatmeal or bran to the bag you can make a body scrub and use it to rub your body near the end of the bathing time.

Another quick method is to use three or four tea bags of herbs available as tea bags such as chamomile or peppermint.

A little more work will give you greater benefits, however. More therapeutic properties will be extracted from the herbs if they are first boiled in a covered saucepan for 15 minutes and the strained liquid is added to your bath water. This decoction can be stored for up to three days in a refrigerator.

Try to keep the bath temperature around body heat because if the bath is too hot the skin will be perspiring and possibly not absorbing the beneficial properties of the herbs, although you will at least be taking them through inhalation. It is known that essential oils (released from the herbs by steam) can pass the skin barrier but there is presently insufficient research to show under what conditions this does or does not happen.

Suitable herbs for the bath are as follows:

Deep cleansing herbs: borage, lemon balm, meadowsweet and sage; also rose petals.

Deodorant herbs: cleavers or goosegrass (*Galium aparine*), lovage, parsley and sage.

Relaxing bath herbs: catnep, hops, meadowsweet, valerian; also flowers of chamomile, cowslips, jasmine, lime blossom, mullein and violets.

Stimulating bath herbs: basil, bay, fennel, lemon verbena, lemon thyme, marjoram, mint, stinging nettles (boiling will remove their sting), pennyroyal, peppermint, pine, rosemary, sage and thyme.

Facial steams

A facial steam is an inexpensive way to provide deep cleansing. The perspiration from the heat improves circulation and helps eliminate toxins and other waste products. The essential oils released by the herbs will benefit the exterior of the skin and be absorbed when inhaling. When the skin is not perspiring, the open pores or hair folicles may absorb the essential oils internally via the skin and lymph system.

Fennel, nettle, rosemary and lime blossom improve circulation and encourage deep cleansing.

Borage, houseleek, lady's mantle, marsh mallow (roots and leaves), parsley, salad burnet, sorrel, violet leaves and flowers, plus cornflowers, are soothing and softening for dry sensitive skin.

Geranium (herb robert), horsetail, sage, yarrow, crushed lupin seeds and calendula petals help refine pores and remove dead skin cells which is especially beneficial to oily skins.

Lemon verbena, dandelion, red clover (leaves and flowers), tansy (leaves and flowers) and elderflowers are used to revive mature or sallow skins.

When giving yourself a facial steam, first tie back your hair, remove your makeup and clean your skin as normal. Put 2 handfuls of fresh leaves (or 3 tbsp [45 ml] dried) in a basin and pour on 3 pts (1.8 l) boiling water. Stir briefly with a wooden spoon. Then hold your face about a foot (30 cm) above the basin (18 in [45 cm] if you have sensitive skin) and make a tent with a towel over your head to confine the steam. Close your eyes and maintain this for 10–15 minutes.

Rinse with tepid water and then cold water a few minutes later to gradually close the pores. Dab on an infusion of peppermint, sage or yarrow leaves or elderflower to tighten the pores. Avoid dramatic changes of temperature for an hour or two.

Do not use a facial steam if you have thread veins, serious skin disorders, asthma or other breathing difficulties, or heart problems.

Making a Herbal Face Pack

Double deep cleaning can be achieved if a face pack is applied after a facial steam and before the pores have closed. It works deeply to draw impurities to the surface and stimulates circulation.

Select any of the above herbs suitable for your skin to make a mask. Soak 2 handfuls of fresh or 3 tbsp (15 ml) dried herbs (soften by soaking in boiled water for several hours) with 2 tbsp (30 ml) pure water and liquidize for a few seconds. Apply this wet mixture as is or add Fuller's earth or ground almonds until a suitable paste is created. Apply it to damp skin and rest with your feet higher than your legs to encourage greater blood supply to the face. Place cooling eye pads of cucumber or cold chamomile tea bags against your closed eyelids. Leave mask for 20–30 minutes before rinsing off with warm water. Finish with a toner of witch hazel or a pore closing infusion such as elderflower water, peppermint, sage or yarrow.

Marsh mallow hand cream

2 oz (50 g) marsh mallow (leaves or root slices)
2 oz (50 g) lady's mantle
2 pts (1.2 l) water
1½ fl oz (40 ml) almond oil
1 oz (25 g) beeswax
1½ tbsp (22.5 ml) clear honey
1 tsp (5 ml) wheatgerm oil
1 tbsp (15 ml) avocado or hazelnut oil to increase penetration (use more wheatgerm or almond if this is not available)
8 drops of geranium, lavender or sandalwood essential oil (optional)

Simmer the herbs in the water for ½ hour in a covered saucepan. Set aside to cool keeping the lid on. Melt the almond oil, avocado or hazelnut oil and beeswax over gentle heat. Remove from heat. Stir in the honey until smooth. Strain the herbal decoction through double muslin or a coffee filter paper and add this with the wheatgerm oil, beating constantly. Stir in the essential oil and pour into a wide mouth jar. Cool, cover, label and date.

Chapped Skin Soother

4 large aloe vera leaves (or 2 tbsp aloe vera gel; or houseleek)
4 leaves lady's mantle
4 leaves comfrey
1 tbsp (15 ml) honey
1 tsp (5 ml) infused comfrey oil (see p.59) or almond oil
oatmeal

Peel the aloe vera leaves and pound together with the lady's mantle and comfrey (which contains allentoin, a protein which encourages cell renewal). With a gentle heat, melt the honey in the infused comfrey (or almond) oil and then beat into the herbs. Add enough of the finely ground oatmeal to make a paste.

Apply thickly to the hands, keep on over night wearing cotten gloves. Store excess for a week to 10 days in a refrigerator.

Ivy Cellulite Cream

1 oz (25 g) ivy
1 cup water
2 tsp (10 ml) beeswax
1 tsp (5 ml) emulsifying wax
1 tbsp (15 ml) hazelnut oil
1 tsp (5 ml) avocado oil
8 drops each of essential oils of fennel, geranium and rosemary (each has a role to play in improving circulation and aiding the removal of cellulite)

Boil the ivy in the water until it is reduced to 4 tbsp (60 ml). Melt the waxes together and stir in the warmed oils, blending thoroughly. Beat in the ivy decoction until smooth, cool a little, stir in the essential oils and pour into a wide mouth jar. Cover, label and date.

Massage this daily into areas of cellulite with a vigorous stroke toward the heart and a lighter stroke outward.

Hair Care

Herb leaves used to condition dry hair include comfrey, marsh mallow, stinging nettles, parsley and sage; plus burdock root and elder flowers. Herbs for greasy hair are horsetail, lemon balm, mints, rosemary, southernwood, witchhazel and yarrow; plus calendula petals, lavender and lemon juice.

Herbs to add body and lustre include goosegrass, horsetail, parsley, rosemary, sage, southernwood, stinging nettle and watercress; plus calendula petals, lime flowers and nasturtium.

These herbs can be used in three ways: as a pre-shampoo oil; in a shampoo and as an after-shampoo rinse.

To make a pre-shampoo lotion, start with an infused herbal oil or macerate a selected herb or herbs in a vegetable oil (see page 59). Alternatively, add a few drops of the essential oil of the chosen herb, if available, to a small amount of vegetable oil. Then pour a little of the warmed herbal oil on to the hands and massage into the scalp drawing the oil out along the hair strands. Cover the head with foil and a shower cap and wrap in a hot towel (wrung out in hot water) replacing the towel as it cools. Maintain this for 20-30 minutes for greatest penetration, then wash off with a mild shampoo.

For shampoo, add a few drops of the essential oil of a selected herb to a bottle of mild, fragrance-free shampoo. For a single shampooing, mix one application of shampoo with a tbsp of a strong decoction in a cup and apply as normal.

Finally, an after-shampoo rinse is made from a strong decoction, cooled to blood heat. The herbs listed above for body and lustre are especially useful for giving extra shine.

To Darken Hair

A strong decoction of sage leaves, sage with rosemary leaves, or sage and dried raspberry leaves can be used as a gentle dark hair rinse. A stronger colour is obtained with walnut shells (see page 37).

Teeth

Rub a sage leaf over your teeth and gums to clean and polish them.

AROMATIC DELIGHTS

The fresh fragrance of herbs may seem like a luxury, something beyond the strictly utilitarian, but the fundamental importance of scent is only beginning to be properly recognized. The power of sweet perfumes to transform our moods is now well documented and to use the natural fresh aromas of herbs is one of the most wholesome ways to lift our spirits.

For those with a garden, the simplest way to have herbal scent around the house is to arrange vases of fresh herbs. These perfume the room and as the plant essences evaporate, they cool and purify the air. The number of ways dried herbs can be used is limited only by your imagination. In the kitchen, dried aromatic herbs can be added to oven mitts or a tea-cosy by tucking them inside the hem or a specially made pocket. Both the handling they receive and the heat they contact will release their fragrance. Use fresh-smelling herbs like mint, lemon thyme, angelica and lemon verbena.

Stick fragrant herbs in saddle bags to fling over the backs of chairs. Each time someone sits they will disturb and release the fragrance. Make two equal sized herb pillow and join with two wide ribbons. You could fill one pillow with 'summer' scents and the other with 'winter' scents and swap when the seasons change. Place santolina, southernwood, wormwood or lavender among old books to discourage worms. Spices and the essential oils of cloves and cinnamon also work well. In fact, the ancient Egyptians protected their papyrus with cinnamon.

Sweet Myrtle Furniture Wax

2 oz (50 g) beeswax
½ pt (300 ml) turpentine
6 fl oz (175 ml) strong infusion of sweet myrtle
¼ oz (7 g) olive oil based soap

Grate beeswax into turpentine and leave to dissolve. This may take a few days. Alternatively, warm beeswax with turpentine carefully over *flameless* heat until wax melts (turpentine can easily burst into flame). Bring the sweet myrtle infusion to boiling point and stir in the grated soap until melted. Allow both mixtures to cool then blend slowly stirring until it resembles thick cream. Stir in a few drops of essential oil if desired. Pour into wide topped container and label.

Aromatic Crafts

Use twigs of aromatic herbs like rosemary, thyme and blades of sweet vernal grass or vanilla grass (*Anthoxanthum odoratum*) to make craft items like woven place mats and baskets.

Pine-scented twigs of the tamarack tree, a variety of larch, are used by the Cree Indian hunters of James Bay, northern Ontario, to make their famous duck decoys. The core of the body is composed of a ball of twigs and then the outer part is shaped like a Canada Goose. As the bird slowly dries the scent fades, but if it is submerged in hot water for 10 to 15 minutes, the fragrance returns. This can be repeated as often as necessary.

Leave any surplus prunings of aromatic herbs in a container near the hearth to throw on the fire to scent and purify the air.

Aromatic Storage

In the bedroom, stick small muslin bags of fragrant leaves in drawers and inside padded coat hangers. Choose the refreshing mint and citrus herbs and perhaps one of the more unusual artemisias like *A. camphorita* for men's clothes. And, most pleasing of all, give yourself sweet dreams by placing fragrant herbs in a sachet under your pillow. Try sweet woodruff, melilot and lady's bedstraw which all smell of new mown hay when they are dried; or dried strawberry leaves, pine needles and oakmoss for the atmosphere of an autumn woodland.

In the linen cupboard, lay them among your sheets and towels, just for the pleasure of rummaging on the shelves. Sprigs of lavender, rosemary, southernwood, alecost, dried lemon peel or root pieces of orris, elecampane, roseroot or sweet flag among clothes will scent the linen and protect it from moths.

Sweet Waters for Rinsing and Scenting Linen

Make a strong decoction of aromatic leaves or flowers in a covered pan, strain well and use as the final rinse for hand-washed articles or add to the final rinse cycle of your washing machine. Use leaves of rosemary, lemon verbena, sweet myrtle, bergamot, sweet marjoram, angelica, bay, alecost and eau-de-cologne mint or powdered root of roseroot or flowers of lavender, violets, pinks and roses. A ½tsp (2.5 ml) of orris root dissolved in the decoction will fix the scent. The mixture can also be sprinkled on clothes before ironing. Alternatively, drops of an essential oil dissolved in a little pure alcohol (or vodka) can be added to the final rinse. Sweet waters can also be used to sprinkle around rooms or as a hair rinse to give it a subtle perfume.

HOUSEHOLD USES

The antibacterial and antifungal properties of many herb leaves give them preservative qualities which can be put to good use. Also, herbs used to discourage insect pests and mice in the kitchen means that the use of toxic chemicals where food is stored, can be avoided.

There are many household uses with more being discovered or rediscovered. The following are some small, simple offerings:

Dried nettle leaves wrapped around moist cheeses, apples, pears and root vegetables will keep the skins smooth and moist for two or three months.

Figs will keep in good condition wrapped in mullein leaves.

Wrap joints in whole bruised sorrel leaves to tenderize meat.

A few bay leaves placed in flour and rice bins or stored with dried pulses will deter weevils.

Mice are repelled by the smell of mint and tansy leaves.

On long sea voyages, pennyroyal was added to kegs of water to help keep it sweet. Its pungent scent also repels ants. Rub a fresh sprig on the surface of a shelf, cupboard or counter top or across the ant's entrance point or route if you know it. Then leave the sprig in the cupboard, or wherever, and disturb it periodically to release more scent. Stronger scent or larger sprigs are needed for bigger ants. It does not kill the ants, but they do not like the smell and will go elsewhere to avoid it. Rue and tansy will also work but avoid touching rue as it gives some skins a nasty, long-lasting rash.

A pot of basil placed on the window is a traditional deterrent to flies, particularly the small-leaved, compact Greek basil. Bouquets of elder, tansy, mint, peppermint, rue, wormwood, mugwort, pennyroyal, hemp agrimony and chamomile can be strategically placed to deter flies. Try rubbing leaves on the woodwork around a window or door frame.

Black Silk Reviver

Boil ivy leaves and mash until water is dark. Strain and use the solution as a rinse for black silk.

Fumigation

To kill fleas and lice, burn leaves of common fleabane (*Pulicaria dysenterica*), greater fleabane (*Inula conyza*), mugwort and wormwood over low embers and encourage the fumes to fill the room (clear everyone, particularly children and pets away and avoid breathing the fumes). Burn the dried leaf of *Eupatoria cannabium* to drive away wasps and flies.

Rust Stain Remover

Place wood sorrel leaves (*Oxalis acetosella*) in a juice extractor. Dab the juice on rust stain and soak for half an hour. Rinse and repeat if necessary.

For rust on white linen, place a slice of lemon between two sheets of tissue paper, place on the white linen rust spots and press with a hot iron; rinse and repeat as necessary.

Thyme Disinfectant

The general prunings of disinfectant herbs like thyme, juniper, eucalyptus, pine, sage, rosemary, lavender or the roots of angelica will provide a germ-killing solution with a fresh, pleasant scent. Boil the leaves and stems in water for half an hour. The higher the ratio of leaves to water, the stronger the disinfectant will be. Strain and use for washing kitchen surfaces, sinks and bathroom facilities. The addition of a little washing-up liquid will remove grease from surfaces. Store any excess in the fridge for up to one week.

GARDEN USES

Sprigs of elder and bog myrtle (*Myrica gale*) in hats minimize summer midges, and lavender or wormwood deter flies.

Comfrey Fertilizer

The excellent quality of a general fertilizer made from comfrey is due to the rich mineral content of the leaves and stems, particularly the Russian comfrey (*Symphytum uplandicum*) which has valuable amounts of potassium, magnesium, iron and calcium. The high quantity of potassium makes it a near perfect food for fruiting tomato and cucumber plants.

Make up a liquid feed by loosely filling a bucket or a water butt with a tap with comfrey leaves and then add water to cover the leaves. The comfrey then ferments in two weeks in hot weather (up to four weeks in cool weather) to produce a very smelly, brown liquid. Extract it from the tap or squeeze and pour it from the bucket and use this as a concentrated feed. Dilute it at the rate of roughly ⅓ cup to 1 gallon (4.5 l) of water.

Nettle is another herb rich in minerals, trace elements, nitrogen and iron. Process leaves in the same way as comfrey.

Elder Leaf Insecticide

Simmer ½ lb (225 g) leaves in 2 pts (1.2 l) of water for ½ hour. Stir well and then strain. Separately dissolve 1 tsp (5 ml) soap flakes or washing-up liquid in 1 pint (600 ml) of warm water. Mix with the elder water to help the solution to stick to the leaves when it is sprayed on. Use a sprayer with relatively large holes as the mixture will clog fine holes. Elder also has fungicidal properties and there are reports of its success against mildew and blackspot on roses. Rhubard leaves roughly chopped can be prepared as an insecticide following the elder recipe. Take care with hygiene when making homemade insecticides and ensure they are properly labelled and kept safely away from children and pets.

Wormwood prepared as above has powerful insecticide properties against larger pests such as caterpillars, flea beetles and moths, as well as aphids. But this should be diluted to half strength and only used on mature plants because of its toxic properties. An easy way to use the pungent scent of wormwood to deter insects is to lay branches of the herb along rows of carrots and onions in the vegetable garden. The leaves lie there and dry out but release their strong scent whenever they are disturbed. This can mask the carrot scent and confuse the carrot fly.

DECORATIVE USES

Botanical wreaths have been used throughout western civilization to celebrate events, honour heros, athletes and academics and to provide a focus for reflection in mourning. Herbs add an extra dimension by introducing fragrance to the wreath and with their range of leaf colour, shape and texture plus their historical connections, they can be used to create something very special.

Making a Wreath

In addition to your herbs, there are two main materials to acquire. The first is a circular base which may be of bound or plaited straw, plain or moss-covered wire, plaited raffia, twisted vine or bound aromatic twigs. These can be home made or bought from a florist. The second is a range of pins, reel (continuous) wire and stubb wires (wires cut to set lengths) for attaching the herbs to the base. These are available from florists and craft shops who should be able to advise you on suitable sizes of stub wires for the stem thickness of the plants you have selected. Once a stub wire is attached to a herb stem it can be bound with gutta-percha tape, a rubber-based tape available in the natural colours of dark green, brown or white.

Fresh or dried herbs can be used but fresh herbs are more flexible and will dry satisfactorily on the wreath.

Often the base is covered with a background material such as sphagnum moss, securely bound in place with fine florist or reel wire. If a circle of one type of leaf is being applied all around the wreath, first make up bunches with a few sprigs cut to the same length. Lay them on the base and bind them with reel wire. Lay the second bunch to overlap the stems of the first facing the same direction and continue binding with the same reel wire. Proceed around the entire circle tucking the stems of the last bunch under the leaves of the first.

To add individual herbs, bend one third of a stub wire around the stem a few times and use the remaining two thirds to extend the stem and pin the herb into the base. For small sprigs like thyme, wire a few stems together with the top one third of a fine stub wire to create a small bunch and use the remainder as a pin to hold the bunch in the base.

When displaying your herbal wreath, try to avoid direct sunlight, moisture and wind, which all shorten its attractive life. Also consider that dried hangings are not fireproof and should be displayed where there is no danger from stray sparks.

If the hanging is part of a permanent display, clean it periodically with a cool blow-dryer or a vacuum cleaner which can be put on reverse so it blows air out. Hold the open end at least 12 in (30 cm) away from the wreath.

To store a wreath, cover it loosely with tissue paper and pack carefully in a box or an opaque plastic bag to hang in a dark dry location. A few sprigs of santolina, lavender, tansy, wormwood or pennyroyal will help keep bugs away.

Making a Garland

A garland is made in a similar fashion to a wreath using a length of string as the centre piece, or rope if the hanging is to be bulky. Measure out the length of the curve where you wish to hang the garland and cut the string to this length, allowing a little extra for a loop at each end to attach it with. Assemble your material and if you are using fresh herbs and flowers, as many garland makers do, mist spray them with water occasionally while working to keep them fresh. This way the herbs should last three days.

Select your material with an eye to colour, fragrance and scale, favouring those which last longer, like the thick leaves of box and sweet myrtle. You might perhaps decide to choose small herb leaves and flowers in soft colours. A good background would be made up of variegated box with the cream flowers of *Santolina* 'Lemon Queen', the blue grey leaves of ecualyptus, the deep-purple flowers of lavender Hidcote, clusters of the tiny, lime-green flowers of lady's mantle (*Alchemilla mollis*, 'the flower arranger's friend'), the ½-in (1.25-cm) long, steel-blue flowers of the thistle *Eryngium tripartitum*, a small cream miniature florabunda rose called 'Cream Serena' (presently available as a cut flower from Italy) and two yarrow flowers, the cream 'Moonshine' and the relatively new 'Salmon Beauty' with apricot flowers.

Tie on the herbs with a continuous length of fuse wire. Larger leaves are put on indivdually while smaller stems, like thyme sprigs, can be bunched together in groups of three or five. Tie on the first group with the flowers facing towards the end and proceed around the base covering the first stems with the second batch, and so on. Vary the colour, leaf size and shape as you progress but maintain an overall harmony. A common error of beginners is to bunch up too many stems at the start of the garland, so try to spread it evenly. Keep turning the garland so that you work in a spiral around the central string to avoid having a front and back.

MEDICINAL USES

Herbs are humanity's most ancient healing aid with a history of several thousand years of continuous use. Even in orthodox medicine today, plants are an important source of therapeutic material. But with the tendency of medical scientists to isolate the active ingredients of herbs in order to create a more powerful medicine the side effects have also become stronger and more serious.

Another change in western medicine has been the move to specialization which means a focusing of the medic's attention on a particular area of the human body. Such work is against one of the original and fundamental ideas of healing, that of rebalancing the basic influences on our body to remove the cause of the illness. Whether these basics are labelled the four humours, the five elements or lifestyle (diet, exercise and stress levels), the principal is the same. For this reason many people are turning to complementary medicines and herbs make a contribution to several of these systems.

To treat illness with herbs, accurate diagnosis is important and to use herbal treatments it is necessary to consult a qualified medical herbalist. Even if you go to an orthodox doctor just for the diagnosis, it is important to see a qualified herbalist for a herbal prescription because individual dosage and blends of herbs vary with the circumstances of each case. Also, the secondary effects of a desirable herb may not be suitable in certain cases and no book written for the lay person can include all these eventualities. When writers describe the attributes of a herb, if there is any record of the plant being harmful to a certain condition, e.g. pregnancy, they must in conscience advise against its use in such circumstances even though thousands may have used it safely. A qualified herbalist, however, is more likely to know if that particular herb would be safe for you by analysing your specific circumstances.

Despite these comments, there are, several herbs which can be safely used for common ailments like colds, sprains, minor burns and sore throats.

Aloe Vera

The leaf of the *Aloe vera* plant (also named *A. barbadensis*) has remarkable healing properties but it is important to have the true *A. vera* (the botanic meaning of vera is 'true, exact') because there are around 350 species and they do not share the same properties. It is a tender, succulent evergreen needing a minimum temperature of 41°F (5°C). It makes a good houseplant as it enjoys the dry air of interiors and it is in the kitchen that it has earned its name as 'the first-aid plant'. It prefers a gritty, well-drained soil and will take sun or light shade. It can be propagated from off-shoots, young plantlets which grow around the base in spring. Separate these, dry for two days and then repot them in compost made of two parts compost to one part sharp sand. Water once a week in summer, once a month in winter and repot annually in spring.

Research has isolated some active substances from the leaf but none are as effective as the fresh sap which includes all the active ingredients. The sap deteriorates rapidly when isolated so the only way to have a constant supply is to grow it at home although several health product firms are working on ways to preserve it.

Inside the leaf is a clear gelatinous sap which has an immediate soothing effect on burns and when applied, forms a clear protective seal allowing healing to take place rapidly. It has been used since at least the fourth century BC and is still commercially grown. It has attracted the interest of governments for its ability to heal radiation burns and there are reports that the US government is stockpiling *Aloe vera* in Texas for use in case of nuclear war.

For minor burns, break or cut off a leaf segment, preferably from a two-year-old plant and touch sap directly to the burn – it instantly relieves pain and any burning sensation, forms a protective skin to stop infection and healing takes place rapidly. For larger areas, split the leaf, open it out, place the sap against the damaged skin and lightly bandage it in place. Renew this every day. Two fresh leaves crushed or sliced can be applied as a poultice for chapped and dry skin, dermatitis, eczema, sunburn, heat and radiation burns. But remember, always seek trained medical personnel for serious burns.

The soothing and healing qualities of *Aloe vera* leaf sap have long been utilized in cosmetic products. It was said to be one of Cleopatra's secret beauty ingredients and is popular today in moisturizers and hand creams, especially for dry skin, in sun-tan lotions for its cooling and healing properties and shampoos where it relieves an itchy scalp.

Comfrey

This is another leaf with remarkable healing properties. Both forms; *Symphytum officinale* and *Symphytum* x *uplandicum*, also known as *S. peregrinum*, are useful.

The leaf contains allentoin, a protein encouraging cell division, which is responsible for its healing properties. It works through the skin when applied in comfrey ointment, as an 'oil' or in a leaf poultice. It has had some remarkable results in speeding the healing of stubborn leg ulcers, sprains and broken bones in humans and animals, particularly horses. The ointment and oil is also healing for patches of rough skin (like those that preceed eczema); aching joints, sores and skin ulcerations; tissue damaged from burns, cuts, acne and other skin conditions; sprains, and is helpful in reducing the swelling around fractures.

The only ingredient involved in making comfrey oil is the comfrey leaf. The resultant liquid which is created feels half way between a water and an oil. To make comfrey 'oil', pick clean dry, undamaged leaves and cut them roughly into small pieces (say 1 in [25 cm] squares). Pack as much as possible into a clean, dark jar, pressing it in around the shoulder.

Apply a screw-top lid, label and date. Store for about two years and do not open it and let air in. Fermentations eventually produce an amber viscous liquid with a sediment. Decant this 'oil' into a smaller container and label. It will keep for months, probably years.

The list of beneficial vitamins and minerals in comfrey is impressive: vitamins A, C and B12 (especially useful for vegetarians, and previously thought to be only available in meat products), calcium, potassium, phosphorous and trace minerals are all to be found. It has more protein in its leaf structure than any other known member of the vegetable kingdom, equal to soya beans and greater than cheddar cheese. Comfrey also has a reputation for remarkable healings in treating gastric ulcers and in bronchial problems, being widely used in natural tuberculosis sanatoriums of Europe and Scandinavia.

For these uses, comfrey was taken internally (as it has been for centuries) with no reported ill effects. In the 1970s, however, there was a report that large concentrated doses were carcinogenic to the liver of rats, causing worry to users. This was relieved by an announcement in the British Medical Journal (3 March 1979, page 593) evaluating the evidence of pharmacists and scientists plus the accumulated reports of herbalists. It concluded that the carcinogenic response in animals was from continuous high dosing over long periods; that liver poisoning preceded tumour development, and that the consumption in man was much lower and no instances of liver poisoning had ever been reported. It concluded that people who have in the past consumed comfrey have no cause for alarm.

Peppermint, Yarrow and Elderflowers

At the first sign of a cold take a mixture of equal parts of peppermint leaves, yarrow leaves and elderflowers (freeze or dry flowers in spring for year-round use). Infuse ½ tsp (2.5 ml) of each, dried, together in a cup of boiling water for 20 minutes. Strain and add 1 tsp (5 ml) honey. It is even more potent if you also add ¼ tsp (1.25 ml) cayenne pepper. This will decrease the intensity and the discomfort of a cold. These three herbs promote perspiration and reduce temperature which makes frequent hot drinks of the combination also a useful treatment for flu.

Sage

Purple sage is wonderful for sore throats. Make an infusion (1 oz [25 g] dried or 2 oz [50 g] fresh herb to 1 pt [570 ml] boiling water) and let it stand for at least 15 minutes. Drink ½ cup, four times a day and gargle with it anytime to relieve discomfort. Do not use sage if you are pregnant as in rare circumstances it can be abortive.

Sage aids digestion, is antiseptic and antifungal. It also contains an oestrogen-like compound which is useful for women to take in the first half of their menstrual cycle as a daily tea especially during the menopause. It is also a nerve and blood tonic but sage should not be taken in large doses for a long period.

CULINARY USES

Herbs are the magic ingredients that can transform a routine meal into a special experience of zesty, crunchy, refreshing flavours and textures. Herbs and spices used to be necessary to preserve food and mask the often unpleasant taste and smell of meat that was less than fresh. But now we can use a much lighter hand and investigate the delicate flavours of herbs like chervil and buckler leaf sorrel with its lemon piquancy and experiment with combinations of flavours.

The aromatic leaves of rosemary, sage and thyme have maintained their popularity with roast meats not only because their flavours enhance those of the meats but also because they aid the digestion of meat fats.

As we grow more adventurous in preparing the cuisine of other cultures we are introduced to an even wider range of exotic flavourings. Oriental dishes are no longer just one category but the specialities of Thailand, Indonesia or Vietnam are created, each with their own distinctive use of herbs and spices.

And, finally, we are encouraged to rediscover recipes from our own national cookery; dishes where the strong flavoured leaves of lovage and smallage add body to soups and casseroles, where fennel is served in a rich sauce with salmon, and lemon balm is rubbed on game or wrapped around chicken before roasting.

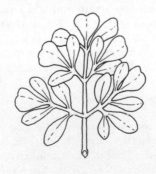

Dinner Party Dishes

PICKLED SAMPHIRE
It is only available for a short season so it is traditionally pickled in vinegar. It can also be served fresh in salads, or cooked in butter as a vegetable.

samphire
white wine vinegar
lemon zest (optional)

Blanch samphire for 10–20 seconds in boiling water. Place in sterilised jars and cover with vinegar. Add a slice of lemon zest to each jar if desired and use within 2 weeks.

If it is to be kept longer, it is necessary to dilute the vinegar as otherwise the vinegar will become dominant. The proportion for storage is 1 part water to 3 parts vinegar.

SMOKED SALMON WITH SAMPHIRE   (Serves 4)
8 thin slices of smoked salmon – get your delicatessen to slice it, it will be thinner than the presliced salmon and it will have more flavour
2 lemons, halved and wrapped in muslin cloth
pickled samphire
12 quail eggs, boiled, shelled with 4 of them cut into half length wise

Place 2 slices of salmon on each large plate. Make a nest of samphire towards the edge of each plate and in it place 2 quail eggs and 2 half eggs. Garnish with the lemon (wrapping the lemon in muslin is a courtesy to prevent the seeds from falling on the salmon).

ROAST POUSSIN WITH HERBS   (Serves 4)
4 poussins (ask your butcher to bone them if your prefer)
1 tbsp (15 ml) fresh thyme (for the stock)
1½ pt (900 ml) good veal stock
4 small sausages
4 slices of bread
1 tsp (5 ml) fresh chives
1 tsp (5 ml) fresh marjoram
1 tsp (5 ml) thyme
(amounts are approximate and governed by taste, but keep the herbs in equal proportions)

Bone each poussin by laying, breast side down, on a chopping board. Slit the skin along the backbone from neck to tail. Working close to the bone, continue cutting down one side of the carcass cutting between the wing bone and thigh bone joints. Work around and up the other side of the rib cage until the meat has been completely removed from the bones. This sounds complicated but if you don't cut the skin, and keep it in one piece the job is not that difficult, and well worth attempting.

Now remove the thigh bone, leaving only one bone in the leg and then sever the first two bones from the wing (use these in the stock), leaving only the upper wing bone. Leaving these bones in the bird helps to reshape the bird before cooking. Set aside until sauce is made.

Roast the bones and add them to the veal stock. Simmer for 1–2 hours. Strain and de-fat the stock. Reduce the stock to form a thick 'sauce'. Strain again, add chopped thyme leaves and season. A few drops of thyme vinegar add a special touch to the sauce.

Skin the sausages, moisten the bread with a little stock, and chop the herbs. Mix together using sufficient herbs to reach the desired aroma. The herbs may be varied: try lemon balm, winter savory, sage or tarragon.

Divide the meat between the birds and reshape them into the original whole bird form. Place on a greased tray and roast at 350°F (180°C) Mark 4 for 15 minutes or until browned and cooked through.

Serve the poussin coated with the sauce and surround with a garland of thyme flowers.

BEEF IN PASTRY *(Serves 2)*

1oz (25 g) butter
12–16 oz (350–450 g) beef fillet
½ lb (225 g) puff pastry
1 large chicken supreme
1 tsp (5 ml) chives finely chopped
10 medium leaves good King Henry (a herb similar to spinach)
2 slices unsmoked bacon

Melt butter in pan, brown beef (approximately 2 minutes) and set aside to cool. Roll out pastry to a thickness of ¼ in (6 mm) in a square. Purée or finely mince the chicken with the chives and good King Henry leaves to form a fine paste, season lightly. Lay the bacon in the middle of the pastry and spread the chicken meat on the bacon to the size of the piece of meat being used. Place the beef on top and wrap the pastry neatly around like a parcel. It is not necessary to moisten the edges to seal the pastry if the dish is cooked immediately.

Cook in a preheated oven at 375°F (190°C) Mark 5 for 20 minutes or until the pastry browns. If the beef is required medium to well-done, the meat must be cooked longer in the browning stage or, for well-done beef, it would be necessary to roast the beef an additional 20 minutes before roasting it in the pastry. Rest for 10 minutes before carving. Serve with a whisky sauce made from cream, meat glaze and whisky reduced to required consistency.

APPLE AND LEMON BALM TERRINE *(Serves 12)*
7 leaves gelatine or ¾ oz (22 g) powdered gelatine
17 fl oz (475 ml) milk
1 vanilla pod
generous handful fresh lemon balm leaves
6 egg yolks
4 oz (100 g) sugar
1 sponge cake – plain
17 fl oz (475 ml) whipped cream
3 apples peeled, sliced and lightly cooked so the pieces remain whole

First soak the gelatine in a little water (or follow packet instructions). Make up a custard by heating the milk and add chopped lemon balm. Leave to infuse for 15 minutes. Reheat and pour over beaten egg yolks and sugar. Return to heat and cook without boiling until it thickens. Strain, add gelatine and set aside to cool.

Line a terrine mould or cake tin with cling film and then with thin slices of the sponge along the base and sides. When the custard is the same temperature as the cream, fold together. Half fill the terrine with the mix and then layer the apples onto the mix. Finally fill to the top, allowing enough room to seal with another layer of the sponge. Cover and chill for 3–4 hours. To serve, unmould onto a flat tray and slice. Serve with a lemon sauce or cream.

LEMON SAUCE
16 fl oz (450 ml) water
8 oz (225 g) sugar
juice of 4 lemons
zest of 1 lemon

Mix the ingredients and bring to the boil to dissolve the sugar. Serve.

RHUBARB SORBET
1 lb (450 g) sugar
1 pt (600 ml) water
2 lb (900 g) rhubarb chopped

Bring all the ingredients to the boil and simmer for 5 minutes. Strain, forcing as much of the fruit through the sieve as possible. When cool, churn in an icecream machine or freeze in trays and churn briefly in a blender, or beat with a fork. Keep bowls, goblets and utensils chilled. Serve in chilled glasses between courses to refresh the palette.

Salads

A quiet revolution is happening to the salads of Britain thanks to people like Joy Larkcom who, in 1976, travelled around Europe on a horticultural scholarship investigating the salad plants of other countries. She collected a wide range of chicories and lettuces and persuaded a few brave seed growers in Britain (like Suffolk Herbs) to begin to offer these varieties. Now the curly leaf of Red Lollo lettuce, first introduced by Joy, is often served in restaurants and is even available in supermarkets.

Herb leaves for a salad can be divided into two groups. First, those herbs which, like lettuce, are used more for a crunchy, fresh texture than flavouring and therefore any amount can be used; such leaves are blanched dandelion, chicory and summer purslane which has a nutty flavour.

Second is the group of sharp-flavoured leaves which should be used only in small quantities as an accent. This would include leaves like basil, chives, lemon thyme, marjoram, mint, nasturtium, sorrel and salad rocket.

For the best flavour, pick at the last minute and only wash if necessary. Small leaves of basil, thyme and marjoram are best left whole while larger ones can be loosely chopped with a stainless steel knife or cut with scissors; tear large basil leaves.

The colourful range of herb leaves can be used to advantage in the presentation of salads. Gold variegated lemon balm can be spread through a green salad to give splashes of colour or a gradual colour change. To create the image of the opening of a giant flower place white chicory in the centre, an inner ring of bright green purslane and lemon balm, an outer ring of stripes of deep green sorrel and, outside, a row of purple salad bowl lettuce.

Flowers and roots are also returning to the salad arena and they are introduced in the flower and root chapters.

Teas

A drink to soothe, solace, heal, and cheer; teas made of aromatic leaves, flowers or roots steeped in water are the most ancient and popular liquid for our consumption. Many herbal tea leaves are easy to grow in our gardens and in addition can be calming and relaxing or stimulating and invigorating. Several herbal teas have specific therapeutic benefits and are used as treatments. Japanese research has discovered that green tea helps prevent stomach cancer.

The word tisane originally meant barley water from the Latin 'ptisana' and the Greek 'ptisane'. In the recent past it has been used to specify unfermented leaves as opposed to the fermented leaves of black tea. But here we use the term 'herb teas'.

HERB LEAVES

It is written in the *Chinese Manual of the Origins of Customs*, that the ceremony of offering tea to a guest began with Kwan Yin, the Goddess of Mercy, during the lifetime in which she was a disciple of Laotse. When he decided to depart to the western mountains she was first at the Han Pass and presented the 'Old Philosopher' with a cup of the golden elixir.

This is one of the most pleasurable aspects of tea, honouring friendship with a lovingly prepared simple drink and here we have much to learn from Eastern cultures.

Herbs can be used fresh or dried. As a rough guide, one part dried equals three parts fresh. Most herb teas are infused, that is, leaves or flowers are put into a warm teapot, boiling water is poured over and the tea is brewed for 3–5 minutes depending on the herb. One tsp (5 ml) of dried or 1 tbsp (15 ml) of fresh herbs is added for each cup of boiling water. Seeds and root are usually ground or pulversized in a pestle and mortar just before use and then made into a decoction; 1 tbsp (15 ml) of crushed root or seeds is put in 2 cups of boiling water and simmered until the water is reduced to 1 cup, approximately 5–20 minutes depending on the herb. Try mint, chamomile, linden, peppermint, rose hip and lemon verbena – as they are all easy to enjoy.

3
HERBAL FLOWERS

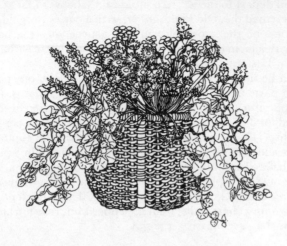

Flowers are the show stoppers of botany; the enchanting, delicate, yet sensuous, pinnacle of a plant's beauty. The flowers of herb plants have a special appeal. They are generally soft colours and shapes flowering in abundance with a blousey innocence that evokes images of old-fashioned cottage gardens. Yet there are a few stunners among them like the Madonna lily whose flowers were once used to treat bruises and epilepsy.

There are flowers for eating in salads, soothing our nerves, cleansing our skin and making fragrant gifts. Among these, the world's favourite flower, the rose, offers all these possibilities and is probably unsurpassed in its range of herbal applications.

While the leaves of herbs provide the permanent structure, colour and continuous pleasure of a herb garden, it is the flowers which, for a brief moment, can make our spirits soar. As the large flower bud of a tall graceful Madonna lily slowly swells, our anticipation grows until the pure-white, elegant petals unfold to assure us that this world is not mundane. The flower with its sweet, penetrating fragrance has been used as a pain killer and a cosmetic. The lily thrives on a sunny slope with good drainage. Unlike other lilies, the Madonna lily only roots from the base of the bulb so it requires just 2 in (5 cm) of soil above the bulb when planting and it shouldn't be allowed to dry out. Start with healthy stock and it will flourish undisturbed for many years. If you get the rich, yellow pollen of the lily on your clothes, you will also discover it is a strong dye.

Lavender is the essence of an English herb garden. Who could ever be without the silver leaves and soft purple flowers alight with white butterflies. It traditionally lines the pathway and promises sweet

82

lavender bags to scent the winter months. To see whole fields of lavender in bloom is an unforgettable treat. It becomes one of those visions tucked in the mind to be called upon in troubled times.

The list of flowers with herbal uses is long indeed. The following are but a few: bergamot, sweet myrtle, marjoram and oregano, rosemary flowers, poppies, elderflower, primrose and cowslip, sage, daisy, nasturtium, mullein, rose, lavender, borage, calendula, chamomile, pyrethrum, chicory, clove pinks, meadowsweet, sweet woodruff, sweet rocket, hops, digitalis, skullcap, roses, violets, lupins, bugloss, musk mallow, goat's rue, jasmine, mock orange, lily, sweet clover, meadow crane's bill, peony and hound's tongue.

THEME GARDENS

In addition to their practical uses, the potent historical and romantic associations of herbal flowers make them a seductive theme for gardens.

Mary Gardens

The rose for pure love and martydom and the lily for purity and innocence are the emblems of Mary Gardens and plantings with these and other herbs associated with Mother Mary have been popular since earliest monastic days. There are medieval references to St Mary Gardens, walled and full of beautiful flowers and 'birds like angels'. At one point they reached near-cult proportions, to the concern of the Catholic hierarchy, and restrictive directives were issued. Many flowers carry the words 'Our Lady' in their name: Our Lady's mantle (*Alchemilla mollis*), Our Lady's smock (*Cardamine pratensis*), Our Lady's bedstraw (*Galium verum*), Our Lady's Garters (ribbon grass), though now the 'Our' is frequently dropped; lady's mantle, lady's smock, etc.

The blue of rosemary flowers is said to have been transformed from white when Mary laid her blue cloak over the plant. A legend relates that the white leaf veins of blessed milk thistle (*Silybum marianum*) came from Mary's milk. The name costamary (*Chrysanthemum balsamita* or *Tanacetum balsamita*), called Our Lady's balsam, comes from 'Costa' or 'kostos' the Greek name for a spicy Oriental plant because of its spicey mint fragrance; and Mary because it was a plant of Mary or women in general. It was also called the bible herb because early American Pilgrims carried the long, slender leaves as book-marks in their bibles both to allay appetites during long sermons and as a long-lasting, green and fragrant bookmark. Forget-me-not, sometimes called 'Mary's eyes' and marigold (*Calendula officinalis*), once known as 'Marygold', claim Marian connections. Others include Our Lady's fingers (*Anthyllis vulneraria*), Our Lady's keys (cowslip), Our Lady's thimble (harebell), Our Lady's tears (lily-of-the-valley), Lady's orchid (*Orchis purpurea*), and

Our Lady's tresses (*Spiranthes spiralis*). A combination of several of these herbs and wild flowers planted together as a Mary Garden could provide a gentle environment for quiet contemplation.

Herb Flowers in a Monastery Garden

The connection between religious orders and herb gardens is an ancient and honourable one. When the Romans came to Britain they introduced around 400 herbs: pot herbs, sweet herbs, salad herbs and their important medicinal plants. They also introduced the system of cultivating plants in enclosed gardens and the idea of a vegetable-medicine garden. When they left, only the hardiest herbs survived without the horticultural skills of the Roman gardeners. Many of the herbs were reintroduced during the Anglo-Saxon invasion of 449 AD and then by the monks who accompanied Augustine to Kent in 597 AD. Credit goes to the monks for restoring and maintaining the gardens of England and the herbs they contained through several bleak and troublesome centuries. They grew healing herbs in the physic garden and provided an area to sit and convalesce in the cloister garden. And in the Paradise gardens were the herbs and flowers for the altar to glorify God.

A monastery garden could include the widest range of herbs. It would also be the perfect place for a central, stone water fountain (the water of life), a vine-covered walkway, a bee hive and the statue of a beloved saint.

One can occasionally find a statue of Saint Fiacre, the patron saint of gardeners, St Francis of Assisi, or Clare of Assisi.

There are saints and holy beings associated with a love of nature, plants and healing in every spiritual movement. From Ancient Greece there is Asclepius, the God of Healing, and his three daughters: Hygieia, Goddess of Health; Iaso, whose name means 'to cure', and Panacea, or 'all-healing'.

Two of my favourites are Kwan Yin and Lady Sengen Sama who is enshrined in a Shinto tablet at the foot of Mount Fuji. She represents the idea that simple, sensitive beauty is a powerful and permanent expression of higher truths and that a garden of peace, harmony and beauty is a focus of spiritual energy as worthy as any temple. What she embodies is encapsulated in the best of Japanese gardens.

There are many herbs mentioned in the Bible, the Koran, the Vedas and other Holy Books and many cultures have sacred plants such as the lotus, arum lily, mistletoe and vervain which could become the starting point or the focal point of a garden for contemplation.

A Garden of Shakespeare's Herbs

The diverse subjects encompassed by Shakespeare's eclectic knowledge included the herbs of his day and their uses and meaning. Over 80 culinary, medicinal and wild flower herbs are sprinkled through his poetry.

If you wanted to create a 'Shakespeare garden'; it could include a knot garden using Shakespeare's 'winter herbs' with perhaps rosemary topiary. This herb can easily be clipped to a neat shape such as a sphere, column or cone, a popular feature of the time. The garden would have geometric paths and regular beds of herbs edged with the smaller evergreens like thyme and pinks. A central statue or fountain; seats; a bank of turf with small flowers growing among the grass, and an arbour or bower of fragrant plants would be suitable. This could be planted with honeysuckle and the several roses mentioned by Shakespeare (the white rose of York (*Rosa alba*); the red rose of Lancaster (*R. gallica officinalis*); the cabbage rose (*R. centifolia*); the damask rose (*R. trigentipetals*); rose of May (Cinnamon rose); the dog rose (*R. canina*), and the 'mingled' damask (*R. mundi*). The garden might be enclosed with a hedge of sweet briar or wattle fencing with rosemary against it. For an informal style to accommodate the wilder herbs mentioned by Shakespeare we can turn to the writings of Francis Bacon.

Bacon's essays include many modern ideas. He was concerned for health and freshness and dismissed a pond as unwholesome, 'full of flies and frogs', unless the water could be perpetually changed. He planned aromatic pockets of rosemary, wild strawberries and thyme and recommended walkways carpeted with sweet-scented herbs.

He also suggested an ancient Chinese garden idea, that of planting for enjoyment in all seasons, and recommended less familiar scents like the fragrance of wild strawberry leaves to scent the autumn air.

Fairie Herbs

In Shakespeare's time the fairies, elves, hobgobblins and sprites who flit through his plays were quite real to his contemporaries. The consensus was that their visible presence had been quite common in the past but that they no longer allowed themselves to be seen.

The writings of Shakespeare did much to change the image of fairies as mischievious, even frightening, creatures of the darkness to childlike creatures of the moonlight.

Herbs from Shakespeare's works associated with fairies and flowery meads include: Forget-me-nots, lawn daisies (*Bellis perennis*), wild thyme, columbine, harebell, wild strawberry, cowslip, primrose, ox-eye daisy, lemon balm, yarrow, borage, saffron crocus, Adonis flower (*Anemone nemorosa*), salad burnet, clover, cuckoo-flowers (*Ranunculus varieties*), daffodils (small wild forms), pinks, fumitory (*Fumaria officinalis*), lady's smock, lark's heel (*Delphinium ajacis*), poppies, pansy, narcissus, mustard and Dian's bud (wormwood).

Sacred Herbs

There are nine herbs listed in an ancient Anglo-Saxon text, the *Lacnunga*, and there is a certain fascination in the belief that they could protect against physical, mental and emotional ailments. The herbs are chervil, crabapple, fennel, mugwort, maythen (chamomile), stime (watercress), waybroed (plantain), wergula (nettle) and the previously unidentified atterlothe. It has now been translated to cockspur grass by the Archaeological Unit in Bury St Edmunds and this is likely the 'Cock's head fitch' (Onobrychis), or sainfoin, of Culpeper's Herbal of 1645. This group of rather unruly and unattractive herbs could be given a bit of style by planting them with paths in the shape of a Celtic knot design with the crabapple tree in the centre.

The six herbs betony, vervain, peony root (named after Paeon, the physician of Olympus), plantain, yarrow and the rose were worn in an amulet to ward off evil and many sacred herbs were burned on hilltops on St John's Day (23 June). It was believed that they purified the air and protected people, livestock and crops. St John's wort was the best known.

FLOWER SYMBOLISM

Flowers are a favourite subject of myths and legends, and since story telling began they have been imbued with personalities and virtues.

The earliest reference to a language of flowers comes in the *Dream Book of Artimedorus* written by a Greek who lived around AD 170. Although this book doesn't give us specific symbols it recounts that each flower in a garland has its own meaning.

The Chinese have a rich folklore of flower signatures. The peach flower represents good luck and happiness while the fruit symbolizes longevity. In art and literature, the plum stands for purity and nobility. The tree peony is the 'king of flowers', the 'most beautiful of the beauties' and represents beauty in paintings, pottery and embroidery. The tall and graceful lily with white flowers is said to embody purity, brightness, freedom and happiness.

The white Arabian jasmine (*Jasminum sambac*) examples shy beauty. Each flower lasts only 12–20 hours, opening at dusk and climaxing around 10 pm, the time to collect them for perfume. The aroma is 'as sweet as roses, as delicate as plums and as exquisite as orchids, pleasing both refined and simple noses.'

The chrysanthemum is a favourite ornamental plant in China where 1000 species have been developed, although it was originally regarded only as an edible and medicinal plant. It is part of the Taoist elixir of immortality and symbolized longevity even before the third century when a physician, Ge Hong, investigated a village of people in Henan province who were noted for living to a ripe old age. He reported that the water they drank was medicated by the roots of the wild chrysanthemum which covered the river valley.

Sacred Flora

Flowers were given religious significance either from their association with a holy person, as mentioned in the theme gardens, or because of their physical attributes, such as the purity of the lotus or the passion flower with its layers of images; the shape of the spear seen in the leaf, the five wounds in the five anthers, the tendrils like the cords and whips, the ovary column as the pillar of the cross, the stamens like hammers and the dark circle of threads symbolizing the crown of thorns. As a simpler statement, the four petalled flowers of the cruciform family (mustard, radish and salad rocket with delicate purple veining on each petal) represent the crucifixion.

The lotus also has a powerful image of nobility and elegance. It emerges from the mud unspoiled to offer its pure colour and pleasing fragrance. It has become a symbol of the process of enlightenment for Buddhists. In Japan, it is the emblem of Paradise and in Hindu theology a different variety of lotus represents the womb which gave birth to the god Brahma. It represents the seven chakras or centres of consciousness in yogic philosophy, too.

The iris was the Christian symbol of royalty and often appears in religious paintings as a garland crown above the Virgin, or as a single flower in the hand of baby Jesus or as a clump growing outside the stable. Other paintings include the columbine (or aquilegia) representing the seven gifts of the spirit. Painters wishing for accurate symbolism would paint seven flowers on the stem. The daisy for innocence, the wild strawberry for righteousness, and the violet for humility can be seen in Botticelli's paintings and in the Unicorn Tapestries.

Elizabethan and Victorian England

A language of flowers surfaced in Britain in early Elizabethan days. A sort of floral alphabet appeared with cowslips for counsel, gilly-flowers for gentleness and marigolds for marriage.

In 1847, a Mr Thomas Miller wrote *The Poetical Language of Flowers; or, The Pilgrimage of Love* in which he compiled Chaucer's, Spencer's, Shakespeare's and Milton's floral meanings. But it was not until Captain Marryat wrote *The Floral Telegraph or Affection's Signals* about 30 years later that enough vocabulary was included (much of it original), to make it possible to send sophisticated messages. As a man of the sea he decided things should be done properly. So the flowers were tied together on a knotted ribbon which was slowly untied to reveal the message as the flowers and the knots between both had meaning.

The idea of secret flower messages became very popular and, of course, commercialized. Floral birthday books and cards, flower symbols for each zodiac sign, flower fairies and a book *The Bible Language of Flowers* were all for sale. A range of postcards appeared with a variety of subtle floral messages for those hoping to bypass the scrutiny of parents and post-men. Even the placing of the postage stamp carried a special meaning until a postcard was published illustrating 'The Language of Stamps'.

Tussie-Mussies

But the most romantic aspect was the sending of messages in a bouquet of flowers called a tussie-mussie. This is a small bouquet of aromatic flowers and leaves sometimes called a posie or a nose-gay. In Eliza-bethan times, and earlier, they were mainly composed of the scented medicinal herbs like rosemary, thyme and rue which had disinfectant properties and were carried to offer some protection against the plague and general unpleasant smells of the day. Judges carried them into courtrooms to prevent them catching gaol fever from prison inmates.

But with meaning attributed to each flower, the planning and giving of posies took on an extra dimension. The idea of using the language of flowers to send a secret message of love reached its peak around 1857 when Arthur Freeling published *Flowers, Their Use and Beauty, Language and Sentiment*. His was a scholarly manual and he included his research on the derivation of each meaning.

Today a tussie-mussie can be used to send a variety of pleasant messages, not just romantic. One of the nicest ideas is to wish someone a speedy recovery is with a posie. It is not only decorative, but the aromatic herbs have soothing and healing properties particularily enjoyable to anyone confined to bed. Flowers and leaves can be chosen to celebrate a birthday. Mother's Day, Father's Day, a wedding, the birth of a baby or to share a sadness.

Making a Tussie-Mussie

It is worth learning to make a tussie-mussie for the pleasure of seeing the delight of your recipient. A tussie-mussie usually has a single flower in the centre, often a rose, a circle of a contrasting leaves, then a circle of another flower or another leaf, building a round bouquet with concentric rings of different coloured leaves and flowers.

Read through the following language of flowers and choose your message. Select your central blossom. Encircle this with a contrasting herb, binding the stems together with florist's tape. If your posie is a large size, you have the choice of creating a dome shape or to maintain a flat shape. If this is the case, the outside stems will be bent almost to right angles. To stop the stem breaking it may be necessary to wire them ahead of time. Mist spray occasionally as you work.

For the outermost ring choose a large-leaved herb with an interesting edge. Lady's mantle, angelica, strawberry, variegated ivy and gardener's garters all give a pleasing shape to the outer edge. The stems can be finished off with a ribbon, a lace doily or a piece of lace. On a card you can note the meaning of the flowers except perhaps for the love messages where the subtlety of the flowers is sufficient.

The tussie-mussie can be kept fresh in water for about a week or hung up to dry in a warm dark dry place where it will eventually assume muted antique tones.

The following are some suggested combinations:

Bridal
New Dawn rose for love
sage for domestic virtue
sweet myrtle for love
rosemary for remembrance
variegated ivy for fidelity

Get Well
lemon verbena for its fresh scent
scarlet geranium for comfort
chamomile for energy in adversity
thyme for courage
lady's mantle for protection
hyssop for cleanliness
lemon balm for sympathy

Posie for a New Baby
tiny pink rose-bud for 'pure
and lovely' in the centre
variegated mint for virtue
thyme for courage
marjoram for blushes
daisy for innocence
lady's mantle for protection
sweet pea for delicate pleasures
wild strawberry for protection

The Language of Flowers

Angelica – inspiration
Apple – temptation
Balm – sympathy
Basil, sweet – good wishes
Bay (leaf) – unchanging affection
Bay tree – glory
Belladonna – silence
Betony – surprise
Birch – meekness
Bluebell – constancy
Borage – bluntness
Box – stoicism
Broom – ardour
Bugloss – falsehood

Buttercup – promises of riches
Carnation – pure love
Cedar – strong and incorruptable
Chamomile – energy in adversity
Chervil – sincerity
Chickweed – rendezvous
Chicory – frugality
Clover – happiness
Coltsfoot – justice
Columbine – folly
Coriander – hidden worth
Cowslip – pensiveness
Crocus – youthful gladness
Daffodil – regret

Daisy – innocence
Dandelion – oracle
Eglantine – simplicity
Elder – zealous
Evening primrose – uncertainty
Fennel – worthy of praise
Flax – domestic industry
Forget-me-not – true love
Foxglove – insincerity
Geranium – comfort
Harebell – grief
Hawthorn – hope
Heartsease – tender thoughts
Holly – domestic happiness
Hollyhock – ambition
Honeysuckle – fidelity
Hop – injustice
Houseleek – domestic energy
Hyssop – cleanliness
Ivy – wedded love
Jacob's ladder – descend
Jasmine – amiability
Juniper – protection
Lavender – acknowledgement of
   love
Lilac – first emotions of love
Lily (white) – purity, modesty
Lily-of-the-valley – return of
   happiness
Lime tree – conjugal love
Lupin – dejection
Marigold (African) – vulgar
   minds
Marigold (French) – jealousy
Marigold (calendula) – sunny
   disposition
Marsh mallow – beneficence
Meadowsweet – uselessness
Mignonette – your qualities
   surpass your charms
Mint – virtue
Motherwort – concealed love

Mugwort – happiness
Myrtle – love
Nasturtium – patriotism
Olive – peace
Orange blossoms – chastity
Parsley – festivity
Passion Flower – religious fervour
Pennyroyal – flee away
Peppermint – warmth of feeling
Pink – perfection
Poppy – sleep and dreams
Primose – early youth
Rocket – rivalry
Rosemary – remembrance
Rose (full bloom) – secrecy
Rose (white) – purity
Rose (pink) – love
Rose (red) – passion
Rue – the herb of grace
Saffron – marriage and mirth
Sage – esteem, domestic virtue
Snowdrop – consolation and hope
Sorrel – affection
Southernwood – jokey, bantering
Spearmint – warmth of sentiment
Star of Bethlehem – reconciliation
Strawberry – perfection
Sweet pea – delicate pleasures
Tansy – I declare war against you
Teasel (Fuller's) – misanthropy
Thyme – activity
Valerian – accommodating
   disposition
Vervain – enchantment
Vine – mirth, intoxication
Violet – faithfulness
Wallflower – fidelity in misfortune
Weeping willow – forsaken
Witch hazel – a spell
Wormwood – absence
Yarrow – war and healing
Yew – sorrow

TREES AND SHRUBS WITH HERBAL FLOWERS

The flowers of many trees and shrubs have a variety of culinary, medicinal and cosmetic uses but the most alluring are those used for their fragrance. Roy Genders, in his *Scented Flora of the World*, lists 300 species of trees, shrubs and climbing plants with scented flowers. The tropical frangipani, gardenia, henna, jasmine, osmanthus and ylang-ylang have rich exotic perfumes highly valued locally to scent body and hair, and internationally in the making of perfumes. Sweet myrtle, whose fresh flowers give us the perfumed water called 'eau d'ange', grows in southern Europe along with the citrus tree family which gives us the orange blossom and its exquisite essential oil, neroli, and the lemon and bergamot trees.

But perfumed shrub flowers are not restricted to hot climates. The lilac, mock orange (Philadelphus), *Viburnam fragrans*, daphne, apple blossom and honeysuckle give us a rainbow of sweet fragrances.

Other flowers with a variety of useful applications include the elder-flower, the blossom of the lime tree, broom flowers and hops. The common elder flower has a muscatel scent used in desserts and wine making. It is also an important part of herbal treatment for colds while the flower infusion is an excellent tonic for oily skins and an attractive aftershave for men. Infused blossoms of the lime tree or linden provides a tea famous in Europe for settling the stomach after a heavy meal.

Golden broom flowers are rich in pollen and attractive to bees. The shrub is called broom because the tough, flexible branches were once used for sweeping. The flower buds, pickled for use in salads, were considered a delicacy in the time of Henry VIII (who also drank an infusion of the flowers to treat gout). Parts of the plant are used in several of today's pharmaceutical drugs, including diuretics.

Newly-opened hop flowers yield a plant essence which is useful in an astringent skin lotion; and the ripe, unpollinated female flowers are used to clear and preserve beer, giving it the characteristic bitterness. The dried flowers with their papery bracts are soporific, or mildly sedative and used in sleep pillows.

But the most significant herbal flower is the rose. There are culinary recipes for soups, salads, meat dishes, desserts, Turkish delight, jams, jellies and drinks using roses. The petals are used fresh, crystallized and made into rose water. Cosmetics and perfumes often use rose essence extracted from the petals; medicinal and nutritional use is made of rose hips, the fruit of the rose; the most basic ingredient of pot pourri is rose petals, and what could be more beautiful in any interior than a bowl of old-fashioned roses.

The predominance of silver plants in a herb garden provides a beautiful foil for roses and can hide their bare stems. The artemisias, santolinas, pinks and the traditional rose companions – lavender and catmint – are especially attractive. The colour of pink roses is enriched by the presence of contrasting blue flowers, particularly the geranium or meadow cranesbill which produces its edible blue flowers at the same time. Another useful plant for concealing the base of roses is parsley which is said to help repel greenfly. Most members of the onion/garlic family also have this reputation and, in addition, garlic is said to increase the scent of the roses which it may do through a root secretion.

THE FUNCTION OF FLOWERS

A herb plant in flower is preparing to reproduce. Most flowers are made up of four concentric parts. The outer part attached to the stem is the calyx (or sepals), which are usually green. When the flower is in bud the calyx forms a protective layer over the corolla (or petals) folded inside – the second layer. The corolla is that which we normally think of as the flower, and is the part used in most recipes. Sometimes the petals are joined together to create a tube as in the foxglove. The next ring, inside the corolla, consists of male stamens which are made up of a filament (or stalk) and the anther (or pollen sac) at the top. Finally, at the centre of the flower is the female carpel which has the ovary at the base and the pistil at the top. The pistil is made up of the style (or stem) and the stigma (or tip).

Pollination occurs when the pollen from the stamens is transferred to the ripe, sticky surface of the stigma. This can be done by wind or insects. Most of the herb flowers which attract our interest are insect pollinated as these are the plants which have evolved bright colours, scent and glands of sweet nectar to entice bees and butterflies and, in passing, entice us, too.

When the pollen lands on the stigma it begins to grow. Each grain develops a tube which grows down the style into the ovary. The tip of this tube carries two pollen cells to be released into a ovule which also contains two cells. One pollen cell joins with the egg cell to create the new seed embryo and the other two cells join to create the food supply, rather like a placenta. The two parts are stored together in the seed coat.

When a bee visits a flower, rumaging for nectar and pollen which it eats, it carries some on its body to the next plant it visits. If the next flower species is too different, the pollen tube will not grow on the alien stigma, so if the bee travels from a thyme flower to a marjoram flower nothing happens. But if the plant is the same variety or very near, cross-fertilization will occur. Sometimes this creates interesting new varieties but it can also create muddy blends. This is the reason fennel and dill should not be planted near each other as cross-fertilization creates a seed without the clear flavour of either parent.

Plant Families

It is mainly by the details of the floral structure and the arrangement of flowers on the stem that botanists classify plants. When a species grows in different climatic and soil conditions, the leaves and stem can differ but the arrangement of the flower parts remains constant, even if their size and colour vary. For example, the Boraginaea family have five-petalled flowers which are often blue like borage and forget-me-not; the Cruciferea family have flowers with four equal petals: like mustard and rocket; and the Labiatae includes two-lipped flowers, which are often aromatic and favoured by bees, such as lavender, thyme and sage.

Perfect Flowers

When a flower contains both the female stigmas and male stamens together, this is botanically called a 'perfect flower'.

The saffron crocus (*crocus sativus*) is one example and it will survive the British climate. From the mid-fourteenth century to the beginning of the twentieth century, it was grown commercially around the town of Saffron Walden in Essex. But the bulb needs a long, hot summer to produce the flowers with their desirable stigmas. The purple flowers open in the autumn and each contains three long, red stigmas next to the orange anthers. The stigmas protrude from the flower and this distinguishes it from the poisonous 'autumn crocus' or 'naked ladies' which are also called meadow saffron (*Colchium autumnale*). Grow the saffron bulb in a rich, well-drained soil in a sheltered spot. If it is on the sunny side of a white wall this will raise the soil temperature significantly. Pick the saffron stigmas as soon as the flower opens.

HARVESTING FLOWERS

Flowers reach perfection and contain the highest proportion of active ingredients as they first open fully so this is the ideal time to pick them. Choose unblemished flowers of good shape as distorted flowers can indicate damage from pests, chemical sprays or a virus. They are best collected at midday in dry weather and it is easiest to pick the whole flowering stem and separate the flowers later indoors, free from wind. If you pick flower-heads, try to avoid touching the petals. Keep them loose in open containers as they bruise easily and soon begin to sweat. Cut flowering stems of lavender and thyme just as the flowers open.

When picking for culinary use, check for insects and dirt and find out if the area has been sprayed with chemicals. Look inside the tube of bergamot flowers as it is an ideal home for small creepy-crawlies. Avoid flowers which will need washing as this will spoil the texture. Very few petals are poisonous; even the daffodil, whose bulb has killed people when mistakenly cooked for an onion, has an edible flower. But of the poisonous plants it is safest to assume that the poisonous principals are also in the flowers so do not eat the following:

Poisonous Plants

Alder buckthorn (*Frangula alnus*)

Baneberry (*Actaea spicata*)

Bittersweet (*Solanum dulcamara*)

Black nightshade (*Solanum nigrum*)

Buckthorn (*Rhamnus cathartica*)

Bryony black (*Tamus communis*)

Bryony white (*Bryonia dioica*)

Buttercup family (*Ranunculus*)

Columbine (*Aquilegia vulgaris*)

Cowbane (*Cicuta virosa*)

Daphne (*Daphne mezereum*)

Darnel rye grass (*Lolium temulentum*)

Deadly nightshade (*Atropa bella-donna*)

Dog's mercury (*Mercurialis perennis*)

Fool's parsley (*Aethusa cynapium*)

Foxglove (*Digitalis purpurea*)

Fritillary (*Fritillaria meleagris*)

Green hellebore (*Helleborus viridis*)

Stinking hellebore (*Helleborus foetidus*)

Hemlock (*Conium maculatum*)

Henbane (*Hyoscyamus niger*)

Ivy (*Hedera helix*)

Laburnum – all varieties

Lily-of-the-valley (*Convallaria majalis*)

Meadow saffron (*Colchicum autumnale*)

Mistletoe (*Viscum album*)

Monkshood (*Aconitum napellus*)

Privet (*Ligustrum vulgare*)

Spindle tree (*Euonymus europaeus*)

Spurges, all (*Euphorbia*)

Spurge-laurel (*Daphne laureola*)

Thorn apple (*Datura stramonium*)

Yew (*Taxus baccata*)

When picking just a few flowers for immediate use, separate them from the calyx, the green backing of the flower which is attached to the stem, as you pick them. With borage, if you hold the flower by the black anthers and twist gently, the whole flower will part from the calyx leaving you with that extraordinarily beautiful blue star in your hand.

The flower part used most often in herbal recipes is the petal. The green sepals, or calyx, is usually removed as it has a bitter taste. For rose petals, other large petals and any with green shading at the base, tear off the bottom section as it may be bitter. For daisy-type flowers, and any with hard centres, pull off their petals and sprinkle them on at the last minute. Small flowers like thyme and marjoram can be left whole.

DRYING FLOWERS

Petals like calendula and roses, and all the flowers for pot pourri, should be dried in a dust-free environment with good ventilation out of direct sunlight. This is usually done by laying petals or whole, small flowers on gauze stretched over a frame so that the air can circulate. At a pinch, they can be laid on newspaper but then they need to be turned occasionally. Make sure the petals do not overlap as they may not dry properly. The ideal temperature for the first day is 90°F (32°C), then 75–80°F (24–28°C) afterwards. Allow four to seven days for small flowers and up to two or three weeks for thick petals. Small rose buds and the thick petals of lilies will need turning once or twice.

Several flowers such as lavender, chamomile, delphiniums, larkspur, love-in-a-mist and the everlasting flowers can be dried on the stem. Either lay the flowering stems on open trays or hang them upside down in small bunches, not more than ten stems together.

If only the lavender flowers are required, say for sweet bags or recipes, they can be rubbed off when wanted but don't discard the stems. Burn them on an open fire for fragrance or make incense by soaking them with 1 tbsp dissolved saltpetre for 30 minutes.

The same drying procedure is used for medicinal and cosmetic recipes. The best quality is necessary for medical, culinary and tea herbs and each variety should be dried separately so that confusion does not arise. Cleanliness must be a priority during drying and storage.

Finally, store the flowers in dark jars or paper bags, with the name and date. Those required for decoration need to be stored flat in a rigid container.

Freezing Flowers

Borage and sweet violet flowers can be captured in an ice-cube to be used as a garnish for cool drinks. Place violets face down and borage flowers with their black anthers upward in the base of an ice-cube container. This way you will see the face of the violet but avoid the black bits of the borage sticking out and looking like a dead fly in your drink. Gently add water to cover and freeze. If you have difficulty keeping the flower in position, just put a little water on the top, freeze and then fill the cube and freeze again.

COSMETIC USES

Flower Waters

Four flower waters have become classic skin tonics as their reputation after hundreds of years of use has not diminished. Lavender water is suitable for delicate and sensitive skins; it is very healing as it speeds cell replacement and is mildly antiseptic to help reduce acne. Orange flower water also has a reputation for stimulating the replacement of old cells; it helps in the treatment of dry skin and broken capillaries and is said to help restore the skin's acid balance. Rose water is a tonic for dry, sensitive and mature skins with a refining and softening effect. Elderflower is good for mature or sallow skins; it softens the texture, helps to smooth wrinkles and fades freckles. It, too, has healing properties and is soothing for sunburn.

The flower waters can be used as they are as an astringent or refresher or they can be mixed with other ingredients for additional benefits such as the following rosewater tonic recipe. Mix 2 parts rosewater with 1 part witch hazel and a few drops of glycerine for its softening properties. It includes distilled witch hazel, made from the leaves and bark of the shrub and is astringent and soothing. The witch hazel from the chemist contains 15 per cent alcohol which means it will keep almost indefinitely. When it is mixed with a water-based liquid the percentage of alcohol is diluted and the preservative qualities with it.

Flower Astringents

Cornflowers and meadowsweet flowers have astringent properties and an infusion makes an effective refresher.

generous handful of cornflowers or meadowsweet flowers
½ pt (300 ml) boiling water
1 tsp (5 ml) witch hazel

Infuse flowers and water and allow to cool. Strain, add witch hazel, bottle and keep refrigerated.

Cornflowers and meadowsweet can also be used in a cleansing milk along with gentle chamomile to soften and lighten the skin (excellent for under-eye shadows). Lime blossom soothes and softens and has a reputation for deep-cleansing, and sweet violets have a gentle soothing astringent action. They can be used individually or blended.

Three Flower Cleansing Milk

½ cup (125 ml) buttermilk
1 tbsp (15 ml) chamomile flowers
1 tbsp (15 ml) lime blossom
1 tbsp (15 ml) elder blossom

Put all the ingredients in a double boiler, and simmer for 30 minutes. Do not allow the milk to boil. Leave to infuse and cool and for a further two hours and strain. Store in the refrigerator and use within a week. Apply with cotton wool and tissue off. Follow with a skin tonic.

Cowslip Cleanser

Cowslip flowers are said to aid deep cleansing, clearing the skin of dirt and perspiration.

small handful of cowslip flowers and stalks
½ pt (300 ml) boiling water
2 tsp (10 ml) witch hazel

Infuse flowers until cool, strain; add witch hazel and use as a cleanser.

Bath Flowers

Tie a handful of flowers in a muslin bag and hang this under your running water as you draw a bath.

Relaxing bath herbal flowers: chamomile, jasmine, lime flowers, meadowsweet
Deep cleansing bath herbal flowers: rose petals
Healing bath herbal flowers (for sun burn or wind burn): calendula, red clover, lavender
Tranquilizing herbal flowers: chamomile, cowslips, jasmine, lavender, lime blossom, mullein, violets
Sauna herbal flowers: rose petals, lavender.

HOUSEHOLD USES

Lavender

The unique, fresh, spicy scent of lavender with its echoes of cleanliness and purity is enjoyed by men and women alike. Among all scents it comes closest to encapsulating the caring and comforting qualities of home.

The name lavender derives from the Latin lavare, 'to wash' and, indeed, its fresh clean scent was the favourite bath water addition of the Greeks and Romans. The laundry man in Edward VI's court manual *The Black Book* was called the lavender man and he was authorized to procure 'sufficient whyte soap tenderly to wasshe the stuffe from the King's propyr person'.

In warm climates, like that of southern Italy where the sun draws the fragrance of the flowers into the air, housewives drape their laundry over bushes of lavender and rosemary to perfume the clothes as they are drying.

It was a popular strewing herb both for its insect-repelling properties and its long-lasting fragrance. Today these qualities are still valued and lavender bags or bundles are tucked into drawers, under pillows, in linen shelves and stored with special garments like a wedding dress. Charles VI of France had lavender filled white satin cushions to lounge upon.

To make a lavender bundle, use fresh lavender as the dried stalks will not bend to create the shape. However, once made they will keep well. A mature plant can provide 1000 spikes.

On a dry day, pick an odd number (usually between 9 and 15

depending on their bulkiness) of well-formed lavender stalks with plump flowers just opened. Strip off their leaves, line up the base of the flower heads and cut the stalks to a uniform length. Select a 3 ft (1 m) piece of ¼ in (6 mm) wide ribbon in a sympathetic colour like mauve or blue. Leave an 8-in (20-cm) tail of ribbon and tie it around the bundle just below the heads. Bend back each of the heads gently to create a cage over the stems. Pull the long piece of ribbon through the outside and weave it in and out of the flower heads in a continuous spiral until the end of the heads is reached. Tie a bow together with the short end of ribbon and either make a loop to hang it by or tie it again at the end of the stalks. The ribbon helps contain the individual flowers if they drop off their stem as they dry.

DECORATIVE AND AROMATIC USES

Pot Pourri

A favourite way of capturing the bounty of the summer herb garden to enjoy through the year is to make pot pourri. This is a colourful, dried mixture of sweet-scented flowers and aromatic leaves. Roses and lavender are the first choice of flower ingredients as they keep their scent for the longest time. Other fragrant flowers are acacia, broom, carnation, elder, freesia, honeysuckle, hyacinth, jasmine, lilac, lily-of-the-valley, linden or lime blossom, meadowsweet, orange blossom and Mexican orange blossom, mignonette, mock orange, narcissus, nicotiana, stock, sweet rocket, violet and wallflower.

To prepare flowers for pot pourri follow the instructions for drying them on pages 94 and 95.

Some flowers are selected for their colour, especially in the blue range, and aromatic leaves make up the remainder of the body of a pot pourri. These often have a stronger or sharper aroma than flowers so they should be chosen carefully to blend with the flowers you have selected. Dry them whole and then crush or crumble them to release their scent. Leave a few whole for a change of scale.

When making your own pot pourri, select from: alecost, balm of Gilead, balsam poplar buds, basil, bay, bearberry, bergamot, lady's bedstraw, lemon balm, lemon verbena, melilot, mints (spearmint, apple, peppermint and especially eau-de-cologne), patchouli, pelargoniums, (rose, lemon, apple, orange, pine, nutmeg and peppermint), rosemary, sage (especially pineapple), southernwood, sweet briar, sweet majoram, sweet myrtle, sweet cicely, tarragon, thymes (lemon and pine), wild strawberry and woodruff.

After leaves and flowers, the third group is spices. Spices, aromatic roots and peel give extra depth and lasting qualities to a pot pourri blend. Again, freshly crush or grind spices in a pestle and mortar and grate nutmeg to release the aroma, but leave a few whole for textural interest. Try alexander seed, allspice, aniseed, cardomom, cinnamon, cloves, coriander, dill seed, ginger, juniper, nutmeg, star anise and vanilla pods.

Roots should be cleaned, peeled, sliced and slowly dried. Then chop, crush or powder them to the desired size. Use the aromatic roots of angelica, elecampane, sweetflag, valerian, cowslip and vetiver (*Vetiveria zizanioides*).

To dry your own peel, take a thin layer of peel with a zester, grater or potato peeler, avoiding any white pith. Dip in orris powder to intensify the scent. Dry slowly, then crush or mince if desired. Use the peel of orange, lemon, lime, bergamot and tangerine.

Wood rasping are particularly exciting to work with as some of their scents are quite new and unusual. Choose from shreds or raspings of cedarwood, rosewood, sandalwood, cassia chips and any of the fruit woods like apple, pear or cherry which have a faint but sweet aroma, and look out for new varieties available. If you discover anything unusual it is worth checking from the supplier if the wood has any skin irritating properties. The highly concentrated essential oils of cassia, cinnamon bark, dwarf pine, thuja, and wintergreen are toxic and should never be applied to skins though the wood chippings, as far as we know, do not irritate the skin when they are handled.

All spices have a strong aroma and should be used sparingly. The ideal quantity is about 1 tbsp (15 ml) to 4 cups of flowers and leaves. Selected spices are usually added in equal proportions. These can give a 'musky' or 'oriental' quality, or suggest a 'masculine' or 'winter' scent.

The final ingredient for a pot pourri is a fixative. This is an aromatic plant part which gives up its fragrance very slowly and thereby lasts longer. In perfume blending it is called a basenote. As the odiferous molecules evaporate more slowly, they slow down the evaporation rate of other scents present, hence they all last longer.

There are various vegetable fixatives. One is orris-root from *Iris florentina* (the most popular as its sweet violet scent doesn't strongly affect a blend); use approximately 1 tbsp (15 ml) per cup of flowers and leaves. Gum benzoin from *Strayx benzoin*, called 'oil of ben' or 'benjamin' in old recipes, has a sweet aromatic scent, a little like vanilla; use about ½ oz (15 gm) to 4–6 cups of flowers and leaves. Tonka bean from *Dipterix odorata* has a strong vanilla scent; use one or two beans per recipe. Storax is from *Liquidamber orientalis*; use as gum benzoin.

A few fragrances double as fixatives and this useful group includes sweet flag root, sweet violet root, sandalwood, patchouli, vetiver (mentioned above) and also frankincense and myrrh (available as oils or resin), and oakmoss. Oakmoss from *Evernia pranastri* is sometimes called chypre or cypre, a name now applied to a group of perfume blends. Use ½ oz (15 gm) to 4 cups of flowers and leaves. Orris and sweet flag can be grown in a temperate climate but purchase the other ingredients from a herb shop.

When you have assembled your ingredients, like the mistress of the 'still room' in Elizabethan times, take a moment to linger over the scent and colour of each flower and leaf. Scented flowers traditionally dominate a pot pourri blend. Choose a theme to harmonize your mixture; say cottage flowers, a woodland blend of musky scents, a fresh mint and citrus blend or a mixture of soothing herbs such as rose petals, lavender, lemon verbena, meadowsweet and chamomile. It is a pleasurable task to educate one's nose to the blending of sweet scents.

Several of the flower, leaf and spice ingredients are available as essential oils and a single drop is a powerful perfume. These can be used with discretion to strengthen a blend or revive a flagging mixture. (Pot pourri boosters for sale are a mixture of real or synthetic essential oils in a carrier such as alcohol.) In the beginning, the temptation is to use too much. So experiment with a few drops first after you have mixed your blend of flowers, leaves and spices, adding it drop by drop and stirring it in between. Put the mixture away in a sealed container in a warm, dry area for six weeks to cure.

When the pot pourri is ready, display it in an open bowl where it can be fingered to release further fragrance and consider the colour and decoration of your containers so they harmonize with the colours and theme of your mixture.

Summer Herb Garden Pot Pourri

Using dried flowers and leaves, the following is a suggested guide to combinations and quantities.

flowers for scent:
2 cups rose petals
1 cup rose buds
2 cups lavender
1 cup clove pinks
½ cup sweet violets

leaves for scent:
½ cup rosemary
½ cup sweet myrtle
½ cup bergamot
½ cup eau-de-cologne mint
¼ cup bay
¼ cup southernwood

flowers for colour:
½ cup bergamot
¼ cup calendula petals
¼ cup borage or forget-me-not
¼ cup deep blue delphinium
¼ cup feverfew flowers
3 Madonna lily whole or separated into petals as an accent

spices:
1 tbsp (15 ml) ground cloves
1 tbsp (15 ml) ground allspice

fixative:
5 tbsp (75 ml) orris root

Decorated Writing Paper

First dry flowers by pressing them between sheets of blotting paper or newsprint set between heavy books. Suitable flowers would be primrose, sweet violet, borage, daisy, gypsophila and forget-me-not, or unusual shapes such as salad burnet, chervil, pelargonium, alpine lady's mantle or sprigs of rosemary, lemon thyme, patchouli and myrtle. When they are thoroughly dried, use a small amount of latex-based glue to fix the herbs to greeting cards, book marks, place cards, tallies, invitations and parcels. When arranging the leaves or sprigs on a surface take into account their natural patterns of growth and try to reflect the elegant curve of a stem or the shy emergence of a flower.

Scented Writing Paper

This is achieved by storing paper with scented herbs in an enclosed space to allow the paper to absorb the fragrance. Place quantities of aromatic dried leaves or lavender flowers, or drops of essential oil between sheets of writing paper in a closed box. Leave for six weeks to absorb the fragrance.

Drawer Lining Paper

The textured back of wallpaper absorbs scent well and can be used to line drawers. Lay thin muslin bags of aromatic herbs and essential oil between layers of lining paper. Roll them up into one cylinder shape and wrap them in cling film for six weeks.

Colour Inks

For red ink, collect 1 cup full of field poppy petals. Pour on a minimum amount of boiling water to cover and steep overnight. Add 15 per cent isopropyl alcohol or vodka to preserve the solution. Strain and bottle. A pale blue ink can be made from cornflowers.

USING FLOWERS IN THE GARDEN

Pyrethrum Insecticide

The herb flower pyrethrum, *Chrysanthemum cinerariifolium*, contains a natural insecticide that is non-toxic to mammals so it can be used to treat pests on the skin of humans and animals, as well as plants. It is non-cumulative and decomposes rapidly. The flowers can be dried and powdered to sprinkle on plants which has some effect but better results are obtained from making a spray. When dealing with pyrethrum flowers, do wear gloves as prolonged contact may cause skin allergies.

To make a spray, the powder must first be steeped in an alcohol, like methylated spirits, and then diluted with water. The active ingredient does not dissolve properly in water. Soak 2 oz (50 g) of powdered pyrethrum flowers in 3 fl oz (75 ml) methylated spirit. Dilute with 6 gals (27 l) water and spray on plants. Keep in a dark container and use quickly as it may deteriorate in the presence of sunlight.

The solution paralyses ants, aphids, bedbugs, cockroaches, flies, mosquitoes and spider mites. Unfortunately it also kills helpful insects and began its life as a fish poison in Malaysia so it shouldn't be used near fish ponds. If you spray pyrethrum at dusk, bees will be safe by morning when they begin working. An extra note: if the active ingredients pyrethin or cinerin are extracted from the flower and therefore concentrated, they *are* toxic to humans and animals so check the labels carefully if you buy it prepared.

Honey Bee Garden

Bees are useful in our gardens because they fertilize the fruit, flowers and vegetables giving us ripe fruit and viable seeds and, of course, somewhere they are making honey and royal jelly.

The flowers of herbs are particularly attractive to bees as many are still the original species with single flowers (not hybridized to create layers of petals which are more difficult for bees to work). Favourites are the Labiatae or lavender family which includes the often aromatic two-lipped flowers such as ajuga, basil, bergamot, hyssop, lavender, lemon balm, mints, marjoram, origano, rosemary, sage, savories and thyme.

Bees also enjoy the normally blue, five-petalled flowers of the Boragineae family like borage, forget-me-not, comfrey and lungwort. They also work the five-petalled flowers of the Malaceae or mallow family which includes hollyhock, marsh mallow, musk mallow, tree mallow and the rose of Sharon.

A few extra considerations make every herb garden safer and more useful for these pollinating insects. A garden specially for bees should be in full sunlight for maximum nectar production with the herbs grown in groups of five or more. A surrounding hedge or fence helps prevent the wind from buffeting the bees. A hedge of holly mixed with ivy is ideal as

the holly supplies nectar in late spring and the ivy in autumn. Yew produces some pollen in early spring while cherry-laurel gives nectar in mid-spring and also produces a sweet fluid on the underside of its leaves which is valuable to hive bees when nectar is scarce. Clovers, lime and fruit trees, oil-seed rape, sainfoin, mustard, charlock, willow herb and dandelion are the most important nectar plants for bees. Try to select herbs to provide nectar and pollen for the longest possible period.

Bumble Bee Garden

The honey bee garden also creates an opportunity to aid our dwindling population of bumble bees. These large, furry, gentle bees begin foraging several weeks earlier than the honey bee and being working earlier in the day often continuing through wind and rain. The familiar buzzing is not produced by the 200 beats per second of the wings but rather by the passage of air through many tiny air holes in the bee's thorax supplying extra oxygen for flight fuel. Several species have already become extinct and more are in danger because their hibernating sites and sources of early nectar (mainly willows) occur on wet lands which vanish as agricultural land is drained.

Try to include a pussy-willow (Salix ssp) somewhere in your garden and plenty of the early spring-flowering deadnettle varieties for early nectar. Bumble bees will obtain nectar from the same plants as honey bees but in addition they work flowers with longer corollas as the bumble bees have a longer probiscis or drinking tube. Lemon balm and bergamot are in this category as well as aquilegia, comfrey, foxglove, honeysuckle, lilac, lupin, nasturtium and wood sage.

MEDICINAL FLOWERS

Cold Remedies

Elderflower is excellent in a cold remedy, especially mixed with yarrow and peppermint leaves (see page 75) and an infusion will help cure a sore throat.

An infusion of ½ oz [15 g] elderflowers and ½ oz [15 g] lime blossom in 1 pt [600 ml] boiling water for 15 minutes will also treat a cold. Take a cupful 3 times a day.

Calendula Cream

Calendula is used to make a healing ointment for rough and cracked skin. Make an infused oil of calendula petals, following the instructions on page 65, repeating with fresh petals several times to increase the potency. Then melt 1 oz (25 g) beeswax, and blend with 4 fl oz (100 ml) of the warmed herbal oil. Add another 1 oz (25 g) of calendula petals and simmer gently for ten minutes, stirring frequently. Strain through double muslin into a wide-necked jar. Stir in a drop of tincture of myrrh or benzoin to extend its life. Don't use borax as it can damage broken skin. Label and date.

A cooled decoction of calendula can be used to soothe burns and a hot poultice to treat bruises. The flower can be crushed and applied to a sting or rubbed on an insect bite for relief.

Floral Infusions

An infusion of lime blossom, chamomile or lavender flowers will also help treat insomnia. Take 1 cup at night before retiring. An infusion of chamomile can also relieve toothache, if repeatedly used to rinse the mouth.

Poisonous Medical Flowers

Foxglove (*Digitalis purpurea*) has provided the primary heart drug for over 200 years and though the main ingredient has been synthesized, the plant is still grown commercially for the pharmaceutical industry. Foxgloves are poisonous and should not be used domestically.

All parts of the opium poppy (*Papaver somniferum*), except the ripe seeds, are dangerous, and should only be used by trained medical personnel.

Poppies have always been considered significant because of their narcotic effect. The opium poppy was a cult plant of the Sumerians 5000 years ago. The name 'somniferum' means 'sleep inducing' and 'opus' is from the Greek for juice. It was one of the first to be investigated with scientific apparatus and represents a turning point in the transition from the magic and religious use of plants to scientific analysis. It also examples the benefits and dangers of reducing plants to chemical components. Morphine and codeine were extracted, providing our most important pain killers, but also heroin, whose side effect outweighs its value. Heroin is in the most toxic class of poisons (super toxic, class 6) and when you read the other members of the group you get a glimpse of what a body taking heroin would have to cope with. The super toxic 'class-mates' include with cyanide, strychnine and nicotine.

The opium latex scraped from the green seed capsules was used to relieve pain, diarrhoea, and some coughs but now it is mainly grown as a source of morphine.

Bach Flower Remedies

Before the First World War, Edward Bach was a renowned physician and bacteriologist with a lucrative practice in Harley Street. His research during the 1920s convinced him of the value of homeopathy so he studied the subject further and moved on to herbalism. With this, he discovered he had an intuitive understanding of the healing qualities of plants, especially their flowers, linking back to very ancient healing systems. He gave up his orthodox practice in 1930 to devote himself full time to flower remedies.

Like most healers, he began with the understanding that the body heals itself and the healer's job is to remove the obstacles or imbalances present in the body which interfere with this healing His concern was with the mental and emotional states of the body; the fear, worry or depression which cause the body to lose its resistance to disease. The plant essence is extracted in a prescribed manner and stored in quality brandy. From this stock bottle, a few drops are added to pure still water to create a dilute solution for each treatment.

In all, he discovered 38 safe and non-addictive wild plants and flowers whose essence would treat the common negative states of mind. These are called the Bach Flower Remedies. Of these remedies, five are combined in a thirty-ninth called rescue remedy. The five are: cherry plum (to reduce uncontrolled irrational thoughts, desperation), clematis (for mental escapism, indifference, absent-mindedness), impatiens (for impatience, irritability), rock rose (scared, panicky, terror, sudden alarm) and star of Bethlehem (for all effects of serious news or fright following an accident. This is an all-purpose, emergency composite for effects of trauma, anguish, bereavement, examinations, etc. It is comforting, calming and reassuring to those distressed by startling experiences.

Animal and Plant Cures

The Handbook of Bach Flower Remedies relates several case histories where animals have been helped with an application of these remedies, particularly the rescue remedy for accident victims. Apparently, plants too showed remarkable recovery rates when watered or sprayed with diluted rescue remedy to help reduce the shock of transplant or to aid recovery from a severe fungal or insect attack.

California and Australian Flower Remedies

The newer California flower remedies and Australian flower remedies work in a similar way using suitable local wild plants for their treatments.

CULINARY USES

Flower cuisine is the celebration of the most beautiful parts of the garden with the skill and pleasure of the kitchen. The very phrase 'edible flowers' conjures up exotic sensory delights, and cooking with flowers is an ancient skill in many countries. Jasmine, peonies and lotus, for example, make their way into an array of oriental dishes. The Chinese use the small garland chrysanthemum (*C. coronarium*) in soups, as a garnish and fry it in batter. Another chrysanthemum (*C. indicum*) is considered a valuable tonic useful to include with 'medicinal meals' and it is part of the Taoist elixer of immortality. Teas are flavoured with osmanthus and jasmine flowers, while lotus and lily buds can be found in soups and delicate savoury dishes.

In Persia and India, the rose has been used to garnish and flavour food for thousands of years. It is mentioned in the first-century Greek cookbook *Banquets for the Learned*. In Arabic countries, the rose is used to flavour every type of dish from soups and savoury courses cooked with dried rose buds, to honey-layered pastries and Turkish delight. Orange flower water from the orange blossom is also used throughout the Middle East in a wide range of delicately flavoured dishes.

But flowers are not alien to the kitchens of Britain. There is a recipe for Saracen sauce which includes roses in the earliest-known English cookbook written in the late fourteenth century by the chefs of Richard II. Salad flowers were popular for centuries and there are old recipes for flowers in soups and sauces, tarts and puddings, and jams and conserves. Pinks in drinks, elderflower champagne and cowslip wine are ancient favourites. Lavender was used to flavour conserves, make lavender vinegar and lavender wine. In 1573, Thomas Tusser in his planting list of 'Seeds and Herbs for the Kitchen' included 'saffron, marigold, primrose and violets of all sorts.'

The flowers of pungent-leaved herbs often have a milder version of the leaves' flavour. Nasturtium, mustard, mint, salad rocket and chive flowers come into this category while sage, thyme and rosemary flowers have a delicate hint of their leaf scent. If rosemary flowers are pounded into sugar and left for a few days, they will impart a light spicyness that goes well with fruit desserts like fools and creams. Calendula, too, has a mild flavour while pinks, roses and sweet violets radiate a little of the perfume for which each is famous. Others, like borage, pansies, daisy petals and mallows, are used more for their unusual colour and texture than their flavour.

Lavender is very strongly flavoured and only tiny amounts are used,

sprinkled sparingly as you might use pepper. It is found in some *Herbs de Provence* mixtures which are prepared for casseroles and stews. This mixture usually includes dried thyme, rosemary, marjoram, savory, oregano, basil, tarragon and a small amount of lavender which gives a light, spicy perfume to the traditional savoury herbs.

Flowers in the Preparation of Salad

Choose when in season from anchusa, basil, bergamot petals, borage, broom (in small quantities only as vast amounts can be toxic), calendula, chicory, common chives and Chinese chives, cowslip, forget-me-nots, garland chrysanthemum (*Chrysanthemum coronarium*), violet, hollyhock petals and flower buds, hounds tongue flowers, lavender (sparingly), lawn daisy (*Bellis perennis*), mallow petals (marsh mallow, musk mallow and tree mallow), marjoram flowers, meadow cranes bill, mint florets (surprisingly pleasant), mustard, nasturtium, pansies, pelargonium, petunia petals, primrose, rose petals, rosemary flowers, sage flowers, salad rocket flowers, salsify, scorzonera, sweet rocket, sweet violet, thyme flowers, verbascum petals and viper's bugloss flowers. Yellow toadflax has an interesting taste rather like a raw courgette.

Some flowers which I have tried that I wouldn't recommend are: single pinks (*D. deltoides*) which are quite bitter; wall germander, wood betony and goat's rue flowers are also a little bitter; clary sage (too sharp for my taste); hyssop, which has an unexpected sweet perfume when the nectar is at maximum production. But there is then a bitter aftertaste.

There is no hard and fast rule to be applied to the art of salad making. Rather, the best approach is to cast an eye over the salad counter of your local supermarket, market stalls or your own garden and by so doing you will soon become aware of the items with the greatest appeal, *i.e.* colour, freshness, originality, etc.

It is best to combine flowers with a basic conventional background of salad leaves as the flower heads are appreciated better when they are not just jumbled together.

When assembling such salads, handle everything as lightly as possible, washing the leaves only when absolutely necessary and making sure they are dry by tossing or swinging them in a dry tea cloth.

Vinaigrette sauces should complement as far as possible the texture and flavour of a salad. Remember to be sparing with the vinegar, as salads are often ruined by the sharp shock of the heavy-handed addition of vinegar. Perhaps you could try a few drops of a flower vinegar.

CRYSTALLIZED FLOWERS

Single petals rather than whole flowers look more elegant, as unless extremely carefully done, the frosting tends to destroy the delicacy of the bloom.

In the case of flower heads, such as elder, which are extremely fragile, it is best to leave them intact, and then gently break off little florets after frosting.

1 egg white
caster sugar

Whisk up the egg white enough to break up the albumen but not as stiffly as for a meringue. Paint the petals using a small paint brush.

Pour a good layer of caster sugar onto a large plate and dip the petals into the sugar. Take care to cover completely as the sugar acts as the preservative. Spread some grease-proof paper on a tray and lay out the petals carefully. Leave for several hours before use, preferably in an airing cupboard or boiler room.

The excess sugar can be re-used in cakes or puddings.

If dried carefully after the frosting process, petals and flowers will keep a reasonable length of time stored between layers of grease-proof paper in a lidded container.

Flower Vinegars

To make floral vinegars follow the recipe on page 60 with a light wine vinegar using any of the perfumed flowers. Choose from broom, clover, elderflower, lavender, nasturiums, clove-scented pinks, rose petals or sweet violets. Sweet-scented floral vinegars are used in special salad dressings, fruit dishes and certain meat dishes cooked with fruits. Some are suitable in cosmetic recipes.

Pickled Flowers

Flowers can be preserved for use in salads or meat dishes by pickling them, although some colour is leached out by the vinegar. Place a layer of flowers in the base of your pickle jar, sprinkle with sugar to cover, repeat flower and sugar layers until jar is filled, compacting them firmly. Boil and cool cider or wine vinegar and cover the layers. Seal and set aside for at least four days to allow flavours to mingle. Try this with calendula, chicory, salsify and scorzonera flowers and rosebuds and broom buds as well as the cowslips, elder and pinks which John Evelyn recommends.

Picnic Dishes

CHERRY AND ROSE PETAL SOUP
(Serves 6–8)

1 good, fragrant rose bloom – pink or red
4 oz (100 g) demerara sugar
large pinch powdered cinnamon
1 pt (600 ml) cold water
1 lb (450 g) fresh stoned cherries (or drained, tinned cherries)
8 fl oz (225 ml) medium-dry white wine
1 tbsp (15 ml) Kirsch
½ pt (300 ml) soured cream

Remove rose petals from the flower head and cut away their bitter white heels. Reserve a few of the smallest and prettiest for decoration.

Combine sugar, cinnamon and water, bring to the boil and add the cherries. Simmer fresh cherries for about ½ hour (tinned cherries for 10 minutes). Add the white wine and the rose petals – not forgetting to leave some for decoration – and allow to stand until cool.

Liquidize or process the soup, then stir in the Kirsch and half the soured cream. Place in the refrigerator to chill thoroughly.

Serve either in a large glass bowl or individual glass dishes. Trickle a swirl of cream on top and scatter with a few rose petals.

CORIANDER AND CALENDULA QUICHE
(Serves 6)
Pastry
(to line an 8-in [20-cm] flan or quiche tin with removable base)
6 oz (175 g) plain flour
large pinch of salt
3 oz (75 g) unsalted butter (or margarine and butter mixed)
1 egg yolk
1 tbsp (15 ml) cold water

Sift flour and salt. Cut cooking fat into small cubes then rub into the flour until the mixture looks like fine breadcrumbs. Sprinkle the egg yolk beaten with the cold water over the flour. Using a table knife, cut and stir to bring the mixture together until it leaves the side of the bowl fairly clean.

Gather together with the hands and rest the pastry for 20 minutes in a cool place before rolling.

In the meantime, switch on the oven set at 350°F (190°C) Mark 4. Grease the pastry tin and lightly dust with flour.

Roll out the pastry and line the tin, making sure that you do not stretch the pastry as you do this – the pastry will shrink back during cooking if it is badly handled. Prick the base all over with a fork.

Line the pastry case with grease-proof paper and weight down with

109

dry beans or pebbles. Bake for 15 minutes in the centre of the oven, then remove the lining, turn down the oven to 325°F (170°C) Mark 3, and place the pastry on the lowest shelf of the oven for a further 5 minutes. This allows the base to dry out a little without risk of over browning.

Remove from oven and allow to cool before filling.

Savoury Custard Filling
2 oz (50 g) grated Gruyere cheese (or a good dry Cheddar)
½ pt (300 ml) single cream
2 large whole eggs
1 egg yolk
petals of 1 large calendula flower
2 tbsp (30 ml) chopped coriander leaves
salt and freshly ground white pepper

Cover the base of the cooked pastry with grated cheese.

Stir beaten eggs into the cream and season. (Do not over-beat the eggs as it spoils the smooth texture of the custard.) Stir in calendula petals and chopped coriander leaves, then gently pour the mixture over the cheese in the pastry shell.

Bake for 35–40 minutes. The top should be set, slightly risen and light brown.

Try to serve straight from the oven as the textures are at their very best when the tart is warm. It is, of course, quite delicious cold.

ROSE LAYERED DESSERT
1 cup loosely-packed, scented rose petals, white heels removed
4 mashed bananas
approx 4 oz (100 g) chopped dates (quantity to equal volume of mashed bananas)
2 tbsp (30 ml) mincemeat
4 tbsp (60 ml) rose petal jam*
juice of 2 oranges
¼ pt (150 ml) double cream

Cover a dish with rose petals – pink and red, preferably. Mix the bananas, dates and mincemeat and make a layer over the petals leaving the petals protruding around the edge. Cover with a layer of rose petal jam.

When ready to serve, pour the orange juice over the top. Add a layer of whipped cream and garnish with crystallized rose petals.
*Rose petal jam is available from good herbalist stores, but it is quite possible to use apple jelly instead.

GOOSEBERRY AND ELDERFLOWER COMPOTE

1 lb (450 g) gooseberries topped and tailed
4 oz (100 g) light muscovada sugar
2 clean heads of elderflower

Place gooseberries and sugar in a heavy saucepan, lay the elderflower heads on the top. Cover the pan and simmer gently until the fruit has softened and almost collapsed. Shake from time to time to prevent sticking. Allow the fruit to cool completely before removing the flower heads.

The fruit can be served just like this as delicious compote, but a little more effort can transform it into a creamy fool or an ice-cream.

GOOSEBERRY FOOL

Stir into the gooseberries two beaten eggs and ½ pt (300 ml) of double cream. Warm gently, stirring continuously, until the mixture thickens. Pour into dishes and garnish with florets of frosted elderflowers.

CREAM HEARTS SCENTED WITH SWEET GERANIUM LEAVES

Perforated porcelain dishes from France, used for draining the cream mixture, are available in England, but not easily found. It is perfectly possible to use empty yogurt or cream cheese cartons with a few holes punched in the bottom – or why not a flower pot?

Do be sure to dampen the muslin (or handkerchieves) before lining as it clings nicely to the shape of the dishes.

1 pt (600 ml) double cream
4 oz (100 g) curd cheese
2 egg whites
8 small, sweet geranium leaves
8 sweet geranium flowers
8 squares of muslin

Combine the cream and the cheese as thoroughly as possible. Whip the egg whites until they are softly peaked but not too dry. If you have a sweet tooth, add just a suggestion of sugar, but it is best left without. Fold egg whites into the cream.

Line your dishes or pots with dampened squares of muslin. Place a small geranium leaf at the bottom of each dish (over the muslin) and spoon in the cream mixture carefully, making sure that all the corners are well-filled. Place dishes on a rack over a plastic tray to drain in the cool. Leave for at least 8 hours.

About an hour before serving, turn out carefully and arrange prettily on a large plate. Decorate each cream with a sweet geranium flower and garnish the plate with frosted red currants.

4
ROOTS AND BULBS WITH HERBAL PROPERTIES

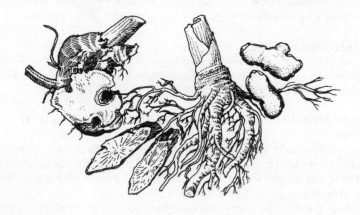

The subject of herbal roots is an area ripe for rediscovery. Among forgotten roots we can find earthy flavours, exotic cosmetics and Biblical aromatics. Like other solid fragrant substances, aromatic roots hold their perfume for years because the odorous molecules evaporate more slowly than in a liquid. This factor made them particularly valuable to ancient civilizations.

As meat became more affordable very few of the edible wild roots made their way into the vegetable gardens and so herbal roots for the cooking pot lost their popularity. In the seventeenth century, there were theories about the windiness, brain damage, melancholy and various negative states caused by eating roots. In his 1636 herbal, *The Historie of Plants*, Gerard writes of turnips which flower in the same year they are sown: 'they are a degenerat kind... causing frensie and giddinesse of the brain for a season.'

Roots made a culinary comeback in 1699, however, when the charming *Acetaria: A Discourse of Sallet* was published by John Evelyn. This book is an adventure in salad-making with instructions for gathering and preparing over 72 herbal roots, stalks, leaves, buds, flowers and fruits. Roots were boiled, sliced and tossed in oil and vinegar, some were boiled in wine, some pickled and others served with a white sauce. Evelyn includes treatment for the roots of beet, carrot, daisy, dandelion, garlic, goat's beard, mallow, onion, parsnips, parsley, radish, rampion, roccombo, salsify, scorzonera, sweet cicely and turnip.

One native root herb not mentioned by John Evelyn and no longer used is the early purple orchid (*Orchis mascula*). It was eaten in difficult times but also used in fertility rites because its double ovoid shape resembles testicles. Indeed the botanic name is from the Greek 'orkhis' meaning testicle. Sadly, this orchid is now rare and we may lose its unusual properties. Richard Mabey points out in *Food For Free* that it would be criminal to dig up any of the dwindling colonies for food. This plant provides a lesson in the valuable potential that can disappear forever when even one plant species is lost. The tubers contain bassorine, a starchy material which is more nutritious than any other single plant product. One ounce of the root, raw or cooked, will sustain a man for a whole day. Its root, dried and powdered, was used to make a thick nourishing drink called salop.

A similar nourishing drink is still served in China. It is made from powdered lotus root which creates a thick, white gelatinous 'drink', served warm and eaten with a spoon. It is very soothing for upset stomachs and ocasionally available at tea houses for visitors suffering from travel sickness. It has little taste and up to a decade ago was flavoured with osmanthus flowers though now sadly it is more likely to be flavoured with something synthetic.

Aromatic roots have strong legendary links. Elecampane (*Inula helenium*) is named after Helen of Troy who was said to have been gathering this herb when she was abducted and spikenard was used by Mary Magdalene to annoint the feet of Jesus.

Today, a herb garden can include many fine roots and bulbs such as: Welsh onion, everlasting onion, garlic, rocambole, wild garlic, marsh mallow, angelica, horseradish, roseroot, elecampane, soapwort, parsley, aniseed, skirret, sweet cicely, scozerona, salsify, lily root, galingale, chicory, dandelion, sea holly (*Eryngo root*), rosemadder, and dong-kwai (*Chinese angelica*). Ginseng needs crisp frost and snow in winter to create a good root so perhaps in the colder parts of Scotland a worthwhile root could be grown.

THE FUNCTION OF ROOTS

The purpose of a root is to absorb water from the soil and with it the dissolved minerals and trace elements it contains making them available to the plant. A root system also anchors the plant and creates the support base necessary to keep the plant upright. Although roots are almost always found underground, there are rare ocassions when plants have aerial roots such as tree orchids, mistletoe and the clinging roots of ivy.

A root sometimes acts as a storage organ for the plant, for example in the two biennials, caraway and carrot. However, not every underground storage organ is classified as a root and this is where some nomenclature is confusing. Bulbs and tubers are forms of storage organs; runners and stolons are stems; and corms and rhizomes are underground stems *and* storage organs. The deciding factor is that underground stems have scale leaves (small leaves like scales at intervals along the stem,) whereas roots have root hairs to collect water.

A bulb is an underground bud with fleshy leaf scales surrounding it and roots which die down annually. In a fully-grown bulb, the flower spike is present inside it in perfect condition and a bulb such as a daffodil can be sliced open in winter to reveal a closed daffodil flower. it will develop perfectly, or otherwise, according to the care it receives when growing. An example of a bulb is the Madonna lily.

A corm has an underground stem with one bud on the top from which both shoots and new roots grow, unlike a bulb which contains a young plant inside. Each year the next year's corm is produced on top of its parent. Montbretia is an example.

A tuber is a storage organ formed from an underground stem like the potato or a thickened fleshy root like the dahlia which helps the plant survive cold or drought.

A rhizome is a swollen, horizontal, creeping, underground stem from which roots, leafy shoots and a flowering stem will grow. Orris, the Florentine iris, grows from a rhizome. 'Rhiza' is Greek for 'root', and 'rhizoma', 'take root' and a rhizotomist was an ancient Greek collector of roots and herbs.

A stolon is a short, horizontal stem that is usually above the soil and grows a new plant at nodes (a joint which contains special cells with the potential of root and shoot growths). Mint is a stolon although it is popularily called a runner. This is an aerial stem producing a new plant at the tip when it comes into contact with moist soil. Strawberries and bramble are two examples.

The two main root shapes are a tap root and a fibrous root. A tap root is a large main root covered with many root hairs. A tap root acts as an anchor while the root hairs absorb the nutrients. In a carrot or caraway there is only one taproot but in a tree or shrub the tap root is the largest of several main roots connected to the tree. A plant with a single tap root is the most difficult to transplant successfully.

Other plants, like shrubby thymes, have a mass of small roots of similar size – a fibrous root system. This type of plant is the easiest to transplant. If several fibrous rooted plants are grown together they help bind the soil and prevent erosion. They also help break up the soil with their growth pattern by creating a myriad of tiny tunnels for oxygen and drainage.

Given ideal soil conditions, a root system will mirror the image of the plant above ground, radiating out the same distance below as the stems above. This becomes significant when visualizing the probable root spread when planning the area a tree will fill or when fertilizing an existing tree. The root hairs which absorb nutrients are mainly located on the outer reaches. This ratio of the amount of below ground roots to above ground growth is particularily important when transplanting. If a substantial amount of the root is cut off when a plant is transplanted, an equal percentage of the top must be pruned as well so that the roots can cope.

A root grows by pushing out new cells with a point of expendable cells on the tip that are rubbed off as it burrows along. They take the easiest route. So, if the soil is loose, not hard and compacted and without obstacles, like stones, the roots (and therefore the foliage) will grow more quickly. Earthworms work 24 hours a day making it easier for roots to grow by creating small tunnels, water courses and pockets for oxygen to collect in, all important to the plant and just one of many reasons to encourage earthworms by spreading good compost. A root will carry on growing all year if the temperature stays above 45°F (7°C) which means it can build a head start for spring foliage.

A plant has no power to select food material. Rather, it is obliged to take up any substance dissolved in the water that is capable of oozing through the vegetable membranes of the root hairs, the tiny threads on each root. These substances continue to pass through the membrane by osmosis until the liquid on the internal side is as highly charged as that on the outside and then the root stops absorbing. If the plant uses any of these materials for plant nutrition, they are withdrawn from the inner surface of the root up into the plant. At this point, the root is able to take up more of the nutrient in dissolved water from the soil. This sysem means that normally the passage of useless or injurious substances into the plant is limited. As soon as the internal liquid in contact with the absorbing surface is as highly charged with the undesirable substance as the external liquid, the absorption stops.

ROOT PROPAGATION

For good-quality roots, a rich, friable (crumbly) loam is important. If straight roots are desired for skirret or salsify, then any obstacles like stones or other rubbish should be removed and the plants thinned out so that the roots do not spiral around each other.

Ginseng can be grown in this climate. It likes a good, rich, moist loam under a shady tree. But it should have crisp winter frosts and snow to force the goodness back into the root each winter and it requires seven years to produce top quality medicinal roots.

Several herbs can be increased by dividing the roots of the plant into sections, each with a growing tip. This also reduces overcrowding of roots. If you inspect a two- or three-year-old primrose or cowslip you will see it appears to be several different small plants. Separate each gently which is easiest to do when the soil is dry. Bistort, chives, costamary, elecampane, good King Henry, lawn chamomile, lemon balm, lovage, lungwort, marjorams, meadowsweet, mugwort, skirret, sorrel, sweet Joe Pye, sweet violet, tansy, tarragon, wall germander and wormwood, as well as the cowslip and primrose, can be propagated this way.

Root sectioning is a simple form of propagation. As the mother plant has already grown the new plants, they only need to be separated. Plants with creeping roots or stolons like mint, bergamot, dwarf comfrey, soapwort and sweet woodruff can be multiplied this way.

Horseradish, skirret and comfrey can be grown from root cuttings. Slice thick lengths of root into 2–3-in (5–8-cm) long pieces and insert them vertically (the same way they were growing) into potting compost with a ¼-in (6-mm) layer of sand on top. Water regularly until shoots appear, then transplant to a permanent site.

HARVESTING AND PRESERVING ROOTS

It is a root's function as a storage organ which mankind has found most useful. The nutritional content of the old pot herbs; carrots, turnips, parsnips, skirret and the flavouring bulbs of onion and garlic are valuable because of the stored principles. Many of these principles have medicinal uses like those of valerian and ginseng. Others are aromatic like sweet flag, orris and rose root. Some are powerful spices like ginger, tumeric and galangal. There are many underground treasures just waiting to be mined.

Perhaps the main resistance to the use of roots is that it appears to end a plant's life by taking the root. But many of these roots, like horseradish and elecampane, spread and it is easy to dig a section of a root for culinary use, and benefit the plant by the pruning. Additionally, any thick piece of root like horseradish, comfrey or marsh mallow left in the ground will grow new shoots.

Roots are usually dug in the autumn when the goodness from the foliage has returned to the root for winter storage or in warm, but early, spring when root circulation is stirring but before it sends goodness back up the stems. When digging a piece of root with the intent of leaving the main part behind so that the plant will continue to grow, sever the piece neatly either with the sharp edge of a spade or a gardener's knife, depending on the size of the root.

Shake or gently rub off as much soil as possible. Then remove fibrous root hairs and scrub to clean. The value of some roots, such as valerian, is in their peel so in general this is not removed, though the roots of marsh mallow and the rhizomes of liquorice are peeled before being dried.

Drying Roots

Cut thick pieces of root lengthwise and then into slices to speed the drying process. Roots need a higher temperature than leaves to dry – about 120°F–150°F (50–60°C) – so they can be dried in a slow oven, turning them frequently until they are fragile and break easily.

When completely dry, store the roots in airtight containers. They will keep for many seasons although the aromatic principles will slowly evaporate. Parsley and angelica root won't last for long, however, as they are hygroscopic, meaning they reabsorb moisture from the air. When they become soft they should be discarded.

Preparing Roots for Use

For an infusion, or decoction, pieces of any convenient size can be used; just bear in mind that the smaller the pieces, the more quickly will the desired principles be extracted to permeate the liquid. When purchasing dried roots, they are usually sold either powdered or in small, pea-sized pieces, very occasionally whole. Fresh ginger is the main exception and its soft texture is easy to grate and slice. For recipes requiring a powder they can be broken up as much as possible in a plastic bag with a rolling pin or hammer and can then be ground with a pestle and mortar. Very small amounts can be powdered in a domestic electric grinder but I have ruined one motor in an attempt to powder enough rhubarb root to use as a hair lightener.

CONTAINER HERBS

A collection of well-grown herbs in pots is a satisfying vision because experience teaches that the daily attention they require in summer indicates an orderly gardener with civilized priorities. To nurture herbs in pots is a labour of love with the extra bonus of convenient fresh herbs – chives for cream cheese before it melts on a baked potato; mint as a sudden inspiration for a blackcurrant tart, or chamomile for a relaxing nightcap.

As most herbs are easy to grow in pots, town dwellers with only a balcony, roof garden or window box can enjoy the delights of a herb garden either outdoors or indoors. Supplying suitable conditions for roots is a main consideration for container herb growers.

Make sure your container has drainage holes and over these place gravel or broken crocks of terracotta. Terracotta is traditionally used because the shards have a little curve so they cover a drainage hole and still keep a little oxygen space, and because terracotta absorbs moisture storing a little extra for the soil mixture. Put a thin layer of grit or fine gravel and a sprinkling of horticultural charcoal granules (if available) over the terracotta. They help keep the soil sweet for herbs which have reached their largest size pot. Then use a good moisture retentive soil mixture.

There are good peat-based mixtures available from garden centres usually with a 'wetting agent' in them. This makes it easier to water the pots when they dry out, but my preference is still for a soil-based mixture. Peat becomes very light when it dries out and pots can be blown over in strong winds. Also, while sterilized soil has all the weed seeds and disease spores steamed out theoretically making it better, to me it feels dusty and lifeless. There is something about a home made mixture (7 parts loam, 3 parts peat, 2 parts sand plus fertilizer) made with a good rich compost, and lots of oxygen incorporated as you mix it like a giant Christmas cake in the wheelbarrow, that is worth putting up with the extra weeding. The herbs themselves discourage many of the diseases so I take my chances with live soil.

The size and condition of the roots of a herb determine when a pot-grown plant needs moving. Seedlings should be moved after they have grown four leaves – that is, their first two 'seed' leaves and two true leaves. By then their root system should be able to stand the shock of moving. Basil plants (like the tomato plants they are so delicious with), benefit from growing in shallow containers because the plant delays making leaf growth while the root is first growing down. The sooner the root hits a base, the earlier its leaves grow.

When you see the roots protruding through the base of a pot, that is the time to move it on to a pot one size larger. Try to use the same soil mixture as before and loosen the edges of the existing clump to help the roots blend into the new soil. Spring is the best time to re-pot as new roots grow most quickly. Avoid late autumn or winter because when the temperature drops below 47°F (7°C) no new roots will grow to anchor the plant.

The mobility of smaller containers gives you the opportunity to change their locations when it pleases you: place culinary herbs at the kitchen window; scented herbs near your favourite seat, and savoury herbs beside the barbeque. You can move them around to catch the sun or avoid the wind and they can be rearranged to enjoy their individual moments of glory. Allow them to migrate indoors for the winter or for one evening to the table so that guests can pick their own fresh garnish. They are also easy to monitor, to see what attention they need, but the flipside is that they require more attention than herbs in the open ground.

Herbs in pots need watering daily in hot weather – sometimes even twice because their roots have nowhere to extend in their search for extra moisture. Larger leaves like basil, lemon balm and sorrel appreciate a mist spray at mid-day in addition to their daily watering on hot days.

If you pick your herbs, try not to take more than one-third of the volume, though the herb will likely survive if even two-thirds is taken. Cropping herbs and the constant watering required by pots leaches the minerals from the pot and so frequent feeding is important for a healthy plant. Use a comfrey or nettle brew every two weeks in peak growing season.

Herbs for the Window Box

Choosing the culinary plants for a small window box is a challenge if you are used to the luxury of a herb garden. First, I think of the herbs I most frequently use fresh and could never be without – parsley and chives. Realistically, if you needed a lot for one recipe (like Tabouleh which takes a cup of chopped parsley) you would have to buy a batch, but for the odd, last-minute garnish and sprinkle I would want a fresh plant. Then I would select a lemon thyme, rosemary and sage which can each be kept small and tidy by judicial pruning. If I could keep the box warm in autumn I would include basil, otherwise I would keep it in a separate pot indoors. In a separate container I would also have a good flavoured spearmint such as Moroccan mint or Red Raripila mint. Allow at least 4×4 in (10×10 cm) for each herb and feed them every two weeks in spring and summer with a dilute liquid fertilizer if you are harvesting the herbs regularly. Try to choose an interesting range of leaf colour and size, such as silver thyme, purple basil and gold sage as there are several forms available of many of the common herbs.

With a larger window box, I could almost manage a herb garden. To the first six mentioned above I would add French tarragon, coriander, marjoram and treat myself to a lemon verbena. And I would tuck in a calendula or nasturtium for salad flowers to cheer me up.

Although a little unusual, lady's mantle in a hanging basket can be quite spectacular. The leaves invite inspection, beautiful green-pleated circles with a glistening crystal dewdrop in each centre. When the delicate pale yellow clusters of tiny flowers outgrow their slender stems they fall gracefully outward in a lacy crinoline around the basket.

COSMETIC USES

Carrots (*Daucus carota* ssp.)

Carrot root pulp appears to have several beneficial attributes for skin care. Dermatologists agree that the most important step for preventing wrinkles is to stop the sun's ultra-violet rays from reaching the skin. Creams with plant material that screens UV light are an important step. Aloe vera leaf gel is the most significant and it appears that carrot root may also contain significant amounts of a sun screening element. A cosmetic company reports that the difficulty has been for laboratories to combine the sun screen material with the other ingredients of a lotion as the sun screen materials either discolour or fail to emulsify. Now, however, they have managed to blend carrot into a moisturizing skin cream and have also produced a macerated carrot oil which can be used as the oil component of your skin lotion recipes.

Carrots contain carotene (provitamin A), which is important for healing, B Vitamin complex, little Vitamin C, potassium salts, and it has antiseptic qualities. In the past it was used as a poultice to treat skin ulcers and cancerous sores and a carrot diet is still taken internally in some European treatment centres to alleviate the pain of cancer. But carrot juice must not be consumed in excess as it induces hypervitaminosis A. The pulp can be used as a face mask to help clear blemishes and to soften rough patches, leaving the skin silky smooth.

To make a face mask, steam roots until soft, cool, mash and stir in 3 drops of wheatgerm oil. Mix with Fuller's earth to create a paste (approx 1 tbsp [15 ml] Fuller's earth to ¼ cup carrot pulp), apply to the face and leave on for 15–30 minutes, resting with your feet higher than your head if possible. Rinse off with tepid water. Pulped marsh mallow root can also be used for its softening and soothing qualities.

Dandelion (*Taraxacum officinale*)

Dandelion is a blood purifier and taken internally to help clear eruptions, sometimes for eczema and to help remove calcium deposits from joints, a problem which can manifest on older hands. A wine glass-full of the decoction is taken twice a day. Externally, it is used along with horseradish root as an effective tonic wash or lotion to clear skin blemishes. The milky juice of the root and stems is said to remove worts. Roots are lifted in late summer, cleaned, then simmered in water for 20 minutes.

Horseradish (*Armoracia rusticana*)

The slice root of horseradish boiled in milk and applied as a lotion will help clear spots and pimples. Lift roots in the autumn as the plant dies back, chop and decoct in milk or put through a juice extractor.

Madonna Lily (*Lilium candidum*)

The bulb of Madonna lily contains a great deal of mucilage which is soothing and softening to skin and it also has astringent properties. An ointment made from the juice of the bulbs has been used to remove inflammation from blemishes and heal the skin, including scars. The herbalist Gerard says 'It bringeth the hairs again upon places which have been burned or scalded, if it be mingled with oil or grease.'

Madonna lily has a reputation as being an effective antiwrinkle pomade which was very popular in Victorian times. Marsh mallow root shares this reputation. Lift bulbs in the autumn for cosmetic use.

To make a lily and marsh mallow rich face cream:

Lily, marsh mallow and carrot are all noted for antiwrinkle properties
1 oz (25 g) marsh mallow root
2 fl oz (50 ml) carrot oil
1 fl oz (25 ml) avocado oil
1 fl oz (25 ml) wheatgerm oil
1 lily bulb
1 oz (25 g) beeswax or anhydrous lanolin or a mixture of the two. Beeswax makes the cream stiffer and shinier, lanolin softer
½ oz (15 g) clear honey
6 drops tincture of myrrh (for healing and keeping qualities)

Crush the marsh mallow root. Blend the three oils together and macerate the marsh mallow root in this for two weeks in a sunny window, stirring daily. Strain off the oils. Put the lily bulb through a juice extractor to obtain about 1 fl oz (25 ml) of liquid.

Melt the wax or lanolin very gently in a double boiler. Remove from heat and add the warmed infused oils slowly drop by drop, stirring the mixture constantly. Slowly add the lily juice, beating constantly at first, then stir slowly until cooled to blood heat. Stir in the tincture of myrrh. Spoon it into a wide-necked, sterilized jar, label and date.

A strong decoction of the lily and marsh mallow root making 1 fl oz (25 ml) in total can be used instead of macerating the oils and juicing the lily bulb.

Marsh Mallow (*Althaea officinalis*)

All the mallow family contains mucilage, a gummy substance which is emollient. This means it is soothing and softening to irritated or inflamed surfaces so it is used internally to smooth inflamed passages in chest complaints and externally on irritated skins, even to soothe inflammed eyes. Marsh mallow has the highest percentage of mucilage in the family and its root can yield half its weight in muscilage. Collect in August and September from plants at least two years old.

Marsh mallow roots do not yield all their desirable principles to boiling water so in many recipes they are soaked in cold water or boiled in wine or oil.

To make a marsh mallow infusion for rough skin: soak crushed root pieces in cold water for 8 hours, then strain and use the liquid. This infusion of mallow can be applied as a compress for rough and chapped hands, dry skin, dry hair and sunburn.

Orris (*Iris florentina*)

The fragrant rhizome of orris is dried and ground down for talcum powder. Three to four-year-old plants are lifted in the autumn, dried and kept for two years during which time their fragrance increases, before being distilled for essential oil. Orris root dry shampoo can be made as follows:

2 tbsp (30 ml) finely powdered orris root
2 tbsp (30 ml) powdered arrowroot or white Fuller's earth

Mix powders together. Part the hair in narrow strips and sprinkle the powder along each row until the whole scalp is covered. Massage lightly with fingertips to encourage absorption. Leave on for 10 minutes to absorb maximum grease and then brush out vigorously and thoroughly until the hair is shiny.

Potato (*Solanum tuberosum*)

The flesh of the common potato has a softening and slight bleaching action on the skin. Peel and wash a freshly-dug potato and slice thinly. Rub several pieces on the face, leave for 30 minutes and wash off.

Rhubarb (*Rheum palmatum* or *R. officinale*)

The dried root is the strongest, natural, hair-blonding agent. The effect is accumulative and the colour becomes softer and deeper gold with each application. Drying the hair in the sun intensifies the lightening action, giving a rich, Titian, golden colour. A golden hair dye is made as follows:

4 tbsp (60 ml) finely chopped rhubarb root
1½ pts (900 ml) water

Prepare a strong decoction by simmering root in water for 20 minutes. Then allow to steep for several hours. This can be used as a rinse, catching the liquid and repeating the rinse action until the colour fades from the liquid. A more effective dye is achieved by making a paste. Add ½ cup kaolin powder (or Fuller's earth) to 1 cup of the decoction. Add 1 tsp (5 ml) of cider vinegar to maintain the hair's acid mantle and 1 tsp (5 ml) glycerine to prevent hair becoming dry. Wear gloves as rhubarb root stains and apply paste evenly throughout the hair. Leave on up to an hour and rinse well or let it dry on the hair and brush out later.

Sweet Flag (*Acorus calamus*)

Calamine lotion is a product of this rhizome; it is frequently dried and ground to create a scented talcum powder. It is also an ingredient of Chypre, the famous French perfume. Roots are lifted in the autumn, cleaned and distilled or dried in low oven and ground.

HOUSEHOLD USES

Agrimony (*Agrimony eupatoria*)

The root and leaves of this common, wayside herb have a faint but pleasant fruity scent like green apple peel. This can be added to pot pourri and sweet bags.

Angelica Root (*Angelica archangelica*)

'To Perfume a House, and Purify the Air' (from *The Toilet of Flora* [1775]), take a root of angelica, dry it in an oven, or before the fire, then bruise it well and infuse it for four or five days in white wine vinegar. When you use it, lay it upon a brick made red hot, and repeat the operation several times.

Elecampane (*Inula helenium*)

When first lifted, the roots of elecampane smell of ripe bananas but as the root dries it acquires a camphorish, violet scent. Burn elecampane root over embers to scent a room or add shavings to pot pourri and sweet bags.

Ginger Family (*Hedychium species*)

This is a family of herbaceous plants from India that is among the most beautiful and sweetly-scented in the world. It is mainly the flowers which radiate such exquisite perfume as to make them almost sacred but several of their roots are also beautifully scented.

Hedychium gardnerianum root supplies a product called Kapur-Kadri which is used in Eastern perfumery, and *Hedychium spicatum* root is dried and used as incense in Hindu worship. It has a strong, sweet, violet/orris scent. Its name is from the Greek for 'sweet snow' because of the white perfumed flowers. The extracted oil resembles the perfume of hyacinths.

Herbal Glue

A strong paper glue can be collected from home grown bluebell bulbs (*Endymion nonscriptus*) by scraping the side with a knife. This produces a thick sticky slime to be used straight away.

Indian Violet Grass (*Andropogon muricatus*)

The root of this herb has a violet perfume used by Eastern women. Another member of the family, *Adropogon nardus*, now reclassified as *Cymbopogon nardus* is highly aromatic in all its parts. The strongly-scented root smells of spikenard (hence the name nardus) and the leaves are the source of oil of citronella, a useful insect repellant.

Orris Root (*Calamus acorus*)

The lovely smell of sweet violets emanates from this dried root and it is the preferred fixative for pot pourris.

Rose Root (*Sedum roseas* or *S. rhodiola*)

The root of this herb is mildly scented of roses when dried. In Elizabethan times it was dried, powdered and soaked, or distilled to create a 'poor man's rose water' to sprinkle over clothes. From historic descriptions it seems the scent from the root used to be stronger, or perhaps a more scented strain was allowed to die out, but the scent in present day roots is very faint.

Soapwort (*Saponaria officinalis*)

The cleaning service of an exclusive London company uses a medieval product on rare fabrics. The secret is soapwort, a cottage flower whose leaves and stems, but mainly roots, produce a detergent-free soap which does a remarkable job of cleaning ancient fabrics. Old skills were redeveloped at the National Trust's Uppark House, West Sussex, by the late Lady Meade-Fetherstonhaugh who found that soapwort not only removes dirt but revitalizes the texture, renewing the depth and brilliance of dyes. These skills are now being introduced to manor houses and museums worldwide.

Boil bruised root, leaves and stems of soapwort for ½-hour in a small amount of rain, soft water or filtered water, enough to keep the herb covered. Strain and use to wash, condition and revive delicate old fabrics, tapestries, silks and lace. Soapwort contains saponins which lubricate natural fabrics and absorb dirt, leaving fabrics with a softness and sheen.

Spikenard (*Valeriana jatamansi*)

This herb has a long history as a valued aromatic and was at one time the most costly fragrance available. The root has a strong, sweet, patchouli-like perfume and is the spikenard of the Bible. It was one of the ingredients in the ointment used by Mary Magdalene to wipe the feet of Jesus whereupon the disciples rebuked her for using such a costly substance. The main reason for its expense was that it only grew in a few remote Himalayan valleys and the transportation problems by camel train through various climates and countries down to the Middle East were enormous.

It is a member of the valerian family and grows easily in Britain if you can find a source of the plant. Dry pieces to add to pot pourri or lay among clothes to perfume them.

Wood Avens or Herb Bennet (*Geum urbanum*)

The root of this herb has a clove like scent which it retains when dried. Place dried root pieces in the linen cupboard or drawers to scent the clothes.

GARDEN USES

Inca Marigold (*Tagetes minuta*)

An important area of research where plants can be used to help or hinder the growth of their neighbours is in the study of root secretions. It seems that some trees pass messages in this way. If a host of caterpillars invades one birch tree, the chemical make-up of the plant changes triggering its neighbours to produce a poison in their leaves that will repel the invaders. Some of the answers to companion planting may be found in this research which is long overdue.

The scent of Tagetes, the French or African marigolds, deters some insect pests and the root secretions have a powerful effect against eelworm. Dutch bulb growers plant it to protect their tulip crops and rose growers to protect roses. The common French and African marigold have some affect against the non-cyst forming eelworm (nematodes) but the most damaging eelworms are clustered 90–500 in cysts or shells which are impervious to chemicals. The most powerful tagetes is *Tagetes minuta*, the Inca marigold which can control these and enabled the Incas to grow potato crops on the same land for hundreds of years, free from the potato eelworm. This is an 8-ft (2½-m) plant (named 'minuta' after the tiny flowers) whose root secretions inhibit the eelworm's ability to sense the correct time to attack the potatos; they 'oversleep' and miss their host plant's appropriate stage.

The root secretions of *Tagetes minuta* have other remarkable effects: they can kill ground elder (*Aegopodium podagraria*), have a strong effect against bindweed (*Calystegia sepium*) and, to a lesser degree, against couch grass (*Agropyron repens*) in a circle around the herb. In Britain, the herb must be started early under glass as this tagetes needs a long growing season. Cut back the weeds in the area to be cleared to give the tagetes a chance to get ahead. When tagetes seedlings are 6-in (15-cm) tall, plant out at 12-in (30-cm) intervals over the area where weeds are to be eliminated. Allow to grow until frost kills them. Seed is available from the Henry Doubleday Association.

Garlic (*Allium sativum*)

Garlic and, to a lesser extent, the entire onion tribe are reported to repel aphids and seem to work in my greenhouse. However, it is not known whether it is the scent of the plants or a root secretion which creates a difference in the plant normally chosen by the aphids; perhaps both. The difference is significant because if it is the scent, then it is wise to plant the garlic near the greenhouse door to deter flying visitors but if it is the root secretions then it is important to plant the cloves near the plant requiring protection. If garlic does increase the scent of roses, as is claimed for this herb, it would make sense of the theory that root secretions of garlic trigger an increased essential oil production in roses.

GINSENG AND TRADITIONAL CHINESE MEDICINE

Ginseng (*Panax ginseng or P. pseudoginseng*)

The oriental 'kingly herb', ginseng is perhaps the most famous herbal root and is the subject of most misunderstanding.

It has an aura of Chinese mystique enhancing the claims that it will make people live longer, improve their memory, stamina and even sex life. Although there is an element of truth in these claims, simplistic thinking inevitably leads to misunderstanding and disappointment.

Ginseng has a wide range of beneficial effects on the body and this is what creates the general vitality so valued by the Chinese. But the wide range is also what confuses conventional western researchers. It makes added energy available to diverse organs (it increases an organ's ability to absorb nutrients which provides it with more available 'fuel') and thereby helps a large variety of health problems. People in the west misconstrued this information and wrongly assumed that it must be a panacea, something that could treat any problem. This would be the ultimate consumer product, so advertisers touted it as a cure-all until eventually it lost credibility. It does not 'treat' any specific problem but rather strengthens the body to deal with all problems. The oriental concept of herbs like ginseng is as an essential tool for maintaining and improving health rather than tackling specific illness. Indeed the Greek goddess and word 'Panacea' represented complete health rather than complete cure.

Unfortunately, orthodox western medicine finds it difficult to classify ginseng because it does not fully comprehend the way in which it works. We have the odd situation where ginseng is not recognized in the British Pharmacopoeia (the country's official pharmaceutical list of therapeutic substances) but on the other hand it is banned by the International Athletics Federation as one of the performance enhancing drugs.

At the moment, scientists test a drug to see if it can achieve a single result; to see for example, if it can cause blood pressure to drop. Paradoxically, ginseng has multiple effects. It can raise or lower blood pressure and it can stimulate or sedate, depending on the circumstances. So new methods of analysis and a new vocabulary become necessary. The term 'adaptogen' was introduced by Professor Israel Brekhman to encompass the results of research into ginseng. It describes a new class of drug which does not affect the body when stress is not present but which returns the body processes to normal when there is stress or damage present. This is a unique idea to western medicine – a drug which has a normalizing effect, which increases the ability of the body to adapt and which only works when needed.

The system of Chinese traditional medicine has been built on 4000 years of empirical knowledge – testing, observing and recording the results of practical experience which is constantly updated and revised. Western drug acceptance relies mainly on the laboratory tests of active ingredients. With western chemical analysis we can learn in more detail how the traditional herbs work and it is being discovered that the empirical knowledge about their values is generally proving to be true. There are added benefits from this chemical analysis; ingredients with specific action are discovered which pinpoint more exactly which group of patients will benefit from a herb, and in other examples a further, previously unknown, active substance is discovered which indicates additional uses for the herb.

However, the reverse process, that is subjecting laboratory western drugs to sufficient years of trial and error, is much more difficult. The dangers of not doing this are increased by the use of 'active ingredients' to create stronger and faster acting drugs because they also create more dangerous side effects. The safety value of the laboratory tests depends on the skill of the testing scientist to imagine every possible danger and test for it. This is clearly difficult, as the Thalidomide and Opren drug disasters have shown. There is no substitute for the years of clinical observation which traditional herbs have undergone.

Nor is it necessary to create potentially dangerous new synthetic drugs for many of the ailments for which drugs are developed. The first line of action should be to investigate existing remedies and the way they are employed within their system. Chinese traditional medicine has herbal compounds for all types of conditions including the chronic ailments which they treat more successfully than western drugs. They even have several for treating a wide range of cancers and AIDS. More and more are being researched and chemically analysed in Britain and in other countries, and this information is available in scientific papers and journals, waiting to be taken up in the West. There are, however, two obstacles.

The first is the expectation level of western patients who want instant cures. We are an impatient race. We want the instant effect of drugs and we will worry about the side effects and the real cause of our problem some other time. A re-adjustment is needed to the idea of a slower, safer, healing process. This will probably be the most difficult task.

The second is the billion dollar pharmaceutical industry whose world wide profits are second only to those of the arms industry. Drug companies do take up this herbal information but they cannot patent plant parts or even isolated plant ingredients and so cannot gain great profits from them. They investigate many herbs; in fact there is presently a massive investigation into folk medicines from around the world. But their aim is to isolate simple active ingredients which can be synthesized and patented. Then they must convince doctors and patients that the original herb is not acceptable, only their synthesized drug is safe.

There is no denying that there are important life-saving synthetic medicines but there are also many valuable herbs which are ignored. Imagine the amount of useful research on herbal ingredients hidden away or destroyed once a company has synthesized the active ingredient of a herb. Rather than wait for a company to isolate, synthesize and patent a compound extracted from Chinese cucumber root, a promising herb for treating AIDS, and then undertake tests for toxicity, why not also adopt the traditional Chinese method of investigating what other herbs are used in combination with it? The compound already exists in the plant and volumes of Chinese literature can specify the side effects of this herb and what herbs are best used with it to strengthen or modify its action.

The valid argument from medical practitioners is that they must have reliable, measurable doses of active ingredients so that they can prescribe proper amounts. But it is certainly possible to organize the availability of herbs at a consistent level of quality. The Korean government does it with ginseng; their approval is required for the site, the fertility of the land, the quantity of plants grown per unit area and the number of years the root is grown. The government only accepts raw ginseng and then they supervise the steaming and drying process.

Information on horticultural and storage techniques, plus the proper methods of preparation to maximize active principles, are well documented and available in oriental countries. Many western people would like to grow good-quality medicinal herbs and technicians can be trained to prepare the herbs in the most efficacious manner.

It is not merely the monopoly of drug companies that causes concern. Many people are worried about the dangers of isolating so-called active ingredients. One danger is that the modifying agents are left out. Modifying agents are part of the make-up of some herbs which render the whole herb safe. These may not appear active in isolated tests but they offset the side effects of the active constituents.

This concept was highlighted in research on common sage which was found to have a component that is toxic. Further research uncovered modifying agents rendering the leaf harmless. It is a similar story with the pyrethrum flower which is a non-toxic insecticide. When the active ingredients of pyrethrin or cinerin are extracted, they are toxic to humans.

Because ginseng has not been recognized in Britain, much of the information on this and many other medicinal herbs comes from the research of other countries, research now recognized by western scientists as excellent quality. One British micro-biologist, reviewing a piece of Chinese research analysis on ginseng declared it to be scientifically faultless. When scientists accept the research, doctors too acknowledge it, and their commitment to health must be stronger than their commitment to drugs, so it is important to have the information disseminated to the appropriate areas and make the herbs, plus training on their proper usage, available.

Ginseng helps fight infections but research on the root found that it was not a 'specific' against any bacteria (a specifc is a herb which fights against a particular problem), rather that it increased the size and number of the macrophages if taken over a prolonged period. Macrophages are fixed cells within different organs of the body (in the liver, lymph nodes, spleen and lungs) that filter out passing bacteria, viruses and toxins.

A clue to the way in which herbs are viewed in the traditional Chinese system can be seen from an explanation in the ancient *Pharmacopoeia of the Heavenly Husbandman*. Those which are mild in effect and not harmful even in large doses are the 'kingly herbs' *e.g.* ginseng, liquorice and jujube (Chinese dates). Interestingly, these are among the few herbs which fall into the new 'adaptogen' category. A second group are called 'ministerial'; they are more powerful and rather more toxic herbs. Finally, a third group are called 'adjutant'; these are the highly powerful herbs which are dangerous; *e.g.* aconite and hellebore.

So, the mildest herbs are the most important and given first rank, while the really powerful are the last-resort drugs to be used only when others fail. This is opposite to western (allopathic) medicine which regards the powerful drugs as the mainstay of medicine and the mild drugs as accessories of little significance. This is partly because of our attitude to healing ourselves. We tend to wait until problems have reached a dramatic stage, before we visit a doctor, even priding ourselves in not going to see one until the last minute. By that time dramatic solutions are needed.

A medical system designed to recognize early problem patterns and give specific advice on diet and lifestyle with gentle treatments such as herbal sedatives or tonics could save later pain and expence. The new, travelling Get Well clinics do part of this, and are to be applauded. In the Far East, ginseng and similar 'kingly herbs' are the primary weapons for maintaining peak fitness.

Ginseng Research

Ginseng contains phosphorous, iron, copper, magnesium, calcium, potassium, sulphur, manganese, silica, sodium, the enzymes amylase and phenolase and vitamins B1 and B2. A team of researchers in Moscow and another in Tokyo have spent two decades trying to isolate the key ingredients of ginseng.

So far, 16 active ingredients (called terpenoidal glycosides) have been identified, appearing to behave like plant hormones in the herb. They are produced in the leaves, flowers and root peel and stored in the root. Japanese researchers have named them ginsenoides and coded them Ra, Rb, Rc, etc. How each affects the body is beginning to be understood but their synergistic effect, the extra benefit of how they function together, still eludes analysis.

The proportion of ginsenoides varies in different plant varieties, different aged roots, and in roots from different locations, but they provide a standard whereby the roots can be judged. A few have been synthesized but most have so far proved impossible to reproduce. The main effects of the first six established are to: mildly increase endocrine activity, mildly increase metabolic activity, mildly stimulate the circulatory system, mildly stimulate the digestive process, prevent adverse reactions to stress and effect homeostasis (returning body processes to normal functioning).

Ginseng and Relief of Stress

This is the area of most potential benefit to western lifestyles. We are contantly subjected to a general background of low-level environmental stress from pollution in air and water, food and radiation. Added to this, our present form of business activities and personal transportation require competitive aggressive actions which keep our adrenalin levels constantly high.

Scientific research repeatedly shows that ginseng helps the body to cope with stress. In experiments with mice, under normal conditions (*i.e.* in the absence of stress) the mice given ginseng showed no difference, but under stressful conditions (some given poisons, depressants, irradiation, alcohol, drugs, infections and stressful environments such as heat, cold, air pressure changes) there was an increase in weight and function of the adrenal glands together with less distress and less abnormal behaviour. Also, the mice given ginseng recovered more quickly from the stressful situations.

One way ginseng reduces stress is by increasing the numbers of red blood cells which help distribute oxygen and white vigilante blood cells patrolling the blood stream looking for infections (virus, bacteria and toxins) which they try to pin down and then dissolve. By increasing the body's ability to rid itself of toxins it reduces the stress on our body leaving more energy to resist specific diseases. And if the body is using less energy, or has a greater ability to fight disease, then we have fewer periods where we feel depressed or down because our body is under attack.

Its action on the central nervous system has also been shown to reverse and block the effects of alcohol and sedative barbiturates.

Other research suggests that ginseng works through the hormones, improving the efficiency of the hormone messenger system probably creating a greater co-ordination in the defence forces of the body. So the improved stamina, alertness and resistance to stress are brought about by more efficient physiological co-ordination – we get higher performance with less fuel.

Ginseng as a Tonic

The Chinese are more interested in taking ginseng for its long-term effects in promoting a better quality of life in later years. It is used to reduce convalescent time and fatigue from illness. It stimulates the body to produce its own hormones and increases body resistance. It helps reduce high blood pressure along with diet and exercise, and helps the metabolism of diabetics to adjust to insulin injections. Russian experience shows it can improve the mental state of the elderly, assisting memory and concentration.

Ginseng as a Stimulant

Soviet research by experts in space medicine, concluded that ginseng was a better stimulant and tonic than the amphetamine drugs used by US astronauts as it increased alertness and performance without a 'hangover'. It stimulates the body systems but is not an excitant so it doesn't cause sleep problems.

Ginseng can save the lives of some seriously ill patients by giving them the energy and stamina to fight disease. In China, someone on their deathbed may be given ginseng to give them the energy to receive their family and arrange their affairs before death.

Korean soldiers used it to sustain the wounded against shock and stress until brought to a field hospital. They also use it as a stimulant for sentry duty.

Russian performance research with double blind tests on the speed and accuracy of proof readers, and Swedish research on students taking exams and others doing heavy physical labour, showed improved reflexes; eyes took less time to adjust to the dark after taking ginseng. These experiments also indicated improved capacity, performance and a general increase in cerebral activity 'with no disturbances in the equilibrium of the cerebral processes'. The conclusion was, 'a good short term stimulant with no unpleasant side effects.'

Ginseng Dosage

There is much literature which suggests ginseng can be taken indefinitely and that no overdose will do any harm, but other practitioners advise that it should not be taken for too long because ginseng acts as a trigger mechanism and there is a limit to how many times or how frequently you should ask the body to increase its red and white blood cell count. Western advice is to take $\frac{1}{25}$ (1 g) twice a day, between meals rather than with food. Orientals might take $\frac{1}{8}$–$\frac{1}{4}$ oz (2–6 g) a day and would advise that the young and healthy shouldn't take it unless under stress. But don't take it for long periods or in high dosage or against medical advice. Most things medicinal have side effects, and excessive ginseng, taken for too long or in too large quantities can produce toxic shock in the heart.

Ginseng is useful in the short term for lowering blood pressure by reducing blood cholesterol, but in the long term it would stress the heart and increase blood pressure. So it would be useful in initial stages of coronary heart disease but not over a long period of time.

Many medicinal roots can be grown in our herb gardens but for treatment it is important to see a specialist for diagnosis and dosage. If this is not possible and you are confident of your herb identification, the advise for self-administration is to take the herb for a short period. Then, if there is no specific benefit from taking it, consult an expert. Also, as a general rule, to get optimum performance from a herb take it for short periods, say two weeks on, two weeks off. Then repeat it for two weeks and then take it off for a month. This way the body maximizes the benefit, reacting in a major way instead of becoming acclimatized to the herb.

Compounds

Traditionally, an oriental herb is rarely used alone. The Chinese system uses a sophisticated combination of plants to target specific problems and to reinforce each other. However, ginseng is one of the most frequently used of all remedies and a Chinese medical book published in 960 lists more than 500 formulae containing ginseng.

Combinations almost always include a main herb for the principal curative action, one or more herbs to counter the side effects, and 'guide herbs' which will direct the drugs to an infection or specific site of disorder. The guide herbs are still an unproven aspect of Chinese medicine but those selected are usually antibiotic and anti-virotic (kill viruses). Substances which kill viruses are rare in western medicine and surely worth investigating. The Chinese give something to surpress a virus long enough for the body's immune system to react to it on its own.

American Ginseng (*Panax quinquefolium*)

This herb was discovered in western Canada by early traders and Jesuits and was a vital export crop, rivalling the fur trade industry until it was almost picked to extinction. Though similar to oriental ginseng, it is considered not as healing and preferred for use in hot climates and in summer. It is not as stimulating as *P. ginseng*, rather slightly sedative.

Siberian Ginseng (*Eleutherococcus senticosus*)

This has similar properties to oriental ginseng, particularly the adaptogen facility. Many consider it much better value as the mystique around ginseng has made the prices unrealistic. It is now often used in the USSR instead of ginseng, especially by Russian sportspersons to speed recovery from stress and exhaustion after intensive activity.

Dong Kwai or Tang-Kuei (*Angelica sinensis*)

Chinese angelica is traditionally used for menstrual disorders but when subjected to modern chemical analysis it was found to have no female hormone action; rather a concentration of folic acid and B12. It therefore alleviates anemia, so helping with a number of menstrual problems.

I have two pieces of dong kwai and it is interesting to see the difference in preparation between them. Perhaps the difference is partly due to the 3,000 years of accumulated knowledge and practice which the Chinese have. The piece from John Hall, a practitioner of traditional Chinese medicine who obtains his supplies from China, is large (about 5 in [12.5 cm] across in section), dried but still flexible, almost 'chewy' and thinly sliced, and is patterned like a piece of marble. The other piece was bought from a herb shop in London. It is from a younger piece of root about 1 in (2.5 cm) in section. The piece has been dried whole and is hard and brittle with a powdery surface.

In Britain, dong kwai can also be purchased chopped in small pieces. In China, the branch roots are separated from the main root because branch root ends are abortive whereas the main section is not, so the practitioner can decide if this is a consideration. If you buy pre-chopped pieces it is not possible to tell if the ends have been chopped with main root, so the mixture should not be taken by a pregnant woman. This again reinforces the importance of seeing a herbalist, eastern or western, to obtain correct dosage and correct plant parts.

Sai-dong-sum (*Codonopsis pilosula*)

This is another ginseng replacement from the bluebell family. It increases the white and red blood cell counts in the same way as Korean ginseng but has a more pronounced effect on reducing adrenalin and therefore stress so it can be particularly useful for westerners. Like Siberian ginseng it is less expensive than Chinese or Korean ginseng.

Wong-Kay or But-Kay (*Astragalus membranaceus*)

As with the previous herb, this root has similar uses to ginseng. It is a tonic, it increases the white and red cell counts and also increases the strength and size of the macrophages (the body's defensive mechanism), so that they are bigger and beefier and can tackle larger cells and bacteria. They take out toxins, almost working like a magnet, and dissolve them. It is used in China similarly to, and often with, sai-dong-sum to treat cancer and would be used to treat AIDS, but kay has the same medicinal effects as dong kwai and sai-dong-sum in that it increases red and white blood cell counts. It also has an effect against immuno-suppressants which are chemical agents released by invading bacteria and viruses to stop our body from reacting to their presence. Wong-kay interferes with that process, so our body resumes its normal activity against invaders and in these circumstances it is more useful than ginseng, though ginseng is also said to have this property.

Wong-kay and sai-dong-sum are often used in combinations to offset the side effects of other more toxic drugs which might be selected for specific problems rather than being selected for their own principal effects. Both are used to alleviate or to offset the side effects, the nausea and reduced red and white blood count of radiotherapy and chemotherapy treatments in cancer so they can be used in conjuction with western medical treatments.

Peony root (*Paeonia officinalis, P. lactiflora*)

The roots of this 'king of flowers', both from the red flowered and the white flowered form, are important herbs in the repertoire of Chinese herbalists. Peony root has antibiotic properties and improves the blood flow, especially to the uterus. It is prescribed for pelvic congestion, uterine infections, uterine congestion, uterine fibroids and is one of a set used to treat uterine cancer. It could be used more in the west.

Yu-chin, Turmeric (*Curcuma longa* and *Curcuma aromatica*)

Turmeric increases the liver's ability to perform its two main functions; to metabolize or break down all the food and drugs we consume into a form usable by the body and to gather toxins from the body for elimination. It is useful for indigestion because it increases the secretion of digestive fluids. Turmeric enhances these actions in the short term but over a prolonged period of time, or if used to excess, it may over-stimulate the liver and upset metabolic processes. Chinese practitioners use a variety of turmeric to treat liver disease up to and including liver cancer.

The Future

Traditional Chinese medicine, along with western herbalism and other complementary medical systems, have much to offer, most of it still unrecognized. It is vitally important that our freedom to choose alternative therapies is maintained, particularily from 1992 when new EEC legislation may attempt to change this situation. It is equally vital that these systems are fairly and objectively tested and the valid aspects consequently integrated into our health system.

WESTERN MEDICINAL ROOTS AND BULBS

Dandelion (*Taraxacum officinale*)

This common weed appears in Arabian herbals of the eleventh century and is still a useful herbal treatment. The root provides one of the safest plant diuretics known (a substances which increases the volume of urine), particularily valuable as it replaces the phosphorus usually lost with increased urination. Juice extracted from the root is used to stimulate the production of bile and a root decoction is drunk as a liver tonic especially for jaundice and the early stages of cirrhosis. It gives some benefit to sufferers of rheumatism and is taken as a mild laxative for chronic constipation. This herb is safe to take in fairly large amounts.

135

Garlic (*Allium sativum*)

Garlic has an ancient reputation as a herb for maintaining health and increasing stamina. This reaches back to records of the daily dose given to Egyptian pyramid builders and early Greek Olympic contenders. Present-day research confirms the historical claims made for this bulb and is discovering new virtues. It has strong antibacterial properties so it gives some protection against infectious diseases such as the common cold, amoeboid dysentery and even typhoid. Garlic lowers blood pressure and is used to treat hypertension and arteriosclerosis. It helps expel fluid from the lungs and is used to treat bronchial catarrh while the fresh juice was once employed as an inhalant for pulmonary tuberculosis. It is mildly fungicide and appears to fight the fungus which causes a fatal form of meningitis and the fungus of athletes' foot. It may also have a role to play in keeping tumours at bay. Unfortunately, the best way to reap the benefits is to eat a fresh clove once or twice a day. Garlic tablets generally have so little actual garlic in them that an enormous number is required to equal a clove. Taken in cooked dishes, garlic will provide most of the benefits so roasted cloves are a good idea. Chew fresh parsley or cardamom seeds at the end of a garlic meal to reduce the tell-tale breath.

Liquorice (*Glycyrrhiza glaba*)

The medical use of this plant stretches back 3000 years to the Assyrians, Egyptians and Chinese. The best roots are at least three years old and they are carefully dug up in late autumn, scrubbed clean and dried. The *British Pharmacopoeia* states that the root must be peeled but other authorities disagree. Liquorice has laxative properties and is used in the relief of Addison's disease but its primary value is in the treatment of coughs, bronchitis and gastric ulcers because of four main attributes. Liquorice root is expectorant – it helps expel phlegm; it is demulcent – smooth and soothing to painful or inflamed areas; it is anti-inflammatory – it relieves inflamed surfaces; and spasmolytic – it relieves pain from spasms. In excessive doses liquorice may cause sodium retention and loss of potassium with resulting water retention, headaches, hypertension and shortness of breath.

Valerian (*Valeriana officinalis*)

The rhizome and roots of two-year-old valerian plants are a powerful nervine, a substance that calms nervous tension. Roots are lifted in September or October, washed and dried. Valerian root is not peeled because an important part of the medical properties resides in the skin. An infusion is made by soaking 1 tsp (5 ml) dried root in cold water for a day, and is drunk for nervous exhaustion, depression, anxiety, headaches, intestinal cramp and chronic insomnia. It is used in combination with other herbs to treat hypertension. Homoeopathic treatment uses a tincture of the fresh root. During the First World War, valerian was used to treat shell shock and, through the Second World War, to help people cope with the stress of constant bomb raids. Valerian should not be taken in addition to other sedative products and it is important to see a medical herbalist for an appropriate dosage. Do not take valerian in strong doses for long periods of time as it can become addictive.

CULINARY ROOTS AND BULBS

Garlic (*Allium sativum*)

The garlic bulb is universally an important seasoning. In its botanic name 'allium' is the name of the onion family and 'sativus' means 'sown, planted, cultivated' – hence also 'crocus sativus', saffron, the cultivated crocus. The bulb is made up of several corms, usually between 8 and 12, and their size and flavour varies with different climates and varieties, the best coming from warm climates.

Garlic is mainly used as a flavouring, but it can be roasted in the oven alongside any meat dish to create a delicious vegetable with a subtle flavour that does not have the pungency normally associated with the bulb. Garlic enhances all meats and fish and blends with most vegetables and herbs, particularly with parsley and mushrooms.

Ginger (*Zingiber officinale*)

Ginger is the warmly-aromatic rhizome of a shade-loving perennial from the tropical jungles of south-east Asia. It has an ancient history as both a culinary herb and a medicine and was perhaps the first spice introduced to the west, long before the Roman empire was expanding. The plant has iris-like leaves and occasionally a flowering stem of white or yellow fragrant sterile flowers with a purple lip. The knobbly, buff rhizome grows like a stubby collection of fingers and at about ten-months-old it is collected and sometimes sold as a 'hand'.

Ginger used to be only available as a powder which was popular in jams (like rhubarb and ginger jam); cakes such as parkin, and biscuits such as gingerbread men and ginger beer, but now the fresh rhizome is available in many supermarkets. It is only when using a plump, fresh 'root' that its true flavour can be appreciated validating its use as the primary spice for savoury dishes in oriental cooking. They use it with all types of meat, and also fish as it helps to transform the unpleasant fishiness of some species.

To use fresh ginger, first peel off the skin. If it will be used to flavour the cooking oil of a stir-fried dish, and then removed before main ingredients are added, it can be quickly sliced. But if it will remain part of the dish, grate it with the finest grade of a hand grater until it is almost like a paste. When buying ginger, choose pieces that have a tight, fresh, unwrinkled skin and store them in a cool, airy vegetable rack. Ginger maintains its life for long periods, so if you use it infrequently it will keep fresh if you plant it in a box of dry sandy soil and water it infrequently; sunlight is not necessary. It may even supply you with fresh green shoots which are the material of crystallized ginger.

Turmeric (*Curcuma longa*)

Turmeric is the fragrant rhizome of a tender perennial from south-east Asia with large lily-like leaves and dense clusters of pale yellow flowers. The rhizome, dug up when about nine months old, has intensely yellow flesh and is washed, boiled, sun-dried and has its skin peeled or rubbed off before being sold as a flavouring. It is usually only available as a powder but this is quite satisfactory as it is a tough root, very hard to pulverize at home, and it is a cheap enough spice so that middlemen are not tempted to adulterate it. It has a mild, 'dry', savoury flavour with a touch of bitterness and is in the same family as ginger. Its presence is mostly noted by the intense yellow colour it gives to curries, piccalilli and some Indian sweet dishes.

Turmeric is also used to dye monks' robes when saffron is too expensive, but it is not colour-fast. It should never be used as a saffron substitute in cooking as its flavour is too pronounced; calendula petals would be better just to supply the colour. In India, it is valued as an antiseptic and in hot climates this attribute gives extra protection to prepared food.

Horseradish (*Armoracia rusticana*)

The perennial root of horseradish grows wild in Britain in patches of moist ground. Locally it can often be found in the short drainage ditches dug out from the minor roads where the land lies low. Horseradish is a member of the mustard (cruciferae) family with dark-green, wavy-edged leaves up to 2 ft (60 cm) long and an occasional flower stem with pointed leaves quite different to the main leaves. The tap root is yellow ochre on the outside with a pungent white flesh. This flesh contains calcium, sodium, magnesium, vitamin C and antibiotic qualities which make it useful for preserving food and protecting the intestinal tract. This is why it is often served with raw fish dishes by the Japanese as raw fish can contain paracites which survive in the human gut.

The root is prepared by scrubbing and then grating it, an experience never forgotten. The grating releases a powerful volatile oil which rushes up the nostrils and can clear sinuses in one breathe. Most of the pungency is in the outer part of the root so peeling would mean the loss of most of the flavour. Only remove damaged or discoloured skin. The root can be grated with a fine grater or scraped off with a knife. Because the pungent oil evaporates so quickly there is little point in adding it to cooked dishes as the flavour will vanish during the cooking process. It can, however, be preserved by immersing the whole root in white wine vinegar.

TRADITIONAL ENGLISH HORSERADISH SAUCE
2 tbsp (30 ml) finely grated horseradish
1 tbsp (15 ml) white wine vinegar or lemon juice
2 tsp (10 ml) castor sugar
¼ tsp (1.25 ml) made-up mustard
salt and pepper to taste
¼ pt (150 ml) cream

Mix all the ingredients together except the cream. Half whip the cream and gradually fold in the horseradish mixture. Chill in the refrigerator until semi-solid and serve cold.

CREAMED HORSERADISH
On the continent, horseradish sauce is generally a lighter sauce made with cream and a little seasoning but without the vinegar of an English mixture.

1 tbsp (15 ml) finely grated horseradish
¼ pt (150 ml) thick cream
dash of lemon juice
salt
few drops olive oil

Gently stir the horseradish into the cream. Add the salt and lemon juice. Beat in the olive oil drop by drop as an emulsifier to keep the mixture thick and smooth.

This is particularly tasty blended with cream cheese, garlic and chives to spread on canapes with smoked fish.

PICKLED HORSERADISH
Pick good sized roots, wash and scrape off any discoloured skin. Mince in a food processor or grate and pack loosely into small jars. Cover with salted vinegar (1 tsp [5 ml] salt to ½ pt [300 ml] vinegar) and seal.

The vinegar from this pickle can also be used as horseradish vinegar if the salt is acceptable to the recipe.

Liquorice (*Glycyrrhiza glabra*)

The dried rhizomes and roots of this hardy perennial herb of the pea family have the characteristic and popular flavour of the sweets named after the plant.

This pretty legume with racemes of small pale-blue flowers, grows in a rich, moist, sandy loam and three- to five-year-old roots are harvested when they have reached an extensive size. The roots are sometimes chewed raw but more often used in powdered form or as an extract. To produce the extract, the rhizomes and roots are ground into pulp, boiled in water and the resulting extract is concentrated by evaporation.

Liquorice flavours sweets, beers, tobacco and snuff. It is also used as a refreshing medicinal tea.

Onion (*Allium cepa*)

The entire onion family is valuable for cooks. There are no known poisonous members of the family, though a few varieties are rather rank. The common onion *Allium cepa* has many forms from spring onions and small pickling onions to giant main crops. The tree onion, also called the Egyptian onion and the Canadian onion (*Allium cepa* Proliferum), is a very hardy form which is easy to grow, producing small, sharply-flavoured onions on the stem tips in mid- and late summer for pickles or garnish.

Bunching Onions

Bunching onions available from herb nurseries in Britain include the everlasting onions (*Allium perutile*) and Welsh onions (*Allium fistulosum*). These form a cluster of small bulbs rather than a single bulb. The everlasting onion was named as such because a few bulbs can be pulled off the side of a cluster and the remainder will stay to clump up again, giving a continuous supply. The everlasting onion is 9–12 in (22–30 cm) high with dark blue-green leaves and does not flower (it can only be propagated by plant division). The Welsh onion (Welsh meaning 'foreign') is a similar, but larger, plant producing a white flower cluster and stronger-flavoured leaves. The young autumn shoots stay green throughout the winter to give a supply of fresh 'chives'. Cut in thin slices with scissors to give rings of green for an attractive garnish.

Cultivars of the bunching onions are the most important onions in the Orient. The base is used like a large spring onion and the stems are blanched (grown with light excluded to produce tender pale shoots) to create the onion greens referred to in Chinese recipes. Two-inch (5-cm) lengths of these blanched stems, briefly stir fried, are often the garnish on take-away meat and rice dishes available from street vendors in China.

Rocambole (*Allium sativum*)

This is a mild form of garlic with a small bulb and a long stem. In a warm summer it produces an attractive head of pinky-mauve flowers which develop into a cluster of tiny bulblets. All parts can be used as garlic and the leaves have a gentle garlic flavour like Chinese chives.

Shallots (*Allium ascalonicum*)

These are popular in French cuisine for their distinctive flavour and blend well with herbs. They grow in clusters and yield a medium-sized bulb which is excellent for pickles.

Dandelion and Chicory Coffee Substitutes

The long, milky, tap root of a dandelion dug when two years old and chicory root dug in the autumn of its first year make acceptable substitutes for coffee giving a similar but slightly more bitter flavour, free from caffeine. Scrub the roots well but do not peel. Cut the chicory into short pieces but leave the dandelion whole and, if possible, dry them in the sun. Roast in a low oven with the door ajar until they are brittle. Store in an airtight tin and when required give them ten minutes further roasting in a hot oven. Grind them in a coffee grinder and use as you would coffee.

Florence Fennel (*Foeniculum vulgare* 'Dulce')

Fennel bulb is the swollen base of the stalks of Florence Fennel (the Latin *dulcis* means sweet or pleasant), and it is also called sweet fennel or Finocchio. This 18-in (45-cm) high form of fennel is grown as an annual and prefers a light, fertile soil. The most common problem is its frequent tendency to bolt whenever a cold or dry spell occurs. 'Zefa Fino' is a relatively new variety which is less prone to bolting. The 'bulb' has a fresh, crunchy texture and a mild, sweet aniseed flavour. It is popular grated or sliced into salads and can be prepared as a baked vegetable.

Salsify (*Tragopogon porrifolius*)

This is a root herb which faded from popularity when meat became cheaper earlier this century. It is a biennial with pretty purple flowers which can be pickled for salads. The root has a strong, individual flavour giving rise to its alternative name of the oyster plant as the taste is reminiscent of sea fish. Peel the long pale roots and steam them. Serve with butter, lemon juice and seasoning. It keeps its flavour well served cold and it can be sliced into salads.

Scorzonera (*Scorzonera hispanica*)

This herb is very similar to salsify but the flowers are yellow, the root has a dark brown skin and the plant is perennial. Prepare as for salsify.

Marsh Mallow (*Althea officinalis*)

Originally, marsh mallow was made from the root of this herb by boiling slices in sugar water to create a soothing sweet paste, but today's marsh mallows have only the sugar in common with the original recipe.

2 oz (50 g) dried powdered marsh mallow root
14 oz (400 g) castor sugar
1 tsp (5 ml) gum tragacanth (available from chemists) or other edible binding muscilage
2½ tbsp (37.5 ml) orange flower water (approx)

Mix the marsh mallow root and sugar together. Stir the gum tragacanth into 2 tbsp (30 ml) of the orange flower water. Add the liquid to the powders and stir. Use just enough orange flower water to bind the mixture together to form little balls. Roll into shape and leave these to dry.

If you cannot get the tragacanth, try soaking the powdered marsh mallow in the orange flower water overnight to draw out the mucilage from the marsh mallow, then add sugar and roll into small balls or, if it is not sticky enough, make into flat cakes, cut into squares and leave to dry.

Elecampane (*Inula helenium*)

This root contains a sweet starchy substance called inulin. In the Middle Ages, apothecaries sold the crystalized root in flat, pink, sugary cakes (coloured with cochineal) which were sucked to relieve asthma and indigestion and to sweeten the breath.

Sea Holly (*Eryngium maritimum*) (Eryngo)

Eryngo root has been a popular flavouring root since Saxon times with its sweet taste and high concentration of mucilage. The root was used medicinally and to make toffee. It is harvested in spring or in the autumn after seeding when it can yield roots up to 6 ft (2 m) long. Roots are washed, parboiled, peeled and either dried or candied. To candy, slice thinly, weigh the eryngo and add an equal weight of sugar. Boil until the sugar becomes syrup, then cool.

SALAD ROOTS

John Evelyn's *Discourse of Sallet* reminds us of many salad roots long forgotten. He suggests chervil roots which should be boiled and eaten cold: 'much commended for Aged Persons'. Sweet cicely was sometimes called chervil and as the annual chervil roots are so tiny it is likely he means sweet cicely root. And they are remarkably tasty. He reports that the young roots of daisy are frequently eaten by Spaniards and Italians from spring until June and that French country people eat the root of dandelion. The history lesson continues with 'and t'was with this homely Sallet the Good-Wife Hecate entertain'd Theseus.'

The 'sallet's' ingredients included garlic, though he adds 'to be sure, 'tis not for Ladies Palats, nor those who court them; a light touch is better supplied by the gentle roccombo'. He lists the roots of Goat's beard (*Tragopogon pratensis*) and scozonera to be stewed and dressed for salads. Goat's beard is the same family as salsify (*Tragopogon porrifolius*) which John Evelyn called viper-grass or salsifex and stated it was 'a very sweet and pleasant sullet; being laid to soak out the bitterness, then peel'd may be eaten raw, but best of all stew'd with Marrow, Spice, and Wine.' Marsh mallow root was boiled to soften it and then sliced and fried. He adds parsnip boiled, cooled and eaten with oil and vinegar and radish whole or sliced.

His highest praise was reserved for skirret; 'exceedingly nourishing, wholesome and delicate; of all the root kind, not subject to be windy and so valued by the Emperor Tiberius that he accepted them for tribute. This excellent root is seldom eaten raw; but being boil'd, stew'd, roasted under the Embers, bak'd in Pies, whole, sliced or in pulp, is very acceptable to all palates. Tis reported they were heretofore something bitter; See what Culture and Education effects!'

SKIRRETS

This recipe appeared in *The Housekeeper's Instructor* (1808) by JC Schebbelie. A timeless process for the cooking of vegetables in a white sauce. 'Wash them [the skirrets] thoroughly clean, and when you have boiled them until they are tender, skin the roots, and cut them into slices. Have ready a little cream, a piece of butter rolled in flour, the yolk of an egg beaten fine, a little grated nutmeg, two or three spoonfuls of white wine, with very little salt, and stir all together. Put your roots into the dish and pour the sauce over them.'

CHERVIL/SWEET CICELY ROOT

Clean and peel the root, cut into strips and boil in salted water until just tender. Drain. While still warm, mix with a well-flavoured vinaigrette. Turn onto a dish and arrange with groups of very finely sliced radishes, peeled shrimps and watercress. The hot radishes and watercress contrast beautifully with the more subtly flavoured roots and shellfish.

JERUSALEM ARTICHOKES

1 lb (450 g) prepared Jerusalem artichokes
1 small onion
1 tbsp (15 ml) vegetable oil
1 tbsp (15 ml) flour
1 garlic clove
small glass of medium dry white wine
approx ½ pt (300 ml) of single cream
salt and fresh ground white pepper
knob of butter
chopped parsley (optional)

Jerusalem artichokes need patience to peel, but it is well worth the effort. As soon as they are peeled, drop them into cold water acidulated with a squeeze of lemon or vinegar to prevent them from discolouring. When everything has been prepared for cooking, drain them and dry gently in a cloth.

Chop onion very finely and fry gently in the oil using a shallow casserole or straight sided frying pan. Sprinkle on the flour and combine well with the onion and oil. Stir in the mashed garlic clove.

Pour in the white wine and stir until smoothly blended. Season the sauce well.

Now add the prepared artichokes and enough cream to cover them. Simmer on the lowest possible heat for about ½ hour. Turn the artichokes occasionally with a spoon, but take great care, for as they soften, they can break up easily.

Either dot with butter and brown under the grill before serving, or sprinkle liberally with chopped parsley.

5
ESSENTIAL OILS

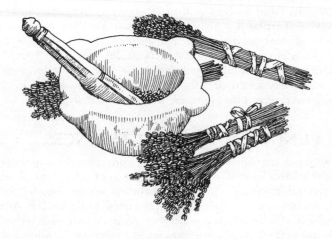

Scent is the first clue to the presence of a plant essence, or essential oil as it is called after it has been extracted by distillation. The plant essence is a cocktail of organic compounds found in minute glands in various parts of plants. It contains the aromatic and therapeutic principles used for flavouring, healing and cosmetics. Plant essences are also used for aromatherapy, the ancient art which uses blended essential oils for both beauty and health. They are mainly applied with massage.

Aromas, fragrances and perfumes are the elusive, desirable, unseen qualities of a plant that have stirred the passions and purse strings of humans through the ages. We have greater access to more of these fragrant treasures now than kings and empresses of any time in history. Of some 400 aromatic plants processed for their oils, at least 50 of the most beautiful are reasonably easy to obtain, from frankincense and myrrh (gifts from the Queen of Sheba to King Solomon 3000 years ago and later presented to the infant Jesus by three Wise Men); to tea-tree (*Melaleuca alternifolia*), a newly discovered oil with antiseptic properties 12-times greater than phenol, the traditional hospital antiseptic. We can create exotic perfumes and effective cosmetics, revive pot pourri, make antiseptic room sprays with real plant perfumes, have aromatic baths, create insect repellants, give relaxing massage treatments for slimming and skin rejuvenation, help prevent stretch marks and cellulite, and treat minor ailments, both physical and mental, with essential oils.

On a world trade basis, the largest quantities of essential oils are used by the food industry; for example, peppermint oil in sweets. Pharmaceutical companies are the second highest consumers using them for products like toothpaste and gargles, although both industries will use a synthetic substitute if they can obtain it cheaper. Third, the oils are vital to the perfume trade which uses synthetics for certain oils for cost reasons but recognizes that the best quality only comes from pure plant essences.

Many of the plants which are processed for their essential oils are grown in our herb gardens; angelica, aniseed, basil, coriander, caraway, clary, chamomile, fennel, hyssop, lavender, melissa (lemon balm), peppermint, rose geranium (pelargonium), rose, rosemary, sage, spearmint, sweet marjoram and thyme. They are also found in the trees growing nearby; in pine, juniper, thuja and eucalyptus.

THE FUNCTION OF PLANT ESSENCES

Plant essences are concentrated aromatic compounds composed of many constituents and located in specialized glands or cells of the plant. When extracted they are usually in a liquid form and although called 'oils', they feel more like water. Some plant essences are found in seeds like coriander and aniseed; many are located in leaves such as rosemary, thyme and sage; several are in flowers like the rose, jasmine and ylang-ylang; some in fruit peel such as orange and lemon; in woods like sandalwood and cedar; in gums and resins like myrrh and frankincense; in bark like cinnamon, and in roots such as orris.

There are plants which yield more than one oil. A North American shrub, *Lindera benzoin*, provides lavender-scented oil from its leaves, a camphor-scented oil from its twigs, an oil with the scent of allspice from its berries and an oil with the scent of wintergreen from its bark. The orange tree gives us orange oil from the fruit peel (classified as sweet orange oil from sweet oranges and bitter orange oil from bitter oranges); it also gives us neroli from the blossom and petitgrain from the twigs.

In the normal activity of a herb, these plant essences are released by warm temperatures and create a protective aura around the plant which resists bacteria, fungi and some viruses and may act as a buffer against extremes of temperature. Though they exist in special cells, it has been found that they migrate around the plant in different seasons and at different times of the day. Russian research has found they participate in the development of the plant, like a sort of vegetable hormone system. Others perceive them on another level. The nineteenth-century German doctor and mystic, Gustav Fechner, describes the plants as communicating with each other through their scents.

The presence of a plant essence around some herbs or herbal trees can be demonstrated by igniting it with a match. From one southern

European tree, the diptani, the leaves exude such a large amount of essence in hot weather that it becomes a natural fire hazard. The haze of plant essence around the herb *Dictamnus albus* (burning bush) on a hot day can sometimes be ignited.

Essential oils are highly volatile. 'Volare' means 'to fly' and it is the number of free electrons flying off which causes the rapid evaporation and gives us the odiferous quality. Different oils evaporate at different rates, resulting in top, middle and base notes which is significant to those composing perfumes. The evaporation rate is scientifically measured but the 'note' also includes a subjective assessment on the strength of odour.

Essential oils are all antiseptic to different degrees and they are soluble in alcohols. However, one constituent of some essential oils, the terpenes, will cloud the alcohol and in order to make a clear perfume, essential oils have to be 'de-terpinated'. They are soluble in ether and only slightly soluble in water (20 per cent) but they mix well with vegetable oils (also called fixed oils or carrier oils). Essential oils are highly flammable which is not a problem with small quantities but definitely a consideration for wholesalers and importers.

METHODS OF EXTRACTING PLANT ESSENCES

The fragrant essence of flowers like lilac, soapwort, osmanthus and jasmine is released to drift in the air. To capture this type of essence, the flower must be processed immediately after it is picked so that the perfume can be absorbed before it is dissipated in the air. To accomplish this, it can be necessary to position the extraction machinery right next to the cultivated plants as is sometimes done with jasmine.

For us to inhale the scent of other flowers like roses, violets and pinks we need to put our noses nearer to the centre of the flower. That is because these flowers release their perfume essence more slowly which allows a reasonable amount of time for harvested flowers to reach the processing stills. But some flowers halt scent production altogether once they are picked and from these it is almost impossible to obtain an essential oil.

Leaves and the hard parts of plants are not so elusive. To smell the aromatic oil in a leaf it only requires a little pressure or rubbing on the surface of the leaf. This action breaks the cell walls of the tiny glands containing the plant essence thereby releasing it to evaporate. The scent pockets of some leaves which are near the surface or have thin cell walls will be released by warm sunlight or the pressure of gentle rain, as happens with the leaves of sweet briar, the eglantine rose. Others, like the oil glands of sweet myrtle, are deeply embedded and need to be pressed quite hard to release their spicy orange scent.

Roots, bark, seeds and wood retain their scent internally for long periods and unless bruised, are seldom fragrant to the casual passing nose. These are generally chopped and then subjected to water or steam distillation.

Expression

This is the simplest form of extraction and may have been in use since Biblical times. A pressing or squeezing system is used to extract the oils from citrus peels and some barks. Up to the 1930s, it was done by the 'sponge process'; oil was extracted by hand and it required great skill to give just the right amount of pressure to obtain all the oil from the rind. It was squeezed onto a sponge and when the sponge was saturated, the oil was squeezed out of it to a container. It was expensive in labour and is now almost all done mechanically.

If you have citrus peel free from sprays or dyes, with pith and pulp removed you can obtain tiny amounts of oil by squeezing pieces with a new, unused garlic press. Allow your extraction to stand and if it is mixed with plant juices the oil will float to the top and can be separated.

Enfleurage

This is another ancient technique for extracting mainly flower essences which has been used for thousands of year. Flowers, like jasmine and rose, which continue to generate scent after they have been picked, are laid on a purified, odourless, cold fat which absorbs their essence. There are many recipes for the fat, often closely-guarded family secrets, but most require a mixture of lard and beef suet.

A sheet of glass is mounted in a rectangular frame and a thin layer of fat is spread onto the glass. A layer of freshly-picked flowers is spread on top of this fat, with another frame to cover. After about 24 hours (the range is 16 to 72 hours depending on the flower) the flowers will have given up all their oils to the fat. The frame is then turned upside down causing the withered flowers to fall off. Another layer of freshly picked blossom is strewn onto the fat and the process goes on for up to 70 days depending on the flowers involved and the quality of the harvest.

When the fat has been completely saturated with perfume it is known as a pomade and given a number; for example 'Pomade 30'. This means that the flowers were changed 30 times. Originally they were used in this form but now further treatment involves washing it in alcohol with mechanical agitation, transfering the oil to the alcohol. After this process, it is called 'Extrait 30'. If the alcohol is then evaporated, the resulting plant essence is called 'absolue de pomade'.

Rose oil, or 'otto' or 'attar' of roses, is expensive because of the labour involved and because it takes around 250 lbs (112 kg) of rose petals to give 1 oz (25 g) of otto of roses. The most valued rose absolute comes from Bulgaria, a reliable exporter as the government of this Eastern bloc country guarantees the purity of its oils.

Although it would be difficult to separate out a useable quantity of essential oils at home, it is possible to persuade the oils out of their plant cells into carrier oils or fats. Experiment with scented jasmine, roses, violets, lily-of-the-valley, hyacinth, jonquil, wall flowers and mignonette using the following method.

Dissolve 1 tsp (5 ml) of alum in 18 fl oz (525 ml) of water. Add ¾ lb (350 g) suet or animal fat and then add ¼ lb (100 g) lard.

Bring to the boil, then strain through two layers of muslin and cool. The fat will form on the surface. Separate this and reheat just to liquid state. Pour half into each of two matching shallow plates and cool. Apply the aromatic flowers in a thick layer, 1–2 in (2.5–5 cm) over the fat of one plate. Invert the second dish over the first ensuring the edges meet to stop the oil evaporating outside the dish. Leave for one to three days, depending on the power of the scent (choose the longer if in doubt). Separate the plates and tip off the withered flowers. Apply another layer. If your supply of one variety runs out, try mixing it with a different sweetly scented flower.

The fat will continue to absorb essences for a month by which time it should be saturated. Scrape the fat into a dark glass jar with a wide top and screw lid. Add an equal amount by volume of alcohol (vodka or ethyl alcohol). Keep the compound in a dark place for eight weeks, shaking the bottle daily. Then strain the mixture through two layers of muslin into a dark glass bottle with a tightly fitting lid. To extend its keeping qualities, add a drop of a fixative oil such as benzoin. It requires a chemical process beyond the domestic scope to separate the oil from the alcohol and produce the pure plant essence.

Maceration

Maceration is used for plants which do not generate oils after harvesting. Flowers, leaves or crushed seed are plunged into hot fat which penetrates the cells of the plant and absorbs the essence. The flowers or other plant parts are then removed either by centrifuge or straining and more fresh flowers or herbs are introduced. This is repeated up to 15 times and the resultant pomade is then treated as for *enfleurage*. A similar technique can be done at home.

Cover bruised herb leaves or aromatic flowers with a scentless oil, such as sweet almond or grape-seed, in a glass jar. Leave a small air space, screw on cap, place in a warm, sunny spot for two weeks and shake daily. Strain the oil, squeezing the herbs or leaves to save every last drop. Refill the jar with fresh flowers or leaves and repeat the process with the original oil. Do this as many times as you have supplies of scented leaves and flowers or until the oil has reached the strength you are satisfied with. Strain, re-bottle in a clean, dark glass jar, seal tightly, label with the oil and date and store in a cool dark space. Fresh and dried herbs can be used together and different herbs can be blended. Lavender and rosemary make a pleasant mix as do lemon verbena and rosemary. This is the same procedure as used for making culinary oils.

Solvent Extraction

This is a complicated but more gentle process with a volatile solvent used to extract the delicate perfumes of rose and jasmine and also for gums and resins. It produces the most concentrated and expensive essences.

For gums and resins the solvent is usually acetone, for flowers usually petroleum, ether or benzine. Plant material is placed in a vessel and covered with solvent. The mixture is slowly heated, usually electrically, and the solvent extracts the odoriferous principle of the material. This is then filtered, giving a dark-coloured paste known as a 'floral concrete'. It contains both natural waxes and odour-bearing matter.

The concrete is then agitated with alcohol and chilled. The aromatic constituents are transferred to the alcohol which is distilled leaving the purest of all perfumes a 'floral absolute', or from the resins and gums, a substance known as a 'resinoid'.

Steam Distillation

This is the normal method of extraction for aromatic leaves and the harder plant parts. Lavender is one of the few flowers which is robust enough to be steam distilled. Britain's last remaining large-scale lavender grower, with just under 100 acres, is located in Heacham in Norfolk and boasts four working stills.

Distillation involves passing hot water or steam through the plant material in a stainless steel or glass still and channelling the produced vapour into a condenser. It is only suitable for flowers, leaves, bark or wood which will not suffer change from the heat. When cooled, the oil floats on the water (very occasionally, visa versa) and is collected as it separates. Tabletop 'stills' are sold mainly as a novelty as the amount one could distill domestically would be measured in drops.

Percolation

Properly called hydradiffusion, this is a new method working rather like an upside-down form of distillation with the steam entering the top. It takes four to five hours, much less time than distillation, and requires less labour and fuel. As the herb is in contact with steam for less time, the cells near the oil glands will not have time to break down (this can add 'impurities' to oils distilled in the normal fashion). Unfortunately, the savings will not come our way as the producers say the new equipment is so expensive that they need the extra profit.

GROWING PLANTS FOR ESSENTIAL OIL

Several factors can influence the quality and amount of essential oil in a plant. First, the species is important. 'Norfolk Lavender' constantly grows new hybrids and then measures the quantity and quality of the essential oil in each variety. For the purpose of harvesting, they must also consider the size and growth pattern of the plant, the average length and number of flower stalks and the time required to reach maturity.

When a particular species is chosen, the soil fertility, drainage, and climate will also influence the quality of oil. This is why oils from certain countries, such as Bulgarian rose or English sage, are considered the best of their kind. There is also a growing conviction that any sprays, such as insecticides, used on the plants are leaving traces in the essential oils so more and more customers are asking for organically grown sources of herb oils.

QUALITY CONTROL

The composition of the essential oils while within the living plant is in constant flux and the oils migrate around the plant at different times of the day and different seasons. Experience and skill are required to select the best time to pick the aromatic parts for oils. Jasmine petals are best collected at midnight when their intoxicating fragrance is most intense.

Then the most suitable method for extracting the oil must be employed. Extractors must decide which plant parts will be put through their machinery. All of the lavender flowering stem can be used as the oil is the same in the leaves, there is just less of it, whereas with other herbs the oil in the stems or leaves may vary in make-up and significantly change a flower or leaf essence.

Once extracted, the oils must be stored correctly. Because of the susceptibility of oils to ultraviolet light, they should be purchased in well-stoppered, dark glass bottles. They should be stored at an even temperature; about 65°F (18°C) is ideal. Plastic and metals may contaminate the oils although plastic is considered acceptable for travel. If bulk oils travel in plastic containers, they must be decanted into glass again as soon as possible.

With the import of essential oils from abroad, in the many transactions from grower to user, opportunities are left for confusion over plant varieties. Secrecy about the country of origin and the general lack of expertise all provide opportunities for the dishonest. This means that even a well-intentioned company may unknowingly be selling adulterated oils. Integrity is required at each step from grower, to distiller, to exporter, to importer, to wholesaler, to retailer.

Each vat of oil must be checked for purity by a gas chromatograph or spectophotometer and several other specific tests with the final test being carried out by a trained 'nose', as in the perfume industry. Reputable and trustworthy suppliers are the vital link to ensure quality.

The retailer must also ensure that shop assistants are aware of the correct handling of oils and understand that they should be stored in airtight, dark glass containers in a cool dark place and never displayed in a sunny window. Most oils correctly stored in their pure state, unopened, will keep for five to ten years, probably longer. The exceptions are oils of the citrus family which are thought to keep their maximum properties for only a few months. After this they are not 'bad', only less beneficial.

From this, it is easy to see at how many stages in the journey from grower to shop an essential oil can be adulterated, misrepresented or impaired, so it is imperative to buy from a reputable dealer who routinely performs checks on the purity of the oils. If you are purchasing oils for therapeutic use (as opposed to just aromatic), check the oils are stored correctly, that the supplier knows the correct botanic name of the plant, that he or she knows which parts of the plant were used for extraction, whether it was organically grown, what system of extraction was used, how long ago they were extracted and the country of origin.

Many shops sell oils labelled 'Aromatherapy oils' which means the bottles contain a mixture of about 2–3 per cent essential oil in a carrier oil mainly meant for massage. It would seem more sensible to label these bottles 'massage oils' to avoid possible confusion. Once essential oils are added to carrier oils their shelf life is dramatically reduced from years down to a few months.

With the increased popularity and use of essential oils there are new small firms starting up to market their own range but it is very expensive to properly test the purity of each batch of oils. If trust is placed in wholesalers, this can be disappointing as they too can be misled by suppliers from other countries.

As a safeguard, make yourself familiar with the price range of essential oils. At the time of writing, camphor is the least expensive with sweet orange and eucalyptus low in price; most oils are around two, three or four times the price of camphor; frankincense and German chamomile are expensive, while rose, jasmine and neroli (orange blossom) are about 150 to 175 times the price of camphor. Tuberose is right off the top of the chart and only used in the most expensive perfumes. Price is the best guide, but beware also of those international city centre clinics who charge exhorbitant prices for oils. There is nothing beyond 100 per cent purity.

AROMATHERAPY

The term 'aromatherapy' was coined by Gattefosse, a French Professor of Chemistry who revived the healing use of essential oils during the First

World War. Madam Maury, a biochemist and keen student of Gattefosse, recognized the potential of essential oils for skin care and was interested in the possibility that the oils could delay the ageing process. It was she who developed the massage techniques and formulae now usually associated with aromatherapy.

In France, where the medical potency of oils is recognized, aromatherapists must also be doctors and it is properly considered a form of healing. In other countries, however, because of the uncertain legal position of complementary medicines, aromatherapy is sometimes listed as a beauty therapy. Such is the healing power of essential oils that even those who enter the field strictly for cosmetic reasons become aware of the greater potential of these vital plant substances.

One definition of aromatherapy is as a healing art which uses essential oils to promote health and beauty of the body and serenity of mind, recognizing that beauty is an aspect of a healthy body and a healthy mind. In this therapy, essential oils are applied in small doses in a carrier oil directly onto the skin with massage. The massage aids the passage of essential oil molecules in their gaseous state through the skin into the lymph system and hence throughout the body.

Aromatherapy works on two levels: first, the aroma is perceived and this has a subtle but beneficial effect on the mind or nervous system and the mood or emotions. Specific oils can be selected to refresh and revive or to relax and soothe. Second, the cosmetic and medicinal properties of the oils (tonic, antiseptic, antispasmodic, etc) work on the physical body. They penetrate the skin and take 20–70 minutes to enter the bloodstream.

The massage itself plays a large part both in relaxation and stress management and as a beauty therapy, improving skin circulation. The essential oils also improve skin quality. It seems that they have a strong influence on the interchange of tissue fluid. This encourages the growth of new cells, helps eliminate old cells more quickly and accelerates toxic elimination. In this way toxic deposits and tissue debris are prevented from infiltrating the connective tissues which maintains an improved tissue state, both in the muscle and the skin. It is difficult to achieve this by any other means.

The following oils have been tested for toxicity, skin irritation and sensitization and are safe, with certain listed reservations, for normal diluted massage applications. All oils are for external use only.

Basil (*Ocimum basilicum*) Avoid internal use as it has some oral toxicity. In moderation it is a tonic, uplifting, energizing and an anti-depressant; it has a clarifying effect on the brain and is good for overworked muscles.

Benzoin (*Styrax benzoin*) (called a resinoid rather than an essential oil). It is penetrating and warming, stimulates circulation and helps heal cracked and chapped skins but has borderline results on skin sensitization.

Bergamot (*Citrus bergamia*) Hazardous on skin sensitization, bergamot has a fresh uplifting scent enjoyed by both men and women and is one of the most important anti-depressants. It is used in pot pourri and sweet bags. It increases the skin's sensitivity to sunlight making it tan faster (this is why it was previously used in sun creams) but this also leads to phototoxicity (a burn on the skin) and is implied in skin cancer. Use only in low percentages (the perfume industry recommends ½–1 per cent) and never apply before going into the sun. In the warm summer of 1989, several cases of bergamot burn were reported. Bitter orange, lemon and lime have similar photosensitizing properties. Bergamot is used to treat depression and anxiety.

Cajuput (*Melaleuca leucadendron*) Tested as safe, though practitioners say it irritates sensitive skins and it should never be allowed to come in contact with the mucous membranes. This is a penetrating camphorous medicinal oil which combats infections. Use it as an inhalent for colds and other respiratory infections but not before bedtime as it is a powerful stimulant. For most of its uses, its cousin niaouli (*Melaleuca viridiflora*), which is non-irritant, can be used instead.

Camphor (White) (*Cinnamomum camphora*) Safe, but brown and yellow camphor with the same botanic name are hazardous for skin irritation. It is cooling and stimulating and used to treat depression, insomnia and shock. It is good for oily skins and acne. Apply in a cold compress to reduce the swelling of bruises and sprains. Use six drops in a bowl with enough cold water to soak a cloth of the size required, squeeze and apply.

Caraway (*Carum carvi*) Safe. This is a stimulant and carminative oil which helps expel intestinal gas and ease the accompanying abdominal pain. It can be used to treat several parasites including scabies and mange in dogs.

Cardamom (*Elettaria cardamomum*) Safe. The plant has many medicinal uses in Indian Vedic medicine and the oil is used in perfumes and incense and claimed as an aphrodisiac in India. It can be used as a refreshing invigorating bath.

Cedarwood (*Cedrus atlantica*, *Juniperus mexicana* and *J. virginianal*) Safe. This oil is a sedative, antiseptic and an insect repellant. It is used to treat anxiety and cystitis but some recommend that it should be avoided in pregnancy.

Chamomile (Roman – *Anthemis nobilis*; German – *Matricaria chamomilla*) Safe. These two oils are a relaxing, refreshing pain reliever for dull aches. They benefit all skin types, especially sensitive, delicate and dry skins and those prone to allergies. They are used to treat depression and insomnia and to assist digestive and menstrual problems. They are very safe and the first choice for treating children.

Citronella (*Cymbopogon nardus*) Borderline hazard on skin sensitization. This oil is used as an insect–repellant and to keep cats off pot plants.

Commercially, it is used in the manufacture of soaps and household disinfectants.

Clary Sage (*Salvia sclarea*) Safe, though some recommend it should not be used during pregnancy. A warming, soothing, nerve tonic used to treat depression, stress and tension, insomnia, asthma and dry skins. It is a powerful muscle relaxant but it can induce intoxication or euphoria and should not be administered to anyone about to drive a vehicle or who is likely to take any alcohol within a few hours.

Coriander (*Coriandrum sativum*) Safe. This is a sweet-scented, uplifting oil used to treat nervous debility, to aid digestion and reduce rheumatic pain.

Cypress (*Cupressus sempervirens*) Safe. A relaxing, refreshing astringent which improves circulation and mature skin. It is used to treat influenza and muscular cramps, and as a bath oil for haemorrhoids and varicose veins. As a deodorant and astringent it is useful for foot boths.

Eucalyptus (*Eucalyptus globulus*) Safe. A stimulating, antiseptic, anti-viral, insect repellant. It is a decongestant and used to treat cold, viruses and respiratory problems. It is an excellent oil to add to a humidifier in the autumn or a room spray. It also helps the formation of skin tissue and is used on cuts, wounds and burns. Eucalyptus oil will remove beach tar from clothes and skin.

Fennel (Sweet-*Foeniculum vulgare* 'dulce') Safe. Fennel is an anti-toxic oil and has been used to treat alcoholics by counter-balancing alcoholic poisoning. It may help prevent the build-up of toxic wastes in joints of the body which preceeds inflammation. It is also used to treat cellulitis by French doctors. Fennel is a diuretic and for this it must only be used by medically trained personel. It contains a precursor of a female hormone and has a role to play in regulating periods, treating painful periods and the menopause. Fennel oil should not be given to epileptics or children under six.

Fennel (Bitter-*Foeniculum vulgare*) Hazardous on skin sensitization.

Frankincense (*Boswellia thurifera*) Safe. This oil is a warming, relaxing, tonic and considered rejuvenating. It is used for respiratory problems as one of the best pulmonary antiseptics, for inflammation and wounds, and for improving mature skins.

Galbanum (*Ferula galbaniflua*) Safe. This oil is mainly used in the perfume industry and not often available to the public. It has the potential for use in treating skin infections and inflammations which are slow to heal.

Geranium (*Pelargonium graveolens*) 'Algerian' and 'Moroc' forms are safe; from 'Reunion' the oil tested as a borderline hazard on skin sensitization. This is a popular oil in aromatherapy which balances the production of sebrum, and normalizes and cleanses all skin types. It is antiseptic and an anti-depressant, a refreshing, relaxing, astringent and an insect repellant. It also assists hormonal balance and is used to relieve premenstrual tension. It stimulates the lymph system so it is useful in cellulite massage and to treat fluid retention.

Hyssop (*Hyssopus officinalis*) Borderline toxicity. Sedative and decongestant. It is used with caution to treat anxiety, hypertension, digestive and respiratory problems. It 'thins out' heavy catarrh so it is easier to expel and is used to normalize circulation. Applied in a cold compress, it is excellent for clearing bruises and has been used for those who have had a face lift. Never give this oil to anyone who suffers from epilepsy.

Jasmine (*Jasminum officinale*) Safe. A relaxing, seductive oil, highly valued in the perfume industry. It is used to treat depression, respiratory problems, uterine pain and is a tonic for sensitive skins.

Juniper (*Juniperus communis*) Safe. It is stimulating, antiseptic, astringent, diuretic and very useful for detoxifying the body in any condition where the toxins should be eliminated. It purifies and tones the urinogenital tract and is used to treat complaints related to this area, especially cystitis. It has a powerful ability to reduce urine retention, though if used in large amounts it will have the opposite effect. It is a good astringent bath oil for treating haemorrhoids and it is used to treat aching muscles and respiratory problems. Juniper is useful for treating several skin conditions; acne, eczema, skin sores and possibly psoriasis. Many also use it for emotional, mental and physic cleansing; therapists and healers put a drop on each wrist to protect themselves from taking on 'negative' energy.

Lavender (*Lavendula angustifolium, L. hybrida* and *L. latifolia*) Safe. An oil with the widest range of applications because it is a normalizing herb. It is sedative, soothing, an anti-depressant, antibiotic, antiseptic, decongestant, an insect repellant and relieves sharp pain. This oil benefits all skin types and aids cell renewal. It is used to treat muscular pains, headaches, infections and colds, indigestion, poor circulation and insomnia. Lavender oil has been used to treat serious burns and war injuries. Two or three drops in a bath will help calm fractious children.

Lemon (*Citrus limonum*) Hazardous on skin sensitization. Lemon is refreshing, invigorating, antiseptic and an insect repellant. It is used to treat respiratory problems and sore throats. It is useful for oily skins, broken capillaries and as a minor bleach in skin care. It stimulates the production of white blood cells which help fight infections and is a powerful bactericide for treating wounds. A 2 per cent solution in water helps to stop bleeding of cuts. Lemon is a tonic to the circulation system and can be used neat to carefully treat a verruca, wort or corn. Apply 1 drop daily taking care to avoid the surrounding skin. Never use more than 1 per cent in a blend because of its possible irritating effect on some skins.

Lemongrass (*Cymbopogon citratus*) Safe. This is a strong tonic and powerful revitalizing antiseptic stimulant with deodorant properties. All the lemon scented herbs have insect repellant properties and this is no

ESSENTIAL OILS

exception. It is useful for treating acne and oily skin though it is better to keep the percentage low as even though it has been tested as safe, some practitioners feel it may cause skin irritation. It is popular for improving circulation and muscle tone and valuable for massaging post-diet saggy skin.

Marjoram Sweet (*Marjorana hortensis* and *Origanum marjorana*) Safe. A calming and warming oil which is used in steam inhalations to treat bronchitis and colds. It has strong sedative properties and is used for several stress-related conditions like insomnia, tension, high blood pressure, headaches and muscular cramp. Do not confuse with origanum, or origano (*Origanum vulgare*) which tested hazardous on skin irritation.

Melissa (Lemon balm—*Melissa officinalis*) No test results available. However, its lemon scent indicates that it should be used in low percentages (1 per cent) in blends in case of skin irritation, and although very popular with aromatherapists, who have used it for decades, they recommend caution as certain blondes and those with fair skins may experience skin irritation. As a bath oil, do not use more than four drops. It is refreshing and an anti-depressant, and calming and soothing. It is used to treat tension, neuralgia, digestion, fevers, painful menstruation, and respiratory problems. It is particularly good for the elderly.

Myrrh (*Commiphora myrrha*) Borderline hazard on toxicity. Myrrh is a tonic that is antiseptic, anti-inflammatory and healing. It is used to treat digestion, loss of appetite, catarrh, bronchitis and skin inflammations.

Neroli (*Citrus aurantium*) Safe. A beautifully scented oil, it is ambrosial, anti-depressant, antiseptic, anti-spasmodic, an aphrodisiac and a sedative. It relieves anxiety, insomnia and emotional problems. It is famous in skin care for stimulating new cells, rejuvenating all skin types and especially for treating dry, sensitive skin.

Niaouli (*Melaleuca viridiflora*) No tests available but considered by practitioners to be tolerated by the skin and mucous membranes and can therefore be used as a gargle (always diluted) and vaginal douche. French doctors use it as an antiseptic in obstetrics and gynaecology. It is safer than its cousin cajuput. It is an antiseptic and disinfectant, and is soothing. The antiseptic and healing qualities resulting from its property of stimulating tissue growth make it useful for treating minor cuts, burns and skin ulcers. It treats respiratory problems, sore throats, colds and is a useful second string for acne. Patricia Davis, an experienced aromatherapist, suggests in *Aromatherapy, an A–Z* that a little-known but valuable use of niaouli is to reduce the severity of radiation burns from cobalt radiation therapy for cancer. A thin layer applied before treatment gives some protection from the burns and has been shown to reduce the severity of the burns.

Nutmeg (*Myristica fragrans*) Safe. Nutmeg is stimulating to the circulation and the heart and though it has been tested as safe, like all the spice

157

oils it must be used with caution. It is a useful warming and toning winter oil to build resistance to colds.

Orange Sweet (*Citrus sinensis*) Safe. This oil is mildy sedative, an anti-depressant and is anti-spasmodic. It can be varied with other sedatives to reduce insomnia. Bitter orange is hazardous on skin sensitization.

Patchouli (*Pogostemon patchouli*) Safe. This is an antiseptic oil which is uplifting and an anti-depressant in small doses and a sedative in larger doses. Its cell-regenerating properties make it excellent in skin care for dry and mature skins. It is also a fungicide and the two properties are useful in treating acne, athletes foot, some skin allergies, eczemas and dandruff.

Pepper Black (*Piper nigrum*) Safe. This is a warming oil which brings the blood to the surface, stimulating circulation. It is used to treat coughs, colds, high temperatures and muscular aches and pains. It is also employed to treat disorders of the digestive tract.

Pettigrain (*Citrus aurantium*) Safe. This oil is from the same tree as neroli with whom it shares several uses though it is less sedative and much less expensive. It is a refreshing bath oil with deodorant properties and a pleasant perfume.

Rose (*Rosa damascena* and *R. centifolia*) Safe. Rose is considered a very feminine oil and is used to treat a range of sexual and menstrual problems. It is cleansing and regulating for the uterus and menstrual cycles. It is also a very powerful healer for emotional problems and assists post-natal depression, stress and sadness. Rose is excellent in skin care for all skin types, especially ageing or sensitive skins. It is a tonic and astringent and regular applications will reduce thread veins. It is also used to improve circulation, digestion and to treat headaches. It is safe to use on children.

Rosemary (*Rosmarinus officinalis*) Safe. This is a toning and invigorating herb that stimulates circulation and brings blood to the surface. It is used for muscular and rheumatic pains. It lifts fatigue and aids digestion and headaches and is used in a range of respiratory ailments. It is said to improve hair growth. It stimulates the brain which has given it its memory strengthening reputation. It should not be used in excess as large amounts may cause epileptic-like fits.

Rosewood (*Aniba rosaeodora*) Safe. This is a pleasant-scented oil for perfuming the home or cosmetics. It is a gentle tonic which fights bacteria and is a useful deodorizing addition to the bath.

Sage (*Salvia officinalis*) Borderline hazard on toxicity. Sage has a powerful, warming, penetrating effect on muscles but it is safer to use clary sage.

Sandalwood (*Santalum album*) Safe. This has long been used in perfumes and body creams and it is well known for its beneficial effect of softening dry skins. Being astringent and antiseptic it is also good for oily skins and acne. Sandalwood is a strong pulmonary antiseptic and a sedative for dry, irritating coughs and chronic bronchitis. It is also used to treat fatigue, diarrhoea and nausea as well as being a strong urinary tract antiseptic.

Spanish Sage (*Salvia lavandulaefolia*) Safe. Although this oil has been tested as safe it may be wider to use clary sage.

Spearmint (*Mentha spicata*) Safe. Do not confuse spearmint with pennyroyal which has high toxicity. Spearmint oil is mainly used in the food and pharmaceutical industry.

Tangerine (*Citrus reticulata*) Safe. A gentle oil, antiseptic, refreshing and pleasant in massage. It is probably an insect repellant.

Tea-Tree (*Melaleuca alternifolia*) Its skin sensitization effect is untested but it is safe on toxicity. However, there are practitioners' reports of sensitive skins reacting to this oil. Although new to essential oil lists, the plant has been used by aboriginies in Australia for thousands of years. It is a powerful antiseptic, the strongest of the known oils, and kills bacteria, fungi and viruses. It stimulates the body's immune system to fight infections and is used for colds, 'flu, catarrh and sinisitus. It can be used to control *Candida albicans* and be used to build up the strength of those scheduled to have an operation. There is also the possibility that it will be useful to AIDS sufferers if it can strengthen their immune system.

Thyme (*Thymus vulgaris*) Borderline on toxicity, hazardous on skin irritation. This strong pulmonary disinfectant is a useful massage oil or inhalant for all respiratory infections, cough, colds and sore throats. It increases white blood cells and therefore helps fight infections. There are forms of thyme oil available from specialist suppliers which are much less toxic and therefore very useful oils.

Vetiver (*Vetiveria zizanoides*) Safe. This is a fragrant scent much enjoyed by men and useful in pot pourri blends and perfumes for a rich woody tone.

Violet Leaf (*Viola odorata*) Safe. Violet leaf is a very expensive oil, seldom seen. It has valuable, skin-healing properties and may have pain-killing qualities.

Ylang-Ylang (*Cananga odorata*) Borderline hazard for skin sensitization. This is a heavy, sweet scent that is sedative, antiseptic and an anti-depressant. It slows down over-rapid breathing and hence it is used to treat anxiety, frustration, shock, fear or great anger. It is used for insomnia and to regulate circulation. This is another oil suitable for both dry and oily skins because of its regulating effect on the production of sebrum. Use ylang-ylang sparingly as too much can cause headaches or nausea.

CARRIER OILS FOR MASSAGE BLENDS

Before application, essential oils are blended with a 'carrier' oil, such as almond or grapeseed oil, chemically known as a fixed oil. Aromatherapy uses only fixed oils of vegetable origin, mainly cold-pressed from seeds. They do not evaporate when warmed, as do essential oils, but they oxidize on exposure to air over a few months and will eventually become unfit for use. This happens more quickly once they are mixed with essential oils. A blend will be at its best for two or three months, so it is wise not to mix more oil than you will use in that time.

The carrier oil should be 100 per cent pure, with little or no smell, an attractive texture for massage, a reasonable price and have some penetrative quality so it does not hinder the essential oil. Mineral oils are not used because they are a barrier oil (hence their use on baby's bottoms), whereas the aromatherapy aim is to have the essential oil pass through the skin barrier. It has been established that skin can absorb fatty substances if their molecular structure is small enough. As essential oils vapourize, their very fine molecules are thought to pass through the hair follicles or sweat glands where they mix with sebum, a sympathetic oily liquid. From there they diffuse into tiny capillaries and on into the blood stream or they are taken up by lymph fluid which continually bathes every cell and transports them along to other parts of the body. Any sceptics need only rub the soles of their feet with a garlic glove and in an hour or two the proof will issue forth on their breath. The following list considers the carrier oils in their order of importance.

Almond Oil This is the most popular carrier oil as it has a very pleasant texture, is almost scentless, is rich in protein and is emollient, nourishing and slow to become rancid. It also helps relieve itching from eczema.
Grapeseed Oil This pleasant light oil is gaining popularity. It is very fine and clear, odourless and has no allergic effects on skin. It gives a satin-smooth finish without a greasy touch. The keeping quality improves with the addition of 5 per cent of an anti-oxidant such as wheatgerm oil. It is one of the least expensive.
Hazelnut Oil (cold pressed) Hazelnut and avocado are the oils which penetrate most easily and deeply. Hazelnut is stimulating to the circulation and nourishing to the skin. The deep penetration is particularly helpful for the massage of muscles aching from sport or exercise. It is used by one famous French company for its range of essential oil skin care products.
Olive Oil (cold pressed, first pressing) This is a calming emollient, good for rheumatism and to relieve the itching of skin ailments. Unfortunately, the scent which can overpower essential oils, is not always appreciated. It is suggested that its nourishing properties are absorbed through the skin of babies.
Apricot Kernel and Peach Kernel Oil (cold pressed) Both have the same properties as sweet almond oil but are more expensive.
Jojoba Oil This is a liquid wax and is very stable because it is

indigestible to bacteria and humans. It dissolves sebum which makes it good for acne and gives a satin-smooth feel to the skin.

Sesame (unbleached) Rich in vitamins A and E and it is a stable oil but the rich colour and odour can be an objection. It is used in Scandinavia for cases of dry eczema and psoriasis and washes out easily from towels and clothing.

Soya Oil Soya has a nice feel and doesn't become sticky with pressure.

Sunflower Sunflower has the least keeping qualities and needs an anti-oxidant but also has Vitamin F and other substances useful for certain skin diseases.

Corn Oil Acceptable.

Groundnut Oil (peanut oil) This has a distinctive odour and oilier feel which makes it less favoured for massage.

Oils to Add in Small Quantities for their Special Qualities

Avocado Oil Along with wheatgerm oil, the most nourishing, and along with hazelnut, the most penetrating; especially useful for fatty areas of skin and muscle preparations. Pleasant to use on small areas but becomes sticky when massaged into a large area. 1 tsp (5 ml) can be added to 2 fl oz (50 ml) of massage mix to increase the oil penetration. It has skin healing properties and is rich in vitamins A, B, D and lecithin. It should not be chilled as some compounds will precipitate.

Calendula It is not possible to buy essential oil of calendula as the petals contain such minute quantities; instead the properties are extracted by macerating them in a stabilized vegetable oil. It has a valuable effect on the skin in any cosmetic preparation, especially for chapped and cracked skin. If you have an abundance of flowers it is worth macerating this oil domestically (see page 59).

Carrot Oil The extraction of this needs expert attention as it consists mainly of water with tiny amounts of oil in suspension. The oil is a tonic and rejuvenating and is particularly good for neck massage. It is a treasure chest of vitamins, being rich in A, B, C, D, E and F.

Evening Primrose Oil An expensive fixed-oil pressed from the seeds and proving very useful medicinally. It contains gamma linoleic acid (GLA), Vitamin F, and is useful for scaly dry skin and dandruff. Research has shown that oil extracted from borage seed and, more recently, oil from blackcurrant pips also contain GLA.

Wheatgerm Oil A natural anti-oxidant. 1 tsp (5 ml) is added to 2 fl oz (50 ml) of massage mix (5 per cent) to extend its keeping qualities. It is nourishing, rich in Vitamin E, especially good for dry skins and helps to heal and reduce scarring from wounds and acne. It is fairly expensive and has a sticky feel, two reasons why it is not used on its own.

AROMATHERAPY AND STRESS RELIEF

The sixteenth-century essayist Michel de Montaigne wrote: 'Physicians might in my opinion draw more use and good from odours than they do. For myself, I have often perceived that according unto their strength and quality, they change and alter and move my spirits and make strange effects in me'.

Scientists and psychiatrists are now investigating the mood-lifting properties of essential oils. Scent passes directly into the brain through the olfactory nerve whose terminal is in the upper nasal cavity. Our scent receptor is within the nasal mucus membrance. It is ¼ in (6 mm) in size (a dog's receptor can cover 10 sq in [25 cm^2]). Our smell receptor is composed of hair cells which are chemical detectors. These only pick up aromatic molecules which are dissolved in the mucus secreted by the nasal membrane. They are sensitive enough to detect 1 part in 30 billion. These receptor hairs pass through tiny holes in the bone at the top of the nose and into the olfactory bulb which is in the brain directly above. This elongated bulb of nerve tissue extends to the olfactory centre in the middle of the brain. So the olfactory nerve brings brain cells into direct contact with the outside world and scent messages pass directly into the brain, which are not edited in any way; hence the memory evoking power of scents. All other messages to the brain from other senses pass through what is called the 'blood brain barrier'. This means other messages arrive at the peripheral of the brain and have to be handed over the brain's private messenger service. This protects and isolates the brain from viruses and other dangerous substances but it also means there is the possibility that the perception of these messages can be altered.

Perhaps the most beneficial medical use of aromatherapy is to relieve stress, the underlying contributor to most illnesses. The massage and oils together bring deep relaxation and serenity creating a situation where the cleared mind can more easily tackle problems.

Dr Annie Coxon is a neurologist with an interest in aromatherapy because of personal experience. At a very stressful time, a low point in her life, she was offered treatment by a friend who was an aromatherapist. She accepted this kindness initially out of politeness as this was something her scientific training made her naturally sceptical of. But she was very surprised by how much she benefitted from the experience and it was evident to her that the effect of relaxation and the subsequent release of energy which she had been greatly lacking was something she could not have achieved with any conventional treatment herself either with medicine or a talk therapy.

She became interested in the possible biology of the nervous system which might account for the effectiveness of aromatherapy. Aromatherapy, massage with essential oils, works in two ways. The light massage on the whole body is a powerful sensory stimulus all over the skin. The relaxation and pleasure relieves stress and works in a similar area of the brain as the accompanying aromatic oils.

With her treatment she was given a bottle of the blended oils to use at home which she religiously did until now she is 'coded' to the mixture and just the scent of the oils makes her feel relaxed even though she does not know what oils were used. She feels it is a kind of learning process, a conditioning, an aspect of biofeedback based on the first powerful aromatherapy memory with its associated mood that was registered by her brain.

Scent and memory are closely related. At the reptilian stage of evolution the scent function dominated the brain. As evolution advanced, a complex set of emotions developed and later a layer of intellect was accumulated including a huge library of memories and visions with which we try to control the emotional layer. This has caused us to 'clog our system' in many ways. Aromatherapy may link us with our buried reptilian brain and reawaken powerful stimulae which are valuable to us.

Dr Annie Coxon feels that there are several groups of patients for whom aromatherapy treatment can be useful and all are stress-related. We live frenetic lives well beyond the pace for which our systems evolved. This alters the whole biochemistry of the body. The biology of stress involves hormones which are released in the same area of the brain (the lymbic system) in which aromatherapy works. This is also associated with the emotional system and neighbours the area for memory which has powerful connections with scent.

The problems of depression, anxiety and bereavement can be assisted by massage with essential oils, as can the physical disorders, disfunctions in various parts of the body caused by the biochemistry of stress, such as sleep problems, hypertension, migraines, ulcers or colitis. If one person suffers from several of these conditions he or she may be taking four or five different pills which could be warring with each other, whereas aromatherapy would get to the root of the problem at the same time as relieving stress immediately through the relaxation of massage. There are benefits from aromatherapy that are not obtained from any pharmaceutical treatments presently available.

Aromatherapy works in a similar way to tranquillizers, but there are also important differences. A tranquillizer works directly on the brain so it has an immediate effect but it takes over the body's system of coping, leaving it dependent on the tranquillizer. Aromatherapy, however, will stimulate the area of the brain which itself produces anti-stress hormones giving a natural protection against stress with better long-term results and without the trap of tranquillizer dependancy.

Aromatherapy can also aid people who would benefit from a period of tranquillity in their life such as women in pregnancy who may experience anxiety because of a previous difficult birth. Those in chronic pain either from known or mysterious causes can be helped by aromatherapy, too. In the biology of pain, the pain runs into the area in which it seems that aromatherapy works.

In aromatherapy, the contact of massage is an important experience both psychologically and biologically. Biologically it is significant because it links into the same area of the brain as the fragrance of the essential oils where brain hormones are stimulated, especially in a stress situation. Psychologically, we can imagine its importance by considering the look of total bliss expressed by a baby being held and given much skin contact. Unfortunately, in our 'civilized' society we have eroticised touch, indeed almost perverted it, which results in our loss of the innocence and simplicity of touch in friendship and family love. Aromatherapy massage restores some of that magic.

It is to be hoped that doctors and scientists will start serious research into the mechanism of action in treatments like aromatherapy because it is a powerful system which has been shown to be beneficial.

The following suggested lists of oils have been mainly arrived at empirically by aromatherapists and other healers observing the effects of essential oils over the centuries in which they have been applied.

Anxiety There are a wide range of sedative oils to choose from, an understanding of their other attributes or scent preference could be the deciding factor for selection. Choose from: jasmine, lavender, marjoram, neroli and basil, bergamot (1 per cent), camphor, chamomile, frankincense, geranium, juniper, melissa, rose and sandalwood.

Apathy Jasmine and rosemary.

Depression Camphor, chamomile, jasmine, basil, bergamot, (1 per cent), clary sage, cypress and geranium.

Insomnia Chamomile, lavender and neroli first choices, benzoin, bergamot (1 per cent), clary sage, juniper, marjoram, neroli, rose, sandalwood and ylang-ylang. Use 4–6 drops as a bath oil before bed, (three for children, premixed with an alcohol or vegetable oil to insure dispersal.) Try one essential oil for two weeks, then if insomnia persists, change to a different sedative oil so that the body doesn't become accustomed to one oil alone.

Mental fatigue Rosemary, basil and peppermint.

Nerves and panic Basil, bergamot (1 per cent), cedarwood, chamomile, geranium, juniper, lavender, marjoram, melissa (use only 4 drops in a bath as it can irritate fair skins), neroli and rose.

Sedatives Chamomile, lavender, lemon and marjoram.

Shock Camphor, melissa, neroli and peppermint.

Stress Neroli, cedarwood and juniper.

TO MAKE UP A MASSAGE OIL OR COSMETIC OIL

Select the essential oil or oils you want to use according to their therapeutic benefits; usually not more than three or four. Select a carrier oil.

Almost fill the bottle with the carrier oil and add 3 per cent of the essential oil. That is between 15 and 30 drops to a 2 fl oz (50 ml) bottle (or 3 drops to a teaspoon or 5 ml teaspoon such as those provided with liquid medicines). Stir with a glass rod, or shake gently to blend, label and date. 2 fl oz (50 ml) will do two to four full body massages. To make a deluxe blend:

A 2 fl oz (50 ml) bottle is made up as follows:

Put 1 tsp (5 ml) wheatgerm oil into the bottle for its preserving qualities. Then put 1 tsp (5 ml) avocado or hazelnut oil into the bottle for its penetrating qualities. Fill up with grapeseed (or other basic carrier) and add the therapeutic element – 3 per cent of selected essential oils. Blend and label.

COSMETIC BENEFITS

Massage and essential oils both work to improve blood circulation and to accelerate the elimination of wastes through the lymph system. These functions help speed the elimination of old cells and encourage growth of new cells giving the skin a smoother and firmer appearance. They help to increase the elasticity of the skin and aid the reduction of scar tissue and stretchmarks. And, finally, they help create a sense of well-being which reflects in appearance.

Oils to Benefit Skins

For all skin types: jasmine, chamomile, rose.
To maintain and improve normal skin: frankinscense, geranium, jasmine, lavender; rose and neroli to normalize all skin types.
For dry skin: chamomile, geranium, clary sage, jasmine, lavender, neroli, patchouli, sandalwood.
For oily skin: cedarwood, juniper, lemon (with caution), ylang-ylang.
For delicate, sensitive skins: chamomile, rose, neroli.
To treat acne: juniper, chamomile, cedarwood, eucalyptus, lavender and lemongrass. Bergamot is excellent but it can make it look worse in the short-term as it drains the skin of excess sebum.
For wrinkles or rejuvenation: try frankincense, neroli and jasmine, patchouli, lavender (for cell renewal); cyprus, black pepper and rosemary stimulate circulation and are useful for mature skins; lemon (with caution).

For thread veins: rose, lemon (with caution). Lemon also has a minor bleaching action.

To improve the elasticity of skin and encourage new cells: lavender, chamomile, calendula, jasmine, frankincense, myrrh, rosemary, cyprus.

For cellulite: try cypress, fennel, geranium, juniper.

For post-diet, sagging skin: lemongrass, pine, sage.

When a slight lift is needed: lavender, lemongrass.

When the skin is pale and anaemic looking: geranium.

When the skin has a puffy look caused by water retention: rosemary.

To reduce or help prevent stretch marks: frankincense, lavender, neroli, mandarin, wheatgerm oil.

Several French cosmetic houses now produce a night facial oil which is composed of essential oils in a carrier oil. It is an expensive cosmetic but one you can make yourself, creating a face or body oil to give you the therapeutic benefits you wish. Choose up to three or four suitable oils from the list above and blend them in a good quality carrier oil with extra wheatgerm and carrot oil as listed in the delux blend on page 165 and apply each night.

Another way to use essential oils cosmetically is to buy a pure, fragrance-free cream or shampoo and add a few drops of essential oil to it. Or make up a basic herbal cosmetic recipe and add a few drops in addition to, or instead of, the herbs required in the recipe.

PERFUMES

Essential oils form the basis of quality perfumes. Some, such as rose, sandalwood and jasmine have been used alone as perfumes and rose is used in 96 per cent of women's perfumes and 42 per cent of men's perfumes.

A 'nose' (a person highly skilled in recognizing and blending aromas) will sit at a scent 'organ' which displays hundreds of fragrances. She or he will select aromatic notes to blend into chords. To evaluate the 'note' of a fragrance, a few drops of oil are placed on a wand to evaporate. If the scent is not detectable after 24 hours it is considered a top note. These are the scents in a perfume that would be noticed first: they are stimulating and uplifting. Basil, bergamot, citrus oils, eucalyptus, peppermint, sage and thyme are top notes. If the oil aroma is still noticeable after 24 hours, but not after 60 hours, it is a middle note. Middle notes form the body and substance of a perfume and provide its dominant character. Chamomile, geranium, lavender, hyssop, fennel, melissa (lemon balm), pine and rosemary are middle notes.

Oils detectable after 60 hours (usually for 6 or 7 days) are the base notes. Base notes are the fixative of a perfume, giving its lasting quality and a different aroma when the top notes have evaporated. Base notes are mainly sedative and calming. Benzoin, camphor, frankincense, myrrh, sandalwood, jasmine, rose and the spices – cinnamon, cloves and ginger.

Perfumes require alcohol to preserve the scent. By definition, perfumes are 15–25 per cent essences in pure (ethol) alcohol. *Parfum de toilette* is 12–15 per cent essential oils blended with over 50 per cent alcohol and some distilled water.

MEDICAL USES OF ESSENTIAL OILS

Essential oils should never be taken internally except when administered by qualified practitioners as they are very powerful substances, even potentially fatal. Taken through the digestive system the oils can be changed considerably by the hydrochloric acid of the stomach. Applied through the skin, mainly with massage or baths, these problems are obviated because the digestive system is bypassed.

They can be used to treat a number of conditions, but a qualified practitioner must be consulted for serious complaints. These oils must never be used neat. When the blended oils are applied with therapeutic massage movements the power of penetration is greater. The time may be 20 to 70 minutes to pass into the skin and then into the bloodstream. Check the general list of essential oils to see where caution is needed.

As Air Purifiers and Antiseptics

A spray of essential oils can kill bacteria, fungi and viruses to varying degrees in the air. Research was undertaken by a Dr Chamberland in 1887 on the antispetic powers of vapourized essential oils, particularly on the anthrax bacillus. He found antigenetic potency (the ability to combat the development of germs and kill them) in decreasing order in: lemon, thyme, orange, bergamot, juniper, clove, citronella, lavender, niaouli, peppermint, rosemary, sandalwood, eucalyptus, and Chinese anise. This list corresponds with the respective terpene strength contained in each. They were most powerful against meningococcus, staphylococcus, and the typhus bacillus. Diphtheric bacillus were more resistant and sadly the spores of anthrax bacillus were not affected at all.

A French researcher L. Cavel published findings in 1918 on the antispectic qualities of several essential oils. He worked with sewage cultures and meat stock cultured in septic tank water, a fertile combination for the multiplication of bacteria. He tested essential oils in direct contact (rather than sprayed) to discover their ability to incapacitate the bacteria, making them infertile. He measured the minimum dose required per 1000cc of this stock to make the bacteria infertile. His results showed thyme to be the strongest at 0.7 parts per 1000, then origanum at 1.0, and then in steps for sweet orange, lemongrass, Chinese cinnamon and rose, down to clove at 2.0;

eucalyptus, peppermint, rose geranium, meadowsweet, Chinese anise, orris, and wild thyme at 4.0; anise, mustard, rosemary, cumin, neroli, birch and lavender at 5.0; melisa, ylang-ylang and juniper at 6.0; sweet fennel, garlic and lemon at 7.0; catjuput, sassafras and heliotrope at 8.0; and turpentine, parsley and violet at 9.0. At the same conditions, phenol made the solution infertile at 5.6 parts per 1000.

Within this information, certain oils work more quickly against specific bacteria. For example, micro-organisms of yellow fever were easily killed by sandalwood and lavender oil. In a further test of the action of essential oils, bacteria usually encountered in the air were exposed to the emanations from essential oils for various periods. The results indicate that many of the bacteria were killed in less than an hour and in some cases after only a few minutes.

More research is required for a precise application. But it can be seen that a great many bacteria will be eliminated by spraying a combination of any of these oils into the air. Room sprays can purify the air of sick rooms, hospitals or doctor's waiting rooms, hair salons, schools, domestic rooms and offer special benefits for those whose immune system is weakened.

Fill 2 fl oz (50 ml) atomiser with 1 fl oz (25 ml) of alcohol (vodka or isoproy). Add 65 drops of essential oil of bergamot, 25 drops of lemon, 25 drops of lavender, 15 drops of orange oil, 15 drops of thyme, 15 drops of clove, 10 drops of juniper, 10 drops of tea-tree, 5 drops of peppermint, 5 drops of rosemary, 5 drops of sandalwood and 5 drops of eucalyptus. (Any combination will be effective.) Top up with distilled water and spray as required.

Immunology

Essential oils may have a future importance in immunology. Recently medicine has taken an increasing interest in T-cells (T for thymus or endocrine gland) and B-cells (B for bone marrow). The T-cells enter the blood and lymphoid tissue where they attack viruses and bacteria. These B-cells are able to move into lymph tissue where they produce antibody molecules that lock onto invaders and incapacitate them. To be really effective, this double-pronged attack needs to be triggered off and it seems that natural enzymes act as catalysts producing the molecular model for the locking-on process. Because of their enzymatic nature, essential oils may provide such a catalytic action.

For Sport and Exercise Routines

Essential oils with massage are said to increase muscular and nervous tone, raise the general body resistance and make possible greater mental and physical effort.

For over-exertion, athletic stiffness or cramp from physical effort –
lavender, marjoram, rosemary (to increase circulation), clary sage (sage
is most penetrating for developed muscles but has toxic principles; use
with caution and for men only). For organic cramp use geranium.

Not for Use

Do not use in pregnancy: pennyroyal is the most dangerous, sage and
oregano next; basil, hyssop, juniper, myrrh, fennel, rosemary and clary
sage, should be avoided until more is known about their actions.

Do not use for a person with skin sensitivity: thyme, basil, lemon,
lemongrass, peppermint, tea-tree, pine.

Do not use in epilepsy: fennel, hyssop, sage.

SUGGESTED FURTHER READING

Gardening
Fertility Without Fertilizers, Lawrence Hills, Henry Doubleday Association, 1975
Nursery Stock Manual, Lamb, Kelly & Bowbrick. Gower Books, London, 1975
Of Gardens, An Essay, 1625, Francis Bacon, John Lane, London, 1902

Culinary
The First Century AD Roman Cookery Book, Apicius, (translated B. Flower and E. Rosenbaum) Harrap, London, 1974
Acetaria: A Discourse on Sallet (1699), John Evelyn, Prospect Books, London, 1982
Edible Flowers, Claire Clifton, Bodley Head, London 1983
Herbs, Spices and Flavourings, Tom Stobard, Penguin, London, 1977
Rose Recipes from Olden times, Eleanour Sinclair Rohde, Dover, New York, 1973
The Salad Garden, Joy Larkcom, Frances Lincoln Windward, 1984

Cosmetic
Feed your Face, Dian Dincin Buchman, Duckworth, London, 1973
Kitty Little's Book of Herbal Beauty, Kitty Little, Penguin, London, 1981
Natural Beauty, Roy Genders, Webb & Bower, 1986

Household
A Book of Pot-Pourri, Gail Duff, Orbis, 1985
Plants with a Purpose, Richard Mabey, Collins, London, 1977
Potpourris and Other Fragrant Delights, Jacqueline Heriteau, Simon and Schuster, New York, 1975

Dyes
A Dyer's Manual, Jill Goodwin, Pelham Books, London, 1982

Herbal Medicine
A Barefoot Doctor's Manual, Health Committee, Hunan Province China, Cloudburst Press, Seattle, 1977
Chinese Medicine, The Web that has no Weaver, Ted J. Kaptchuk, Century Hutchinson, 1983
The Holistic Herbal, David Hoffmann, The Findhorn Press, 1986
The Home Herbal, Barbara Griggs, Norman & Hobhouse, 1982
Handbook of the Bach Flower Remedies, Philip M. Chancellor, The C.W. Daniel Company, 1973
Bach Flower Therapy, Mechthild Scheffer, Thorsons, 1988

SUGGESTED FURTHER READING

Flower Essences by Gurudas, Brotherhood of Life Inc., USA, 1983 (California Flower remedies)

Ginseng: The Magical Herb of the East, Stephen Fulder M.A. Ph.D, Thorsons

Hygieia: A Woman's Herbal, Jeanninev Parvati, Wildwood House, London, 1979

Natural Medicine (A Study of Alternative Therapies), Brian Inglis, Collins, London, 1979

Essential Oils & Aromatherapy

Aromatherapy, An A–Z, Patricia Davis, C.W. Daniel, 1988

The Practice of Aromatherapy, Dr Jean Valnet, C.W. Daniel Co., Saffron Walden, 1980

The Power of Holistic Aromatherapy, Christine Stead, Javelin Books, 1986

The Art of Aromatherapy, Robert Tisserand, C.W. Daniel Co., 1977

Practical Aromatherapy, Shirley Price, Thorsons, 1983

The Essential Oil Safety Data Manual, Robert Tisserand, privately published, 1985

General

The Golden Age of Herbs and Herbals, Rosetta Clarkson, Constable, London, 1973

The Folk-Lore of Plants, T.F. Thisleton Dyer, Appleton, New York, 1889

A Modern Herbal, M. Grieve, Peregrine, London, 1979

Kayas Muskekeya: Herbs of Long Ago (Indians of Western Canada), Luke Chalifoux and Dr Anne Anderson, University of Alberta, 1982

The Complete Book of Herbs, Lesley Bremness, Dorling Kindersley, 1988

The Complete Book of Herbs & Spices, Claire Lowenfeld & Philippa Back, David & Charles, London, 1974

Flower Favourites, Their Legends, Symbolism & Significance, Lizzie Deas, George Allen, London, 1898

Scented Flora of the World, Roy Genders, Robert Hale, London, 1977

The Shakespeare Garden, Esther Singleton, Methuen, London, 1923

Shakespeare's Wild Flowers, Fairy Lore, Gardens, Herbs. Gatherers of Simples & Bee Lore, Eleanour Sinclair Rohde, Medici, London, 1935

The Encyclopedia of Herbs and Herbalism, Malcolm Stuart, Orbis, London, 1979

The Herb and Spice Book, Sarah Garland, Windward, London, 1979

The Illustrated Book of Herbs, Stodola, Jiri and Volak Octopus, London, 1984

INDEX

agrimony, 123
air purifiers, 168
almond oil, 28, 160
aloe vera, 73–4, 119; chapped skin soother, 65
American ginseng, 133
angelica, 123, 133–4
animals, Bach flower remedies, 105
aniseed, 38
antiseptics, 167–8
anxiety, 163, 164
apathy, 164
aphids, 126
apple and lemon balm terrine, 79
apricot kernel oil, 29, 160
Aristotle, 11–12
aromatherapy, 145, 152–65
Asclepius, 10–11, 18, 84
astringents, flower, 96
attar of roses, 148–9
Australian flower remedies, 105
Avicenna, 13
avocado oil, 29, 161

babies, tussie-mussies for, 89
Bach flower remedies, 104–5
Bacon, Francis, 85
bananas, rose layered dessert, 110
barbeque dishes, 49–50
basil oil, 153
baths, herbal, 62–3, 97
bay leaves, 58–9
bee gardens, 102–3
beef in pastry, 78–9
benzoin, 153
bergamot oil, 154
biscuits, 41
black silk reviver, 69
bluebells, glue, 124
bouquets, tussie-mussies, 88–9
bread, 41
breath sweeteners, 37
Brekhman, Israel, 127
bridal bouquets, 89
broom flowers, 91
Buddhism, 87
bulbs, 114
bumble bee gardens, 103
bunching onions, 140–1
burns, *Aloe vera* and, 74
but-kay, 134
butters, herb, 60

cajuput oil, 154
calamine lotion, 123
calendula: coriander and calendula quiche, 109; cream, 103; oil, 161
California flower remedies, 105
camphor oil, 154
caraway seeds, 19, 38–9; oil, 154

cardamom seed, 19–20; oil, 154; rhubarb scented with, 50
carrier oils, aromatherapy, 159–61
carrots: cosmetic uses, 119–20; oil, 29, 161
Cavel, L., 167–8
cedarwood oil, 154
cellulite cream, ivy, 65
Chamberland, Dr, 167
chamomile oil, 154
chapped skin soother, 65
cheese, herb, 60
cherry and rose petal soup, 108
chervil roots, 144
chicken, roast poussin with herbs, 77–8
chicory, coffee substitutes, 141
China, 81, 85, 86, 113, 126–35
chlorophyll, 52
Christianity, 87
chrysanthemums, 86–7, 105
chypre, 99, 123
citronella oil, 154–5
clary sage oil, 155
classification of plants, 93
cleanser, cowslip, 96–7
cleansing milk, 96
coconut palm oil, 29
coffee substitutes, 141
cold remedies, 103
coloured inks, 101
comfrey, 70, 74–5
compost, potting, 118
compounds, 133
container herbs, 117–19
cooking: with flowers, 105–11; with leaves, 76–81; roots and bulbs, 137–44; with seeds, 39–50
coriander, 19, 38; coriander and calendula quiche, 109; coriander mushrooms, 48; oil, 155
corms, 114
corn oil, 29–30, 161
cornflower astringent, 96
cosmetics: essential oils, 165–7; flowers, 95–7; leaves, 61–5; oil extracts, 35–8; roots, 119–23
cowslip cleanser, 96–7
Coxon, Dr Annie, 162–3
cream hearts scented with sweet geranium leaves, 111
creamed horseradish, 139
Cree Indians, 67
crocuses, saffron, 93
crystallized flowers, 107
curry dishes, 45–7
curry powder, 44
cuttings, 55–7
cypress oil, 155

daffodils, 114
daisy roots, 143

dandelion, 120, 135, 141, 143
dates, rose layered dessert, 110
Davis, Patricia, 157
decoction, 62
deodorants, 63
depression, 163, 164
digestive aids, 38–9
dill seeds, 37, 38, 39; dill pickles, 42; dill
    water, 39; nail bath, 38
Dioscorides, 12, 18
diptani, 147
disinfectant, thyme, 69–70
distillation, essential oils, 150
dong kwai, 133–4
dormancy, seeds, 21–2
drawer lining paper, 101
Dream Book of Artimedorus, 86
drug companies, 128
drying: flowers, 94–5; leaves, 58–9;
    roots, 117
duck decoys, 67
dyes: fabric, 38; hair, 37, 122

early puple orchid, 113
eelworms, 125
elder leaf insecticide, 70
elderflowers, 91; cold remedies, 103;
    elderflower water, 95–6; gooseberry and
    elderflower compote, 110; medicinal
    properties, 75
elecampane, 113, 123, 142
enfleurage, essential oils, 148–9
essential oils *see* oils, essential
eucalpytus oil, 155
evaporation, essential oils, 147
Evelyn, John, 10, 112–13, 143
evening primrose oil, 30, 39, 161
evergreen herbs, 53–4
expression, essential oils, 148

fabric dyes, 38
face cream, lily and marshmallow, 121
face masks, 64, 120
facial steams, 63–4
fairies, 85
Fechner, Gustav, 146
fennel, Florence, 141
fennel seeds, 38; crown roast of lamb, 47–
    8; oil, 155
fenugreek seed, 37, 38
fertilizers, comfrey, 70
fixatives, pot pourri, 99
Florence fennel, 141
flowers, 82–111; cosmetics, 95–7;
    crystallized, 107; culinary uses, 105–11;
    decorative and aromatic uses, 98–101;
    drying, 94–5; extracting essences, 147;
    flower waters, 95–6; freezing, 95;
    functions, 92–3; garden uses, 101–3;
    harvesting, 93–4; household uses, 97–8;
    language of, 87–90; medicinal uses, 103–
    5; pickled, 108; pressing, 101;

symbolism, 86–90; theme gardens, 83–6;
    trees and shrubs, 91–2; vinegars, 108
fool, gooseberry, 110
foxglove, 104
fragrance: brain's perception of, 162;
    essential oils, 145, 147; flowers, 91;
    leaves, 51–2, 66–8; making perfumes,
    166–7; and memory, 162, 163
frankincense, 155
Freeling, Arthur, 88
freezing: flowers, 95; herbs, 58
fruit salads, 41
fumigation, 69
furniture wax, sweet myrtle, 67

galbanum oil, 155
Galen, 12, 36
gardens, 22–8, 54–7; fertilizers, 70; theme
    gardens, 83–6; using flowers in, 101–3;
    using roots in, 125–6
garlands, 72
garlic: cooking with, 48, 137, 143; in the
    garden, 126; medicinal properties, 136
Gattefosse, 152–3
Ge Hong, 86–7
Genders, Roy, 91
geranium oil, 155–6
Gerard, John, 112, 120
gherkins, dill pickles, 42
germination, 22–3
get well posies, 89
ginger, 123, 137–8
ginseng, 113, 115, 126–33
glue, 124
goat's beard, 143
gooseberries: fool, 111; gooseberry and
    elderflower compote, 111
grapeseed oil, 30, 160
groundnut oil, 30, 161
gum benzoin, 99

hair: dyes, 37, 66, 122; hair care products,
    37, 65–6
Hall, John, 133
hand cream, 64–5
harvesting: flowers, 93–4; leaves, 57; roots,
    116–17; seeds, 26–7
hazelnut oil, 30, 160
hedges, 54
Helen of Troy, 113
herb bennet, 125
herb gardens, 27–8, 51, 113
herbalists, 73
heroin, 104
Hinduism, 87
Hippocrates, 11, 20
history, 9–16
homoeopathy, 13, 15
honey bee gardens, 102
hops, 91
hormones, 131, 163
horseradish, 120, 138–9; creamed, 139;

pickled, 139–40; traditional English horseradish sauce, 139
horsetail, nail bath, 38
household uses: flowers, 97–8; leaves, 68–70; roots, 123–5; seeds, 38
Hypatia, 12
hyssop oil, 156

immunology, 168–9
Inca marigold, 125–6
Indian violet grass, 124
infusions, 59–60, 61–2, 104
inks, coloured, 101
insecticides, 68–9, 70–1, 101–2
insomnia, 164
ivy cellulite cream, 65

Japan, 84, 87
jasmine, 86, 147, 148, 151
jasmine oil, 156
Jerusalem artichokes, 144
jojoba oil, 31, 160–1
juniper berries: barbeque sauce, 49; oil, 156

knot gardens, 54–5
kofta sauce, 46
koftas, 45
Kwan Yin, 81, 84

lamb, crown roast of, 47–8
language of flowers, 87–90
Larkcom, Joy, 80
lavender, 83, 95, 97–8, 106, 150, 151; lavender water, 95; oil, 156
leaves, 51–81; culinary uses, 76–81; decorative uses, 71–2; extracting essences, 147; fragrance, 66–8; functions, 52–4; garden uses, 70–1; growing, 54–7; hair care, 65–6; harvesting, 57; household uses, 68–70; medicinal uses, 72–6; pot pourri, 98; preserving, 57–9; skin care, 61–5
lemon balm, 157; apple and lemon balm terrine, 79
lemon oil, 156
lemon sauce, 79
lemongrass oil, 156–7
Lindera benzoin, 146
linen, rinsing and scenting, 68
linen cupboards, 68
linseed oil, 31
liquorice, 136, 140
lotus, 87, 113

Mabey, Richard, 113
maceration, 62, 149–50
Madonna lily, 82–3, 120–1; lily and marsh mallow face cream, 121
marigolds, Inca, 125–6
marjoram oil, 157
Marryat, Captain, 87

marsh mallow, 121; hand cream, 64–5; lily and marsh mallow face cream, 121; sweets, 142
Mary gardens, 83–4
massage, aromatherapy, 152–3
Maury, Madam, 153
Meade-Fetherstonhaugh, Lady, 124
meadowsweet astringent, 96
meat balls, koftas, 45
medicines, 10–13, Chinese, 126–35; essential oils, 167–9; flowers, 103–5; leaves, 72–6; roots, 135–7; seeds, 38–9
melissa oil, 157
memory, scent and, 162, 163
mental fatigue, 164
Miller, Thomas, 87
modifying agents, 129
monastery gardens, 84
Montaigne, Michel de, 162
morphine, 104
mouse bait, 38
mucilage, 120, 121
mushrooms, coriander, 48
mustard seed, 18–19, 38, 43–4; oil, 31; poultices, 39
myrrh, 157

nail baths, 38
nasturtium seeds, pickled, 43
neroli oil, 157
nervous problems, 164–5
nervous system, 162, 163
niaouli oil, 157
nose-gays, 88–9
nutmeg oil, 157–8

oakmoss, 99
oils, essential, 145–69; aromatherapy, 152–65; carrier, 159–61; cosmetic uses, 165–7; extracting, 28–36, 147–50; functions, 146–7; growing plants for, 151; herbal baths, 62, 63; infusing, 59–60; medicinal uses, 167–9; perfumes, 166–7; quality control, 151–2; for sport and exercise routines, 169; storage, 152
olive oil, 31–2, 160
onions, 126, 140–1
opium poppies, 104
orange, 146; oil, 158; orange flower water, 95, 106; oranges with sweet cicely, 49–50
orchids, 113
orris root, 99, 114, 122, 124
otto of roses, 148–9

pain, 164
pan cleansers, 38
panic attacks, 164–5
Paracelsus, 15
passion flower, 87
patchouli oil, 158
peach kernel oil, 29, 160

peanut oil, 30, 161
peel, in pot pourri, 99
peony root, 135
pepper oil, 158
peppermint, 75
percolation, essential oils, 150
'perfect flowers', 93
perfumes, essential oils, 166–7; *see also* fragrance
pettigrain oil, 158
pharmaceutical companies, 128
Pharmacopoeia of the Heavenly Husbandman, 129
photosynthesis, 52, 53
pickled flowers, 108
pickled horseradish, 139–40
pickled samphire, 77
pickles, dill, 42
pickling spice, 42
pillows, herb, 67, 68
pine nut oil, 32
poisonous plants, 93–4, 104
pollination, 92
poppies, 104; oil, 32
pork skewers, 49
posies, 88–9
pot pourri, 98–100
potatoes, 122, 125
pots, growing herbs in, 117–19
potting compost, 118
potting on, 25–6
poultices, mustard, 39
pregnancy, 164, 169
preserving leaves, 57–9
pressed flowers, 101
propagation: cuttings, 55–7; roots, 115–16
pulverizing herbs, 61
pumpkin seed oil, 33
pyrethrum, 101–2, 129
Pythagorus, 11

quiche, coriander and calendula, 109

rape seed oil, 33
rhizomes, 114
rhubarb: hair dye, 122; insecticide, 70; rhubarb root hair dye, 122; rhubarb sorbet, 79; scented with cardamom, 50
rice, spiced, 46
rocambole, 141
Romans, 84
roots, 112–44; Chinese medicine, 126–35; cosmetic uses, 119–23; culinary uses, 137–44; drying, 117; extracting essences, 147–8; functions, 113–15; garden uses, 125–6; ginseng, 126–33; harvesting, 116–17; household uses, 123–5; medicines, 135–7; pot pourri, 99; preparation, 117; propagation, 115–16
rose root, 124
rosemary, 106; oil, 158
roses, 85, 91, 106, 126, 147, 148, 166;

cherry and rose petal soup, 108; rose layered dessert, 110; rose oil, 148–9, 158; rose water, 95
rosewood oil, 158
rust stain remover, 69

sacred flowers, 87
sacred herbs, 86
safflower oil, 33
saffron, 93
sage: medicinal properties, 75–6; oil, 158
sai-dong-sum, 134
salads: flowers, 106–7; herb seeds in, 41; leaves, 80; roots, 143–4
salmon, smoked, with samphire, 77
salsify, 141–2, 143
samphire: pickled, 77: smoked salmon with, 77
sandalwood oil, 158–9
sauces: barbeque, 49; kofta, 46; lemon, 79; traditional English horseradish, 139
scarification, seeds, 22
scent *see* fragrance
scented writing paper, 101
Schebbelie, J.C., 144
scorzonera, 142
sea holly, 142–3
sedatives, 164
seedlings, potting on, 118
seeds, 18–50; cosmetic uses, 35–8; culinary uses, 39–50; functions, 20–3; harvesting, 26–7; household uses, 38; medicinal uses, 38–9; oil extracts, 28–36; potting on, 25–6; sowing, 23–5
Sengen Sama, Lady, 84
sesame oil, 33–4, 161
Shakespeare, William, 84–5, 87
shallots, 141
shampoos, 66, 122
shock, 165
shrubs, 91–2
Siberian ginseng, 133
silk, black silk reviver, 69
silver plants, 91–2
skin care, 61–5, 119–20, 165–6
skin cream, 36–7
skirret, 143–4
sleep problems, 164
smoked salmon with samphire, 77
soapwort, 124
solvent extraction, essential oils, 150
sorbet, rhubarb, 79
soup, cherry and rose petal, 108
sowing seeds, 23–5
soya oil, 34–5, 161
Spanish sage oil, 159
spearmint oil, 159
spices, 20, 41–2, 98–9
spikenard, 113, 125
spinach, spicy, 47
sports, essential oils and, 168–9
sprouting seeds, 39–40

stain removers, for rust, 69
steam distillation, essential oils, 150
steams, facial, 63–4
stimulants, ginseng, 131–2
stolons, 114
storage: aromatic, 68; essential oils, 152
storax, 99
stratification, seeds, 22
stress: aromatherapy and, 162–5; ginseng and, 130–1
sunflower oil, 35, 161
sweet cicely: oranges with, 49–50; roots, 143, 144
sweet flag, 123
sweet geranium, cream hearts scented with, 110–11
sweet myrtle, furniture wax, 67
sweet waters, 68
sweets, marsh mallows, 142
symbolism, flowers, 86–90

Tagetes, 125–6
tandoori mix, 44
tang-kuei, 133–4
tangerine oil, 159
Taoisim, 86, 105
tea-tree oil, 145, 159, 168, 169
teas, herb, 80–1
terpenes, 147
theme gardens, 83–6
Theophrastus, 12, 18
thyme, 52; disinfectant, 69–70; oil, 159
tisanes, 80–1
tonics, ginseng, 131
tonka beans, 99

tooth care, 66
tranquillizers, 163–4
transpiration, 53
trees, 91–2
tubers, 114
turmeric, 135, 138
Tusser, Thomas, 106
tussie-mussies, 88–9

valerian, 136–7
vetiver oil, 159
vinaigrette sauces, 107
vinegars, 60, 108
violet leaf oil, 159
vitamins, 61

walnut oil, 35
walnut shell dyes, 37, 38
waters, flower, 95–6
wax, furniture, 67
wedding bouquets, 89
wheatgerm oil, 35, 161–2
window boxes, 119
Wolsey, Cardinal, 51
wong-kay, 134
wood avens, 125
wood raspings, in pot pourri, 99
wormwood, insecticide, 70–1
wreaths, 71–2
writing paper, 101

yarrow, 75
ylang-ylang oil, 159
yu-chin turmeric, 135